D0198848

FIELD GUIDE TO MYSTERIOUS PLACES

OF THE PACIFIC COAST

FIELD GUIDE TO

MYSTERIOUS PLACES

OF THE PACIFIC COAST

SALVATORE M. TRENTO

AN OWL BOOK   HENRY HOLT AND COMPANY   NEW YORK

Henry Holt and Company, Inc.
Publishers since 1866
115 West 18th Street
New York, New York 10011

Henry Holt® is a registered trademark of
Henry Holt and Company, Inc.

Copyright © 1997 by Salvatore M. Trento
All rights reserved.
Published in Canada by Fitzhenry & Whiteside Ltd.,
195 Allstate Parkway, Markham, Ontario L3R 4T8.

Library of Congress Cataloging-in-Publication Data
Trento, Salvatore Michael.
Field guide to mysterious places of the Pacific Coast /
Salvatore M. Trento.—1st ed.
          p.   cm.
Includes bibliographical references and index.
ISBN 0-8050-4450-7 (acid-free paper)
1. Pacific Coast (U.S.)—Guidebooks.   2. Curiosities and wonders—
Pacific Coast (U.S.)—Guidebooks.   3. Pacific Coast (U.S.)—
Antiquities—Guidebooks.   I. Title.
                F852.T75   1997
        917.9504'43—dc21   97-8313

Henry Holt books are available for special promotions
and premiums. For details contact: Director, Special Markets.

First Edition 1997

Designed by Kate Nichols

Printed in the United States of America

All first editions are printed on acid-free paper ∞

1   3   5   7   9   10   8   6   4   2

When you remove yourself from the forest
it becomes unknown.

When you're faced with the unknown
you face fear.

—*Conversation overheard in a coffeehouse,
Mount Shasta, California*

Contents

Acknowledgments

Wandering along the insanely gorgeous Pacific Coast introduced me to a staggering array of weird places and cool people. I owe this book to the many individuals who evolved from gracious hosts, to traveling buddies, and finally to friends.

First and foremost, a hearty thanks, again, goes to Cassandra Leoncini, my agent and sounding board. You sure know how to read a contract!

To publisher Jim Pruett for taking a chance and following through on an idea. A 1,001 thanks, Jim, for getting this project off the ground with *Field Guide to Mysterious Places of the West.*

To my traveling compadre, Hayden Hirschfeld, for photographing our Northern California-Oregon-western Washington trip while searching for large, fur-laden hominids. I'll never forget those mystical moments in the gigantic redwoods, the strange spirits at Fern Cave, or the setting sun's golden rays at the base of Shasta. And of course, thanks for your all-too-accurate musings about home in Colorado while driving through the heart of volcanic darkness: "It's nice to know the Rocky Mountains aren't going to blow up." What a strange trip that was, ole bean!

To my Lesley College colleague, master storyteller Rebecca Chamberlain, for letting me into her Pacific Coast world of myth. I owe you.

To my old friend Claire Lofrese, who provided early leads on many Californian mysteries. Has it really been over twenty years since those halcyon days in Vermont searching for ruins?

To Kathy Anderson for all that great information on the Channeled Scablands. To Vince Eberly and John Anderson for sharing the wealth of

Spokane's ancient past during those gorgeous afternoons after our research class.

To Alessandra Bocco and the rest of the crew at Henry Holt. Thanks for making me look good!

To all my colleagues, friends, and students at Graland, Metropolitan State, and Lesley Colleges. You've been great the past few years listening to all these stories and escapades.

To my lovely wife, Leslie, who has supported me in countless ways during these field guide adventures. And finally to Reane and Sarah. Here's another book of adventures for you to dream about as you grow older.

Note to the Reader

This collection of mysterious places is not a definitive atlas. There are far too many sites to list in one volume, so consider this book to be a sampling of the best that's out there. Don't be disappointed if a special place I list is now a parking lot or a multistoried townhouse. All too often developers know not what they have on their land. And those that do sometimes don't care about all this "mumbo-jumbo," to quote one intellectually challenged individual I met in the San Joaquin Valley.

Some of the sites in this book are near the ocean. Beware—the Pacific is tricky. It can be violent, powerful, and overwhelming. Never turn your back on it while in the splash zone. You could be swept away by a sudden killer wave. And watch those cliffside trails. Severe winter storms can erode the foundation of your footing—and usually you'll discover this when it's too late. Be careful even at a sandy beach, like the few at the base of the Big Sur area. If you wander around the coast during the summer months, the water can be a powerful lure. Please don't swim in areas that are unsupervised! The Pacific Coast is infamous for its relentless riptides and undertows.

All maps are oriented with north at the top, unless otherwise depicted. The statement "a significant drop (or increase) in geomagnetic field" refers to a change of over 500 milligauss units.

A word about cameras. If you plan on visiting the amazing places in this book, then do bring along a few flash cameras and film with speeds ranging from 100 to 400 ASA. Also handy are portable optical "slaves," hand-held units that sense your camera's flash and flash independently. They're useful in low-light places like caves and tunnels. In cases that bar the transport of bulky lighting rigs they are the only way to shoot a dark cavern's paintings, for instance. Also, never trust your super-sophisticated, computer-assisted expensive camera. If you plan on visiting most of these sites, then plan on it failing at a crucial moment. I'm not denying the convenience and beauty of these "idiot-proof" machines—I own several—but dust, humidity. and the simple act of transport sometimes messes up the camera's computer chip. I've been saved many times by my backup: a simple, manual-focus, no-frills 35mm camera. Most people long ago traded in these workhorses for the simplicity of point and shoot. That's good news for you. Check out your local camera store or pawnshop—you may be able to buy a used manual camera for pennies. And if the thought of a manual camera gives you a headache, then at least take along those one-time-only throwaway cameras as backups. They take surprisingly good pictures and, unlike their costly cousins, rarely break!

Finally, if you come across anything intriguing, perplexing, or unusual in your travels, give a call or write me via the publisher:

> Sal Trento/Mysterious Places
> c/o Henry Holt and Company, Inc.
> 115 West 18th Street
> New York, NY 10011

Thanks, and enjoy what follows!

FIELD GUIDE TO MYSTERIOUS PLACES

OF THE PACIFIC COAST

Introduction

Soon after the publication of *Field Guide to Mysterious Places of the West*,[1] which detailed weird anomalies in seven states bordering the Rocky Mountains, and the release of *Field Guide to Mysterious Places of Eastern North America*,[2] which described unusual sites from Nova Scotia to North Carolina, hundreds of people phoned, faxed, and visited claiming to have even stranger sites in their neighborhoods. As the reports continued to flood my desk, it was evident that *something* was out there. Armed with maps, reference guides, laptops, and survey equipment, once again I headed out in the field in search of mysterious places. Because a good number of the reports were coming from the Pacific coastal states of Washington, Oregon, and California, I decided to concentrate on that region. The trek was well worth the effort.

This book is the third in a series of field guides dedicated to mapping out strange and unusual places. The series is distinguished by its focus on uncovering *why* a site is mysterious: Is it modern-day hype, ancient legends, or something more tangible, like the location or the ground itself?

This book, like the others in the series, starts with a synopsis, or "snapshot" summary of a site. Detailed directions to each locale are provided in map and text form. Any extenuating or dangerous circumstances like private property or military restrictions or the threat of wild animals are noted. Background and historical information set the context of a site. Extra contact information is provided. Any unusual magnetic field aberration associated with a mysterious place is noted. And finally, any other weird places in the general vicinity are described briefly.

When I was researching strange locales in the East, I noticed something bizarre. I found that many of the ancient, so-called sacred sites scattered

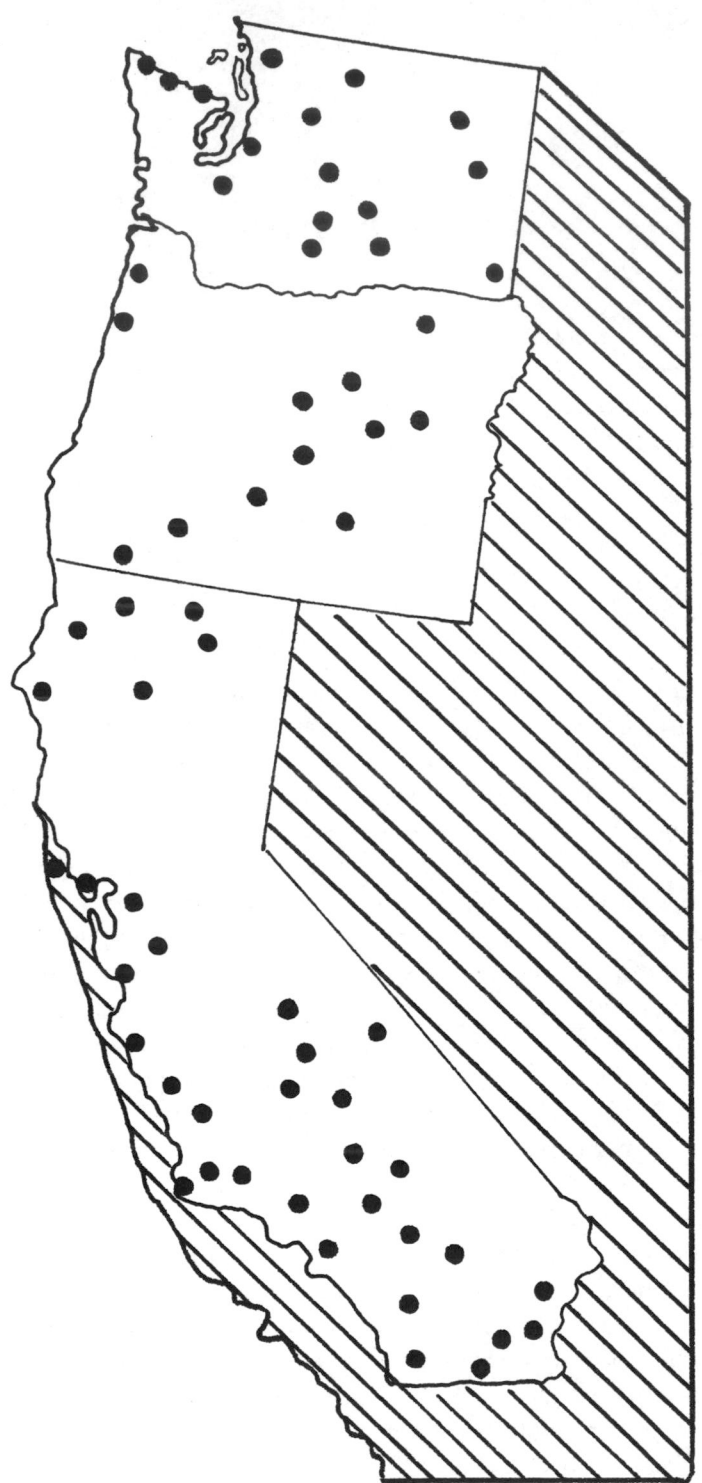

Mysterious sites along the Pacific West Coast

throughout the hills and valleys were located in places that had unusual magnetic fields.

The earth is like a massive electromagnet. As the planet spins, a magnetic field is generated from deep within the earth's crust. Theoretically, this field should be the same over wide stretches of earth, but this is not so due to the density, composition, and other variations within the crust. For years oil geologists have known about these broad magnetic field aberrations and have used this information in rather innovative ways to find new sources of fossil fuel.

With a device called a magnetometer, I surveyed the natural magnetic field in a region. This established a base-line reading, or the *total magnetic field*. With the same instrument I also measured the angle the field makes with the horizon as it leaves the ground—the *angle of inclination*. Once I calculated the base-line readings I then moved toward the sacred site. Inevitably, as I approached it, the magnetic field and the angle of inclination radically changed. In many cases the magnetic field, measured in milligauss units, went up or down dramatically; the angle skewed inward or outward. As I collected more data from around the country, the pattern became clear. Ancient peoples chose a *specific location* for their inscriptions, their standing stones, their stone chambers. Many sites had been built *on top of aberrant magnetic fields*! But *how* and *why*?

An exhaustive review of the physiological literature provided some of the answers. Over the past fifteen years researchers discovered that electromagnetic fields can influence different brain chemicals, which in turn influence general behavior. The secretion of neurotransmitters, like serotonin or melatonin, produced in the pineal gland at the base of the brain, can be increased or decreased depending on the flux of a magnetic field. In short, your mood, body cycle, and general perception of the world could be altered in a laboratory setting. Could this also happen out in the field or at a sacred site? Did prehistoric shamans select a particular place because it made them feel different, be it better or worse? Did they direct the placement of some structure or inscription to enhance the experience? The data collected in my Eastern North America book suggested they did just that.

Could the same methods have been used at mysterious places in the western states? For example, at the site of the strange Chumash Indian cave paintings in the mountains above Santa Barbara, California? Yes, and they can be experienced today by following the maps provided in this book.

Some of the sacred places of Washington and California have traditionally been used in puberty rites. Perhaps the extreme geomagnetic flux associated with these locales stimulated a cascade of pineal gland chemicals that altered cognition. No doubt this chemical flood, filtered through the cultural lens of indigenous tribes, expressed itself in many ways, such as the vision quest. These sacred sites still exist and can be visited. But why do we need to go to the mountains to feel anything? Why do we need tips on how to relate to the natural world?

Our society today is totally out of touch with the earth's magnetic rhythms. There are conflicting, artificial magnetic fields all over the place—from toaster ovens to car phones to television sets. Each one resonates, pulsating its own electromagnetic vibrations that mask the subtleties streaming forth from the earth's core. I feel the conflict myself as I write this using the heavily laced electromagnetic aberration of my computer and monitor. The conflict is Faustian: experience the comfort and ease of modern life at the price of never understanding one's place on earth because we *never relate* to it, *we never feel its magic.* Most of us are missing out on the earth's mysteries.

Could these manmade fields also be endangering our long-term health? The scientific jury is still out on that one, but some studies do suggest that daily exposure to powerful electrical systems may interfere with cellular growth, leading to cancer and sterility. Perhaps unwittingly we are causing our own slow extinction. To heal the spirit, if not body, we need to reconnect with our surroundings in ways that go beyond Earth Day celebrations and tree hugging. We must learn to feel what the planet is offering. But to do that we need to experience it firsthand.

The following is a compilation of some of the weirder places I've visited within the Pacific coastal states. Almost all are on public lands and accessible, but sometimes you may need to get a landowner's permission to visit a site. Some of the places listed are easy to get to, while others demand intensive study of road and topographic maps. Be forewarned. But don't give up—there's a mysterious world out there ready to overwhelm all who look and feel. Have fun seeking the unusual!

ONE

Background and Overview

The Pacific Coast of North America is a strange, unique place. Formed several million years ago by massive continental slabs of rock pushing and sliding under each other, the land is a complicated array of stone on stone. The more you know about this place the more difficult it is to fully comprehend the churning tectonic forces that created it: the once-violent volcanoes that masquerade as sleepy mountains or the gentle-looking folded hills that still whisper of impending earthquakes. How does one live among the tremors of San Francisco, or in Seattle near the shadow of Mount Rainier, without completely succumbing to fear? By denial? By the eternity of youth? The geography is young and restless, like a good deal of the population of the Pacific Coast.

Washington and Oregon are the result of 200 million years of the North American continental plate smashing into the Pacific Ocean floor. As the denser ocean plate sank beneath the lighter continental plate, rifts in the crust allowed great masses of lava to spew across the terrain. Geologists calculate that about 35 million years ago the volcanoes that make up today's western Cascades began to erupt, sending clouds of ash and explosive rock into the air. This went on day and night, continuously, for close to 10 million years. Nothing organic survived this epic holocaust. Much later in time when the lava cooled and solidified, the ground repopulated with wind-dispersed seeds. Today both states are a mixture of mountains, lava flows, grasslands, and lakes. The gentle hills hide a sleeping giant miles below the ground's surface.

While most of the country thinks only of California's floods, earthquakes, fires, and riots, there are many good reasons why people continue to live along this western edge of the United States. To start, it's beautiful. Sitting atop a

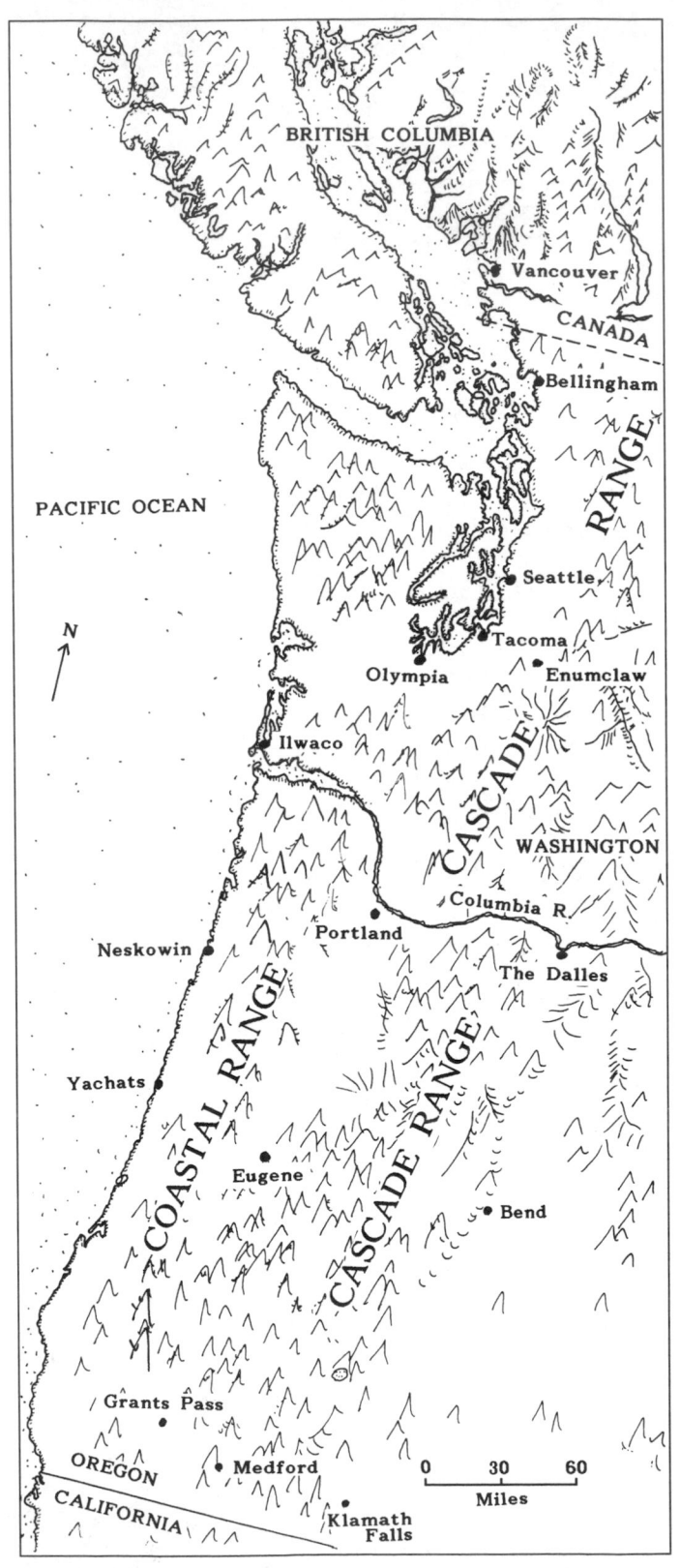

Geographical overview of the Pacific Northwest

Some of the Indian tribes inhabiting the West Coast at the time of European contact

mountain overlooking giant waves crashing into Big Sur is a mystical experience. Feeling the sun warm your soul while the scent of a vast ocean wafts past can be a sublime moment. While the geologist can easily explain this topography, to experience it firsthand makes one more appreciative of living with the danger inherent in the land.

Stretching for over 2,700 miles, the Pacific shore does not slope down gently to the sea as it does on the Atlantic Coast. Rather, mountains come to an abrupt halt when they meet the ocean. The drama of steep-sided cliffs rimmed by giant redwood trees first impressed early sailors as they tacked south hugging the shore. The feeling is still there today. As you travel down the coast from Washington to California, the rugged coastal landscape gives little indication of the mixed terrain located east of the inland mountains. You see a coastline savaged by powerful waves carrying the force of 4,500 miles of open ocean behind them. These high ranges, which go by the names of the Olympiads, Cascades, and Sierra Nevadas, trap cold Pacific moisture along their western slopes. As a result, the land east of the mountains is dry and arid, unlike the wet, rainforestlike northwestern tip of Washington State.

Houses of indigenous tribes of the Pacific Northwest at the time of European contact

Beyond the sea cliffs the land slopes downward, creating a central valley of sorts between the mountains that begin again to the east. Scattered throughout this expanse are the remnants of ancient times. Depending on which reports you believe, the land was traversed by early peoples somewhere between 10,000 to 15,000 years ago. The hunters who came to the land enjoyed a mild climate that was filled with game. In the southern part of what eventually would become California, the lakes had not yet dried out. Ancient, lake-shore terraces can be seen there today, showing where these Paleolithic hunters camped.

Over time the climate changed and the water dried up. A large part of Southern California today is desert, with huge depressions filled with salt and gypsum—the sites of Ice Age lakes.

Scattered throughout this strangely inviting landscape are the quiet remains of peoples who first scouted the high mountains and climbed into water-strewn valleys. Caves, cracks, and rock crevices found throughout the coastal mountain ranges are covered with the painted remnants of these ancient peoples. Some of these sites are accessible to all. Others are the domain

of the many Indian reservations located throughout the region. The mystery of these ancients becomes evident when one visits a painted cave. The symbols are unlike anything found elsewhere in America. Much has been written about their meaning, but few understand their original intent. All we have today are snippets of oral legends to interpret them.

The dry, barren, moonscape of southeastern California is wrought with controversy. Based on some intriguing stones excavated over a twenty-year period, a clutch of researchers claim there is definitive proof that an early form of human lived and made tools there. How early? Between 40,000 and 200,000 years ago! (Conventional archaeological dogma puts man in the Americas between 12,000 and, at the most, 15,000 years ago.) And just who are these scientists who spout such archaeological heresy? The famed paleontologist Dr. Louis Leakey, who spent over twenty years at Olduvai Gorge in East Africa uncovering ancestors to man millions of years old, stunning the academic community in the mid-1960s, is one of those scientists. Leakey claimed that stone tools found in the Calico Hills of California were thousands of years older than anything ever found in this country. American archaeologists scoffed at the data. Leakey persisted until his death. The debate continues today.

The Pacific coastal states are filled with weird and unusual sites. Follow me on a journey throughout this varied and intriguing landscape to mysterious places.

TWO

Washington

First-time visitors to Washington are always fooled. While images of the evergreen, snowcapped Cascades are certainly true, a drive across the state from west to east reveals something much more startling. Incoming moist Pacific air is blocked by the high Cascade Range. The expanse of evergreen and Douglas fir trees clinging to the western slopes thrive on this sea moisture. It rains a lot here. But just east of the mountains the land settles down to rolling plains of wheat fields and irrigated apple orchards. The rainy season of the coast is replaced by a dry, flat landscape. Most drivers immediately conclude that the state has a dual personality. They are correct.

Coastal Native Americans had an easy time getting by: the mild climate, abundance of seafood, and cedars made it a pleasure to live in the western Washington area. These people were able to stay in the same area all year. They didn't need to follow the game or move to warmer climates. As a result, they didn't have to spend most of their time hunting for food. They had a lot of time on their hands.

East of the Cascades it was (and still is) another story. The region gets very little of the ocean storms due to the height of the mountains. Native tribes in this area of the state needed to hunt game like deer, bear, squirrel, and rabbit. They couldn't stay in one place too long. They needed to roam the vast plains in search of food and warmer shelter.

In the 1700s, Spain sent an expedition to the Pacific Northwest to check out the terrain. Not much happened. Vitus Bering (famed for the Bering Strait, the waterway separating Alaska from Russia) sailed along the Pacific Coast and brought back reports of beavers and sea otters. This information led to the establishment of Russian fur-trapping colonies all along the coast. The English also got involved in the area, courtesy of George Vancouver, who tacked around the future Puget Sound area searching for the mythical Northwest Passage across America. Vancouver took detailed notes of the terrain, eventually naming many of the prominent volcanoes and islands, such as Mount Rainier, Mount Baker, and Whidbey Island.

By 1805, Lewis and Clark had ventured all the way to the mouth of the Columbia River, along Washington's eventual southern boundary, before returning to the East. John Astor's fur-trading business set up shop in 1811 and successfully traded beaver and otter skins for many years. This company formed the foundation of the great Astor family fortune that accrued throughout the nineteenth century.

Westward movement into the great Oregon Territory, as the entire Pacific Northwest was then known, began in the 1840s when Congress passed a set of laws that essentially gave away a 640-acre plot of land (one square mile) to any adult white male who staked a claim, marked the boundaries, and built a cabin. Moving out of the densely populated eastern states became the driving force in this incredible migration. Thousands of people hauled their families across the "Great American Desert" of the plains in covered wagons. Many never made it. But those who did got the land they always dreamed of—and more.

Unfortunately, no one told Congress that the land was already occupied, by Native Americans. Many of the tribes inhabiting eastern and western Washington were not about to give up a good thing—archaeological excavations suggest that the land had been traversed by the natives' ancestors 10,000 to 15,000 years ago, or earlier. The atrocities on both sides were many. Eventually the United States Army was called in to protect the newly arriving settlers. Dissident Indian warriors and their families were either massacred or shipped off to reservations thousands of miles from their homelands. Hundreds of treaties signed between Congress and various tribes were systematically broken as land-hungry settlers demanded more.

In many parts of the Northwest, white-Indian relationships are still reeling from the betrayals of the past. Gambling on reservations hasn't helped. Because a reservation is a separate legal entity under U.S. law, many western tribes have built casinos on their land to garner money for their people. Many of these establishments have been remarkably successful. Too successful, according to some whites. Local governments want a piece of the revenue, but they can't get it: the reservations are tax-free. White businessmen who want to start gaming operations sometimes can't due to local restrictions and covenants that don't apply to the reservations. In some parts of the West, this economic war is the latest stage of friction stretching back hundreds of years.

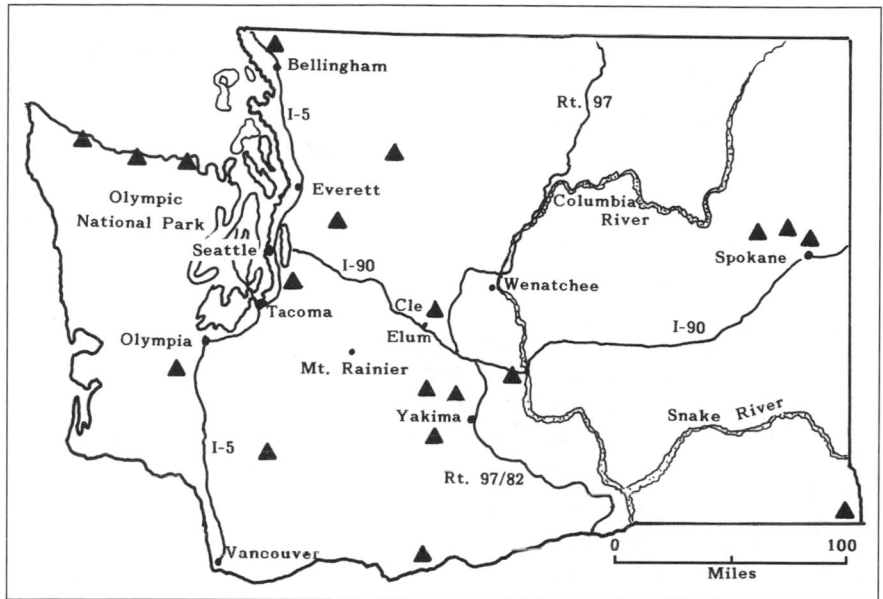

Mysterious sites in Washington

WESTERN WASHINGTON

Western Washington was a land of plenty for the original inhabitants. By the 1700s white traders had discovered the enormous fur-bearing sea creatures in the region, making fortunes for those willing to put up with the hardships of isolation.

When the first party of Oregon Trail emigrants set sail for the Duwamish River Valley in 1851, just south of the present city of Seattle, they didn't know what they were getting into. But tales of land and the region's great bounty attracted these pioneers from Illinois. The pioneers had a vision of developing the Puget Sound area into the New York City of the West. The idea started becoming a reality when the settlers discovered their fortunes in the vast expanse of lumber just east of the Sound. Logging became the lifeblood of the fledgling city of Seattle. Railroad connections with the city, as well as the Great Klondike Gold Rush, gave Seattle premier port-supply status for the thousands who passed through on their way to the northern Yukon Territories of Canada. Outfitting the mass of gold-fever prospectors made Seattle very wealthy.

Unfortunately, while all this hullabaloo was going on the Native Americans who for centuries had lived in and around the Sound went unnoticed. True, the city *was* named for the Suquamish's Chief Seattle, but little

View of Seattle in the Washington Territory, 1870, (Somerville, The Mediterranean of the Pacific

good that did the people who lived near the Duwamish River a few miles south of the blossoming city. If anyone *had* taken notice back in the 1800s, we would know a tad more about the unusual places found scattered around western Washington.

SACRED MOUND
Tukwila, Washington

Site Synopsis
On a nondescript spot about 300 feet from the Duwamish River in south Seattle is an eroded hill that may be the center of the world. According to traditional Native American folklore, the earth was created at this very spot. The accuracy of the myth with respect to time is uncanny. After every rainstorm 30-million-year-old fossils leach out of its sloping sides. Of all the hills in the area, why is this one such a special place?

Location

Take Route 5 south from Seattle. Turn off at exit 158. Continue on down the ramp going west on Pacific Highway. At the first stop sign, make a sharp left onto East Marginal Way. In less than half a mile turn left (east) onto South 115th Street. Park on the right side of the road parallel to the Duwamish River. The mound is on the north side of the road.

Considerations

This mound is private property. Be sure to look for the current landowner signs stapled to fences and trees in the area. Call up the owner and request permission to walk on the site. Also, leave all fossils at the mound. Take nothing but pictures. This is sacred land!

The best place to see fossils is along the northern portion of the mound. There are many steep paths where rainwater has washed away years of accumulating sand and mud. Look carefully at the ground.

A quick climb to the top of the hill will astonish all. On a clear day, Mount

Rainier can be seen to the southeast. It's an awesome sight. The juxtaposition of modern buildings with the primeval settings of the surrounding view is overwhelming. Look at the nearby Duwamish River. For untold centuries Native Americans fished and canoed along that winding path. Imagine what it must have been like during their time. Now think back even further to a time when *Homo sapiens* were just a twinkle in the eye of some primitive mammal.

History/Background

The mound is technically in the city of Tukwila, where it's called Poverty Hill. Long known as a thrill-filled motorcycle run for local youth, this place, according to storyteller Rebecca Chamberlain, an honorary member of the Upper Skagit tribe who's fluent in the Native American Lushootseed language, is where story, myth, and legend fit together with science and paleontology.

Chamberlain first heard about the site from a geologist who described the ancient marine life found there. His description matched a local origin story she knew. Visiting the site convinced her that Poverty Hill was of mythological importance.

According to the legend, two Native American animal spirits, Muskrat and Beaver, dove to the bottom of the ocean, where they gathered up mud. The mud brought to the surface was piled into a heap, which was the start of Earth. But it took Grandmother to make the world a pleasant place for people to live. According to Chamberlain, the old woman may have stood on this very mound to call to the four winds, her sons. She told North Wind to leave, to go farther north and not to visit too often. This was difficult to do. It was her son. But she needed to fashion a place for her future people, the Indians. The tears in her eyes saved the fledgling earth from eternal winter by melting the cold, brutal ice of North Wind.

A close examination of the mini-ravines and clay runoff on this hill reveals a seemingly strange past of fossil scattered throughout the dirt: miniature clams, ancient shark teeth, fish vertebrae, and curiously spiraled seashells. The remnants of this ancient life ooze out of the earth after every storm. For over 50 years it's been a special place for geologists at the University of Washington, who have cataloged up to fifty species of 30-million-year-old fossils. But it's also been a sacred place for many Native American elders still living in the vicinity. Special forces created this mound. Special forces protected it, they claim.

They may be right. Geologists marvel at the mound's existence. When the sea level dropped over 30 million years ago, this pile of dirt, ensconced with ancient life, lay on the newly created shore. It should have been leveled during the advance of the last Ice Age, but for unknown reasons, a tongue of the

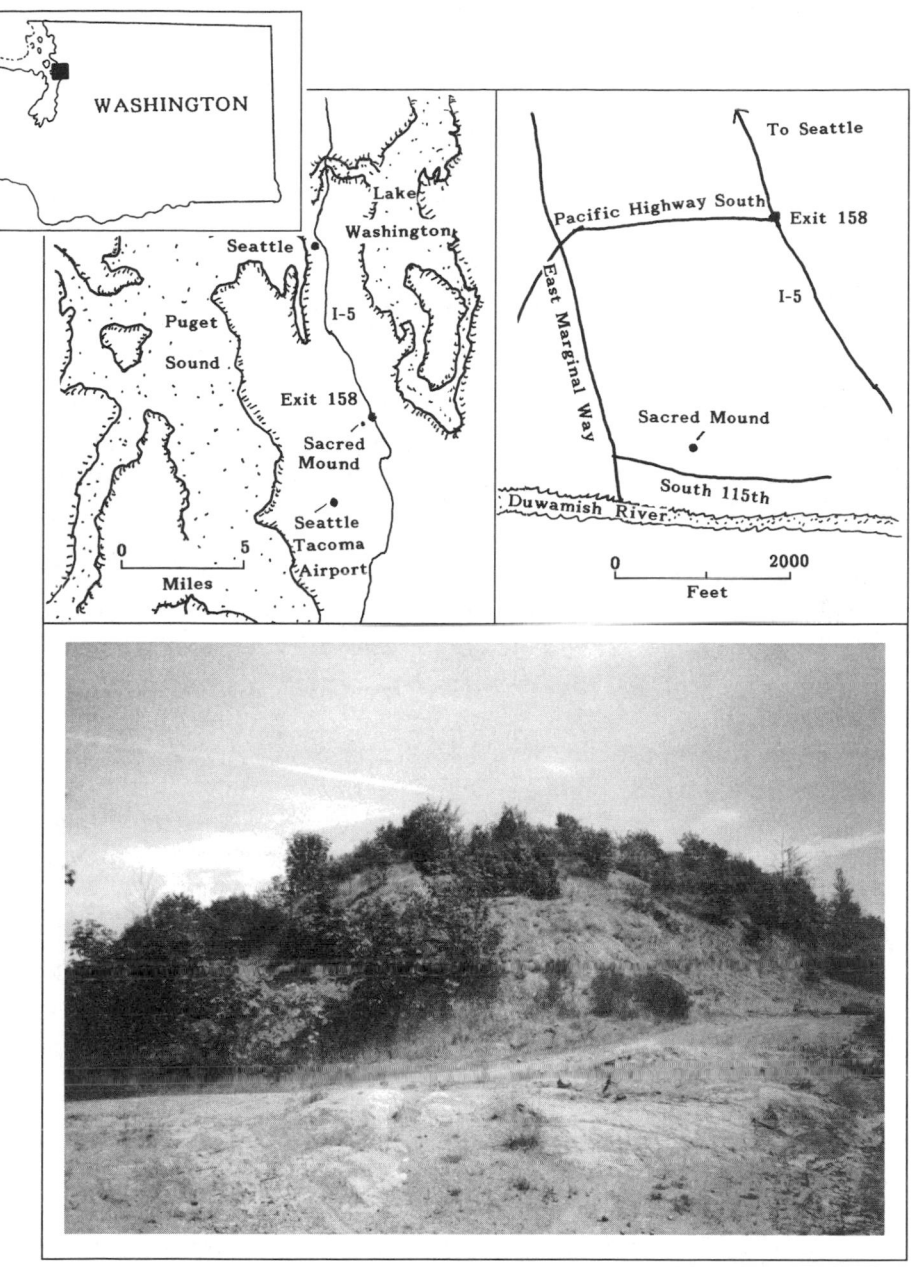

ensuing glacier must have warmed up, split, and bypassed this chunk of antiquity. The geology of the region suggests this happened along the north side of
the hill. Eventually the climate warmed and the glaciers retreated, leaving dirt,
debris, and accumulations of rock chaos in their wake. The melting ice spared
the mound. Scientists can't explain why, but Native American legend can.

Contact Person (s)/Organization
The University of Washington
The Burke Museum
Seattle, Washington 98195

Total Magnetic Field/Inclination Angle
     This mound of earth had an intriguing geomagnetic field. The top of the
mound, where Grandmother sorrowfully called to her sons, has the lowest
total magnetic field recording of any area. In short, as you climb the mound
the magnetic field progressively drops. The significant geomagnetic aberration
here would make this spot a very powerful place. The change in feelings
and/or perceptions here may have stimulated the early inhabitants of the
Duwamish River Valley to attribute special importance to the site.

Further Investigations in Area
     South and west of Seattle are a variety of strange dimplelike bumps on the
soil. Called the Mima Mounds, these small, rounded hills have been the subject of dozens of theories as to their origin. Some researchers claimed prehistoric gophers left them; others argued that melting ice or seismic motion did
the work. To get there take Interstate 5 south from Seattle through Olympia
and Tumwater. Eight miles south of Tumwater turn off at exit 95. At the bottom of the ramp continue west (straight ahead) toward Littlerock, not Route
121. Once in Littlerock, follow 128th Avenue—the main road through
town—for a mile to the junction with Waddell Creek Road. Turn north
(right) at this junction. The mounds are about a mile up the road on your left.
This is a protected preserve. The gates open at 8:00 A.M. and close at dusk.
For detailed information about the mounds' origin see the first in this field
guide series, *Field Guide to Mysterious Places of the West.*[1]
     About 100 miles south of Seattle is the infamous Mount St. Helens that
erupted on May 18, 1980. The entire north face of the volcano blew away,
dumping 800-degree mud flows 17 miles down the Toutle River. Over 150
square miles of forest were destroyed when a 15-mile-high blast of ash and
molten rock burst through the newly formed crater.
     Few people today realize that this pre-eruption, perfectly symmetrical
"mountain" peak was once known not for its devastation but for the strange
ape men who roamed its slope (see Northern California section, page 81).
Early miners claimed a strange breed of ape creatures roamed this densely
forested area. A holdover from this time can be seen today along the south and
southeastern slopes of the volcano. Ape Cave is one of the longest underground lava tube trails in the country; at 12,810 feet in length, it is startling.
Lava tubes form when the outer layer of molten lava hardens while the inner
section continues to flow until it runs out. (See Oregon Caves section, page 51.)

Nearby Ape Canyon is another reminder of the strange creatures that may have once roamed this eerie countryside.

Several years ago journalist Loren Bliss surveyed a variety of odd mounds and outcroppings in the western Washington region. At the time Bliss believed he had uncovered a vast prehistoric grid system, or alignments and orientations. He even spent a summer excavating a site. His early work did, however, turn up some intriguing archaeological finds: rocks with cuplike markings and a stone bench. The field surveys included areas around Des Moines, Clayton Beach, and Lake Tapps.

On a curious geological note, north of Seattle just outside of the town of Bellingham are some fine examples of weird weathering. Although this honeycomb weathering is common in many parts of the world on igneous and metamorphic rocks, geologists haven't a clue as to how it happens here. This distinctive weathering pattern is characterized by walls of honeycomb-like erosion. This is odd, considering that this type of weathering occurs most often in rock that is of the same mixture—it's homogeneous, as geologists like to say. If the rock were made up of different stones of differing types and density, it would be easy to explain. But the Bellingham rocks, as well as other examples throughout the country, are homogeneous. How did this happen?

Along the beaches of the Olympic Peninsula's north shore are remnants of the last Ice Age. The cliffs that line the Strait of Juan de Fuca are slowing eroding and depositing amazing amounts of beach treasure along the shore. As you travel west from the town of Sequim, prominent bluffs overlook the water. Over 15,000 years ago when the sea level was 400 feet lower than it is today, the land continued all the way to Canada. As the glaciers melted, tons of debris formerly locked up in the ice was deposited on the scarred landscape. Water filled up the Strait and Puget Sound, and the erosion of the resulting beaches began. In these glacial till beaches are the teeth, ivory tusks, and bones from animals that lived there during the Ice Age. Winter storms and high surf cut into these beaches to expose these treasures. Often they are found along the splash zone—where the water meets the sand. If you get to the beaches during low tide, look carefully: you may uncover the prehistoric artifacts that killed these ancient creatures. Do respect private property!

EASTERN WASHINGTON

East of the Cascades could be another world. The land seems softer, gentler, much more mellow than the craggy volcanoes to the west. Gone are the giant Douglas firs and rugged peaks. In their place are gentle hills, rolling prairies of wheat, and rounded hillsides of apple orchards. Just past Wenatchee and the Columbia River the landscape changes dramatically. Chaotic valleys are carved into vast, U-shaped gorges. The land seems ravaged, plundered, and littered with gigantic boulders alien to the region. Called the Scablands, this terrifying terrain causes unknowing travelers to gasp and ask, "What caused this?" The answer: one of the most catastrophic events ever to gouge the face of the earth.

The more unusual legends of the Pacific Coast involve massive water inundation. In 1878, the journal *American Antiquarian* summarized these curious tales:

> Many of the Native Americans in the Pacific Northwest, for example, have a tradition of a flood. The Twanas on Puget Sound speak of it and that only good Indians were saved, though there were quite a number of them. It occurred because of a great rain and all the country was overflowed. The Indians went in their canoes to the highest mountains near them which is in the Olympic range. And as the waters rose above the top of it, they tied their canoes to the tops of the trees so that they wouldn't float away. Their ropes were made of the limbs of the cedar trees. The waters continued to rise, however, above the tops of the trees, until the whole length of their ropes was reached. Just when they thought they might have to cut the ropes and drift off to some unknown place, the waters began to recede. Some canoes, however, broke from their fastenings and drifted to the west, where they say their descendants now live—a tribe who speaks a language similar to that of the Twanas. This, they also say, accounts for the present small number of the tribes. . . .
>
> The Clallams, whose country adjoins that of the Twanas, also have a tradition of a flood. . . . The Lummi Indians, who live very near the northern line of Washington Territory, also speak of a flood.
>
> The Puyallop Indians, near Tacoma, say the flood overflowed all the country except one high mound near Steilacoom—and this mound is called *The Old Land* because it was not overflowed. . . .
>
> The Makah Indians, who lived at Neah Bay, in the northwest corner of Washington, next to the Pacific Ocean, as well as the Chemakums and Kuilleyutes, speak of . . . Indians . . . [drifting] off in their canoes to the north. Others floated in large circles until they came down on the many trees in the region. Many lives were lost.[2]

Why are there so many legends of a flood? Did someone actually see a mind-numbing water catastrophe and live to tell about it? There's good reason to bet on it. Somewhere between 12,000 and 16,000 years ago, as the glaciers advanced southward over Montana and Idaho, sections of ice formed *ice dams*—narrow valleys in which huge chunks of ice accumulate, preventing the flow of glacial meltwater. At times massive lakes formed behind this natural barrier. Lake Missoula was such a glacial formation. Based on still-visible mountainside wave cuts, it had a depth of nearly 2,000 feet. Present-day Lake Superior is less than 1,000 feet deep. Furthermore, Lake Missoula covered over 3,000 square miles—about half of Lake Michigan![3] This was a massive body of water.

About 70 miles northeast of Spokane at the mouth of the Clark River near the Idaho-Montana border a major ice plug developed sometime during the last glacial period. When increasing worldwide temperatures caused the northern glaciers to melt faster than they were advancing, the unthinkable happened. The weight and pressure of the water undercut the dam, releasing all 500 cubic miles of water locked up in Lake Missoula. Gigantic waves rushed southwest through the Spokane Valley. The chaos that ensued is almost unfathomable, for the lake drained at a rate unmatched by any known flood today. Astonishingly, this did not happen once. Geologists estimate that in the 4,000-year period beginning 16,000 years ago the glacial Lake Missoula filled up and roared out of its enclave 85 times.[4] According to telltale evidence scattered across Washington State, the deepest and most catastrophic flood happened between 12,000 and 13,000 years ago.[5]

This was no ordinary water flow. To give some idea of how fast the water was traveling, consider these figures: At the breached dam, the rate of flow was estimated to have reached 400 million cubic feet per second. The world's largest river, the Amazon, flows at 6 million cubic feet per second. At the narrowest point along the Columbia River, at the Dalles Gorge in Oregon, the average is but 195,000 cubic feet per second.[6]

At these rates water poured through the Spokane Valley plucking away bedrock, lifting boulders, and carving up massive blocks of basalt, some measuring over thirty feet across. Floodwaters rushed westward into the Columbia River Gorge, carving out the channel even farther before cascading into the Portland area and into the Pacific Ocean. A giant 400-foot lake suddenly appeared in the Willamette Valley to the south. Anyone living there would have been swamped by tidal waves.

The geological scenario describes what actually happened, but was anyone around to see it? Persistent Northwest legends seem to suggest that was the case. So the question is simple: Were there any people in the Northwest between 12,000 and 13,000 years ago?

In the late 1970s on a farm outside of the town of Sequim in the northeastern section of the Olympic Peninsula, archaeologists found mastodon bones they dated as being between 12,000 and 14,000 years old. Even more intriguing was the extinct elephant's rib they found that still had a bone spear point stuck inside it. Mastodons were being successfully killed more than 13,000 years ago. The time frame puts us well into the chronological boundaries of the last great Ice Age flood. Clearly someone saw this devastation and lived to tell about the horror.

RUNIC STONE
North of Spokane, Washington

Site Synopsis

On a volcanic rock outcropping north of Spokane are a series of strange painted symbols. Early residents of the city thought the symbols were Viking runes. Preliminary investigation suggests the symbols are American Indian in origin.

Location

From Interstate 90, take exit 281, near downtown Spokane, to Route 2/395 north for three miles. Exit west on Route 291. Travel for about a mile, exiting north on Indian Trail Road. In a little more than half a mile the Excelsior Youth Center will be on the right. Turn into the driveway and park near the main office. The outcropping can be seen from the parking lot.

Considerations

As the site is located on the grounds of the Excelsior Youth Center, please stop at the office to get permission to visit it.

History/Background

The first trading post in the Spokane area was built around 1810. Not much settlement took place in this eastern part of Washington Territory until the early 1870s. In the ten-year period between 1880 and 1890, when the Northern Pacific Railroad came through town, the population went from 350 to over 20,000. Farming and gold and silver strikes throughout the Northwest led to the city's rapid growth.

It was during these boom years that one Robert McKinley and his family arrived in the Spokane area to homestead. In 1926, McKinley noticed some weird markings under a rock overhang on his property. A chain of events then occurred in which well-meaning people misrepresented an unusual event. The local historical society was called in. Then came the newspapers publicizing the event. Big-city presses picked up the story, and suddenly backwater Spokane was making international headlines. Incredibly, tourists, scientists, and others were allowed to chip off sections of the painted markings. Why all the interest?

One of the scholars who visited the Spokane site was Professor Oluf

Opsjon, at the time an internationally acclaimed expert on Viking runes—the syllabary of those early Nordic warriors. Opsjon examined the markings and stated with absolute authority that the strange symbols on a rock in eastern Washington were a history of Viking exploration of North America. The good professor set about to decode the runic pictures and symbols as an eager public awaited his interpretation. The markings told the tale of 24 Viking men and 7 women who trekked across early America in A.D. 1010. They stopped in the Spokane area to drink some water from the stream near the rock. Local Indians apparently were also thirsty, and the two groups got into a fight. Many of the Norse people were killed. After the battle a few Vikings who had escaped returned to bury their dead and to document the horror.

Many people thought this explanation was perfectly reasonable. Compounding the plausibility was the local Indian response to the paintings' origin: they claimed to know nothing about who painted the marks and what they said. And then there was an elderly Spokane Indian woman's story about big blond men visiting western British Columbia 800 years before her time.

Amateur excavation near the rock site exposed human bones and stone arrowheads. The place seemed to be a burial ground, so why not a Viking one?

Simply put, the rock symbols have nothing to do with Vikings and are not Viking runes. Their style is indicative of other painted petroglyph sites throughout the Pacific Northwest. The good professor's interpretation was a function of the times. During the 1920s people were finding Viking runes in all sorts of places: the northeastern coast of America, New Jersey, Minnesota, South Dakota—and Spokane, Washington. Although many of the symbols were vaguely suggestive of runes, they clearly were not runes. But popular theories of the time created the mind-set for such flotsam.

Intriguingly, the painted symbols seem oriented toward the winter solstice sunrise on December 21. A person at the rock outcropping on the shortest day of the year would observe the sunrise dramatically striking the markings. The bones found at the mound no doubt were Native American, though unfortunately, the location of the material is nowhere to be found. And for years after the discovery, people continued to deface the symbols with bullets, twentieth-century carvings, and chipped-off souvenirs. Today an iron gate protects the remaining marks.

When you visit this site walk around the volcanic outcropping. On one side you'll notice "pillow lava." This is liquid rock that flowed into a water source, creating a telltale "puffy" form. Look on the ground and you'll notice remnants of the stream, which was an important place for Native Americans. And look over the remaining markings very carefully. The painted symbols have become part of the rock matrix itself. But what did these symbols once mean? Unless some of the stolen rock slabs turn up elsewhere over the next few years, we will never know the full extent of the symbols.

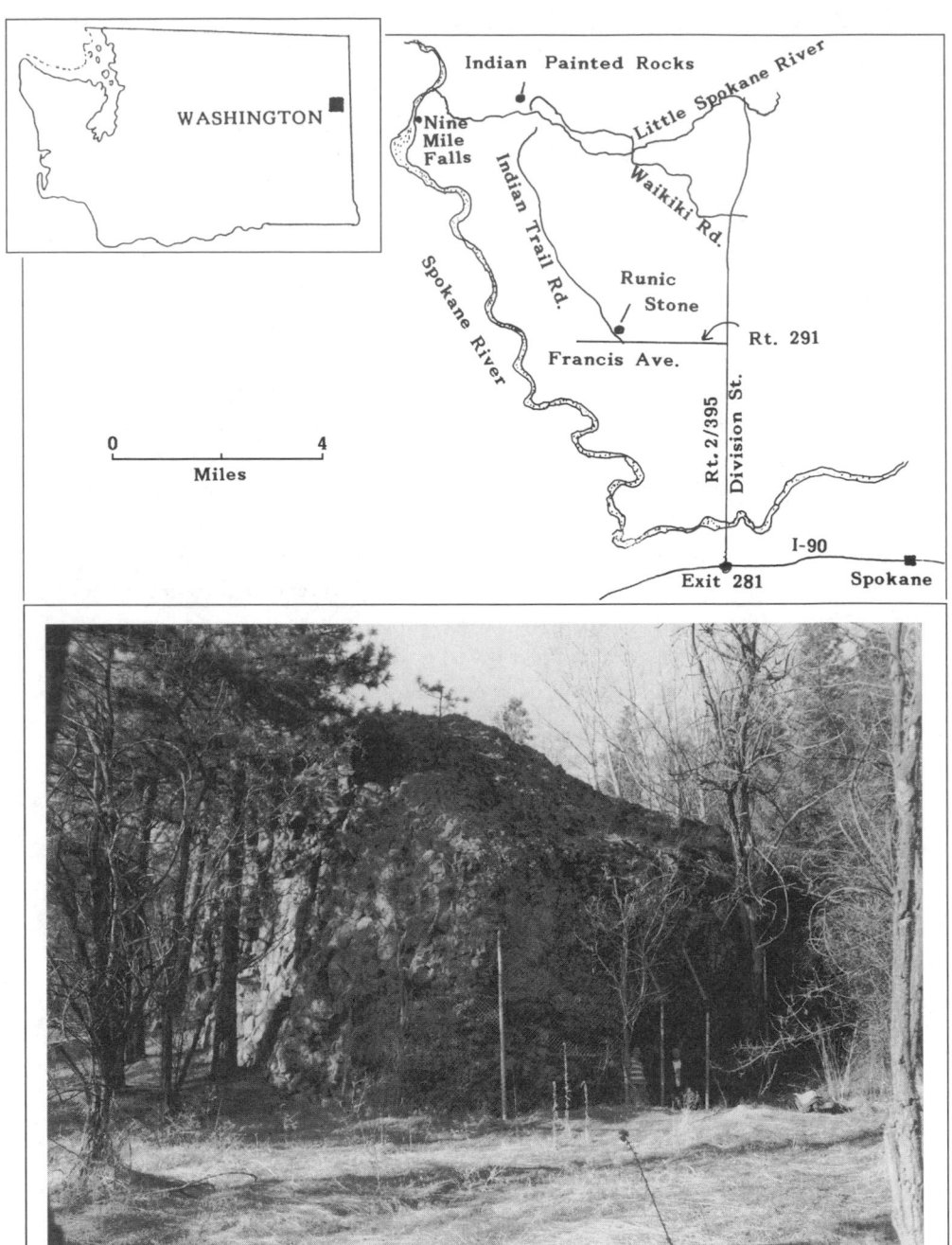

Contact Person(s)/Organization
Excelsior Youth Center
3754 West Indian Trail Road
Spokane, Washington 99208–47736
(509) 328–7041

Total Magnetic Field/Inclination Angle
Geomagnetic data dropped significantly as I took readings closer to the rock site. There seemed to be a specific pattern of placement: only the painted side of this volcanic outcropping showed any anomaly.

Further Investigations in Area
Northwest of Spokane on the Spokane River are the Long Lake pictographs. To get there take Route 291 north out of Spokane for 28 miles toward the town of Tumtum. Pull off into the parking area and take a walk along the trails. Two separate painting areas can be seen at this intriguing site. Fence gratings protect each site.

INDIAN PAINTED ROCKS
Nine Mile Falls, Washington

Site Synopsis
Along a road curiously named Indian Trail, some five miles from the Runic Stone site, is another outcropping of volcanic rock. Behind a steel gate are the symbolic remnants of a people who lived near this area for thousands of years.

Location
From Interstate 90, exit 281, near downtown Spokane, take Route 2/395 north for three miles. Exit west on Route 291. In a little less than six miles you'll drive over the Little Spokane River. Just over the bridge on the left is the site.

Considerations
The site is part of the Washington State Parks and Recreation Commission. Please observe all trail markers and cautions.

History/Background
Indian Trail Road was not named by some clever developer. The name is a holdover from the first settlement of the region. Early Spokane made its money from milling—the river provided the much needed waterpower for timber mills. For many years early homesteaders and Native Americans coexisted peacefully. Relations became strained, however, when thousands stopped at this lovely valley to stake their future.

A researcher points toward a strange, red-painted thunderbird image on the Runic Stone.

The Painted Rocks site is interesting for many reasons. Its similarity both in form and location to the Runic Stone site is astonishing—but then, perhaps the site was painted by the same people who put paint to the Runic site. The outcropping is similar, and so is the orientation—the Painted Rocks site seems positioned to observe the winter solstice sunrise!

Archaeologists know very little about this specific site. The meaning of the strange symbols has been lost to history. About all any researcher can say is: "The pictographs are in a style common to the northeast of Washington." Great. Wander around this place and try to get a feel for the people who took the time to paint these symbols. Ask, why here? I suspect the geomagnetic aberration data has something to do with this particular volcanic outcrop.

Contact Person(s)/Organization
Eastern Washington State Historical Society
(The Cheney Cowles Memorial Museum)
2316 West 1st Avenue
Spokane, Washington 99204–1006
(509) 456–3931
Open Tuesday through Saturday, 10:00 A.M.–5:00 P.M.; also open Sunday afternoons after noon. Admission fee.

Total Magnetic Field/Inclination Angle

As at the Runic Stone site I noticed a significant drop in geomagnetic field as I approached the painted rock face.

Further Investigations in Area

Walk through the woods near this site. If you are lucky and have keen eyesight, you may spot the remnant artifacts from another time. (See also the associated section under the Runic Stone heading.)

SACRED SYMBOLS: INDIAN PAINTED ROCKS
Yakima, Washington

Site Synopsis

Northwest of Yakima just off Route 12 a volcanic cliff looms over the traffic below. All along the base of this basalt upthrust are white and red paintings of faces with rays and halos. Some of the walls are blank while other sections of the cliff face are densely covered with these mysterious images. What do they mean?

Location

West of Yakima. From Route 82 take Route 12 west for 3.6 miles. Turn left (south) on Ackley Road. At the end of Ackley turn right (west) on Powerhouse Road. Park off to the right well away from the road traffic. The site is across the road at the base of the large cliff.

Considerations

If you wander around this site you'll see the graffiti "art" of the late twentieth century: *John loves Mary, Peace,* and so on. This place is a hangout for kids who like to smoke, drink, and decorate stone with spray paint. As far as I can tell, most of this activity takes place well beyond the boundaries of the cordoned-off area of paintings, which is fortunate. I find it intriguing that some in the community gravitate toward this cliff that was used thousands of years ago by ancients to paint *their* images. It was an attempt then to represent some other type of reality. Our teenagers today alter their perception with alcohol and nicotine—did the ancients use various substances to enhance *their* perception? Curiously, most people who see these pictographs and others scattered throughout the Pacific Coast ask, "What were these people smoking?" Their images do have the marks of hallucinogenic perceptions.

But maybe our modern artists gravitate to this cliff for reasons other than a desire to paint. Perhaps they come because they simply *like* this place. Maybe it makes them feel good to be "away" from everything—even though they

really aren't: a major road is a few yards away. Curiously, there may be some-thing to feeling good at this place. The geomagnetic data collected here has some peculiar attributes that may contribute to the draw.

Sadly, part of this cliff face was destroyed several years ago for an irrigation project. But the remaining shell contains enough data for speculation.

Detail of the red-colored Indian Painted Rocks, seen behind metal gate, Nine Mile, Washington

History/Background

Early white settlement in and around the Yakima Valley was difficult: the Yakima Indians wanted no part of this encroachment. They were happy with their territory and in no way did they want to leave it. This is understandable, as the valley has an allure of its own. It must have been even more charming before the Yakima River was diverted for agriculture. By the late 1850s, after a grueling Indian war, the Yakima accepted a large tract of reservation land just south of the present-day city of Yakima. They apparently negotiated a better set of terms than their brothers to the south, the Modocs of northeastern California, who were forced to relocate in Oklahoma.

West of the Yakima River an Indian trail ran through the valley to the Wenas Mountains. Like almost all native trails in America, it was followed by the invading whites to enter the countryside. This same trail was used in the 1850s by miners en route to the Canadian gold fields. Later a stagecoach line followed it as the first white settlers in the region turned from cattle ranching to cultivating fruit trees.

Just south of this ancient trail, at the base of a stunning cliff face made up of solidified, prism-shaped basalt, are dozens of white and red paintings. A closer inspection of this site shows that many of the images are like human faces decorated with halo-styled "rays" pulsating from the head. Some areas of the cliff have one or two white and red faces. Other spots along the cliff face have multiple images overlapping one another.

Technically these paintings are classified as the Yakima polychrome style. The motif is associated with red and white facial images with rayed heads, concentric circles, and triangular abstractions.[7] Researchers believe the style developed more than 1,200 years ago along the Columbia River in northern Oregon. It presumably spread north from there into the Yakima Valley. Why these paintings are true polychrome (multicolored) is unknown.

And what do these rayed designs mean? Difficult to say, but a few researchers believe it has something to do with the supernatural power that a person possessed. My gut reaction at this site was that people came here to experience the mystical. Once they saw a vision, perhaps through a vision quest, they then attempted to record it.

Some organic hallucinogens allow the user to see auras, or halos, around people. Why this is so is not known, but many psychoactive-drug explorers have reported such. Did the Yakima—or whoever drew these designs—have a market on hallucinogenic substances? Perhaps. But no one on the nearby reservation is talking today. I suspect that there was some other substance mixed into this stylistic stew at Yakima.

At one time it was thought that Native American paintings like those at Yakima had to be quite recent: little or no wear, erosion, or fading was noted by early investigators. We now know, however, that the combination of painting techniques and certain types of rock resulted in pigments that became part of the rock itself. Historical sources state that Pacific Coast Indians used a variety of mineral pigments: crushed iron oxides for reds, copper oxides for blue-green colors, and manganese oxide and charcoal for blacks. White pigments were formed by collecting specific mud clays. The collected mineral pigments were mixed with organic binders such as egg, animal fat, plant sap, or urine. The application of such a mixture to porous rock allowed the colors to seep into the rock, thereby becoming intricately mixed with the hard surface. Furthermore, in a marvelous stroke of good luck (or some might argue, planning), the placement of the painted images sometimes allowed rain-soaked minerals surrounding the image to leach out and coat the pigments with a transparent protective film. The end result of all this is that many paintings, thought only a short while ago to be of recent origin, are in fact several thousands of years old.

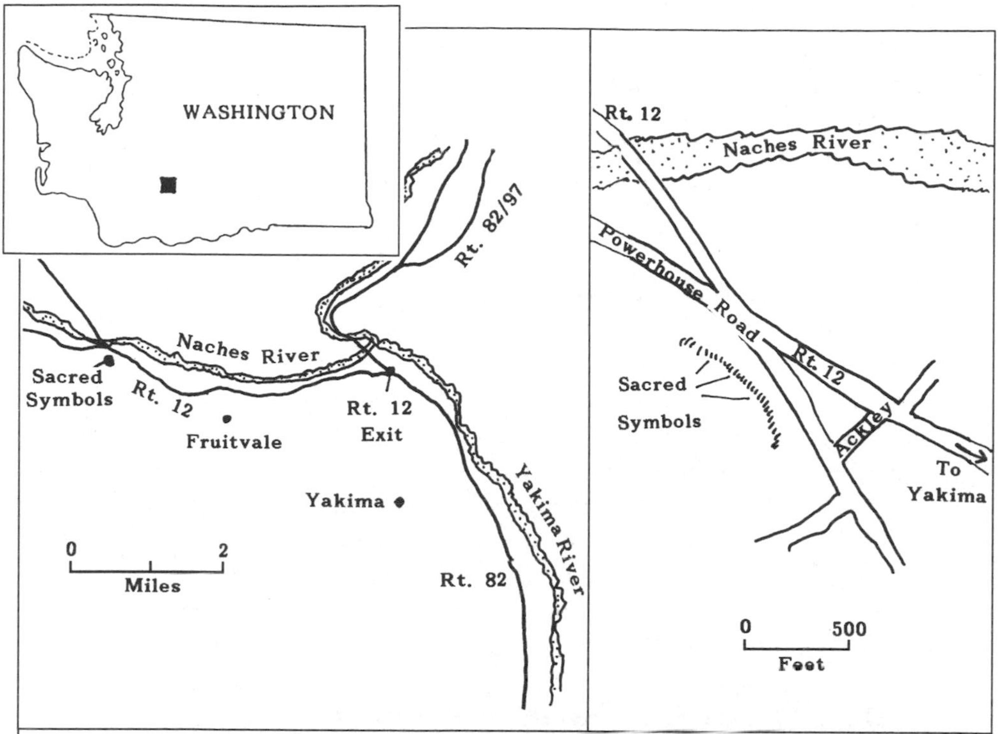

WASHINGTON

Naches River

Sacred
Symbols

Rt. 12

Fruitvale

Rt. 12
Exit

Yakima

Rt. 82/97

Yakima River

Rt. 82

0   2
Miles

Rt. 12

Naches River

Powerhouse Road

Sacred
Symbols

Rt. 12

Ackley

To
Yakima

0   500
Feet

Contact Person(s)/Organization
Yakima Valley Museum
2105 Tieton Drive
Yakima, Washington 98902–3766
(509) 248–0747

Total Magnetic Field/Inclination Angle

This was one of the most intriguing sites I've ever recorded. Twenty feet from the cliff I noticed a very high total magnetic field and a constant angle of incidence. (This refers to the angle the magnetic field makes with the earth as it leaves the ground.) But at the base of the cliff and below the paintings things changed—the total magnetic field across the basaltic base dropped. The lowest total magnetic field recordings occurred at the highest cluster of rayed paintings. In other words, every time I came across a jumble of heads all squeezed onto one rock panel, I recorded a radically low milligauss reading. Moving but two feet away to a panel with only one face, the total magnetic field shot upward. Moving again to a densely clustered panel, the total magnetic field dropped.

The bottom line? The artists chose specific locations along the cliff face to paint multiple images. These locations had lower geomagnetic fields. It is known that changing geomagnetic fields can change the way people feel. The

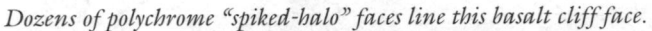

Dozens of polychrome "spiked-halo" faces line this basalt cliff face.

Detail of the sacred faces painted at the base of a cliff just outside Yakima, Washington

The eyes and halo spikes of the multicolored faces make for an eerie setting.

connection seems logical: these were places that "felt right." Or in the tribe's tradition perhaps it felt like a place of power. In any event, the paintings at this Yakima sacred site were *not* randomly placed; there was a purpose to where they were positioned.

Further Investigations in Area

South of the Indian Painted Rocks site, Cowiche Creek flows into the Naches River. Along the basalt outcroppings in this area are several mysterious polychrome pictographs.

In the late 1970s, a fire control officer at Sopelia Lookout Tower near the south end of the Yakima Indian Reservation heard seven hours of unexplained sounds coming from deep within the earth. The officer likened the sound to underground turbines or engines. Her dog showed signs of trepidation upon being let outside. The weird sounds had also been heard earlier in the year by the same officer.[8]

What did this woman and dog hear? It's difficult to say, but similar unexplained sounds occur throughout the entire country. Explanations have ranged from pre-earthquake tremors to auditory delusions on the part of the witness. For example, in Taos, New Mexico, longtime residents report a "hum" during certain times of the year. Sound specialists have actually measured the sound, but they cannot say where it is coming from. There is no doubt that the fire control officer and her dog heard and felt the vibrations of sounds, but the explanation remains buried deep within the ground. The reservation land around Yakima remains a powerful place where mysterious events continue to take place.

A few years ago I received a rather vague report of medicinal lake mud somewhere in or near the Yakima Indian reservation. Supposedly the mud from this lake has been used for thousands of years to cure a variety of illnesses. While this may sound crazy, there are other examples of healing mud from other parts of the country. In northern New Mexico, at the Hispanic hill town of Chimayo, there's an early nineteenth-century Catholic church built on top of an ancient Tewa Indian healing site. For centuries the Tewa Indians have used mud from a source near the church to cure diseases. Today thousands of people visit this sanctuary hoping the mud will cure them of their problems.

When the Wanapum Dam was built across the Columbia River in the late 1950s many petroglyph sites were inundated with water. While these underwater rock carvings are hidden from vandals, they cannot be seen by anyone today. Several concerned citizens at the time thought it important to document the carvings of the ancient people who lived in this region. At the Ginkgo Petrified Forest State Park in Vantage are several examples of indecipherable petroglyphs. The most intriguing are the so-called twins motif. These are images that always appear in pairs.

*"Twin" petroglyph at
Ginkgo Petrified
Forest State Park
Museum, Vantage,
Washington*

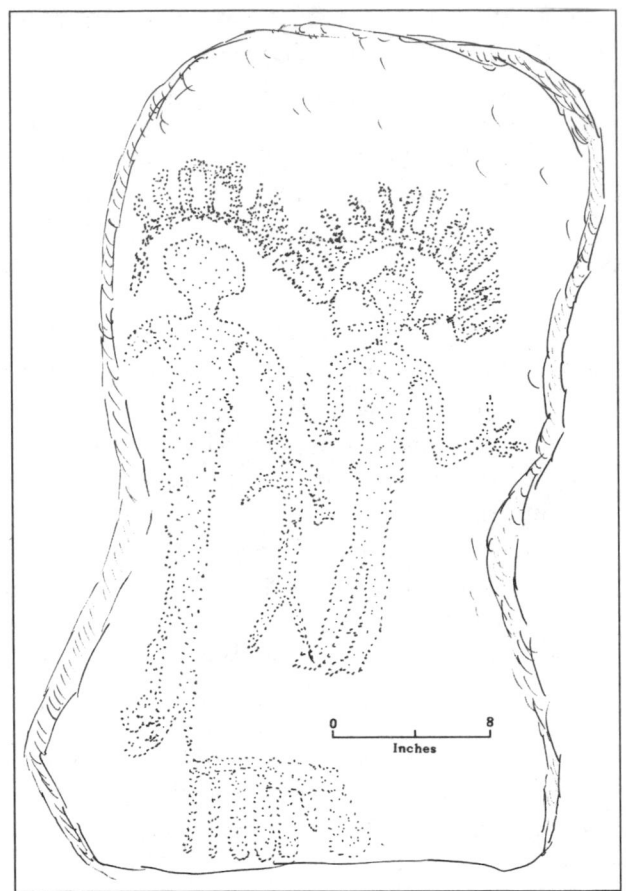

About 90 miles southwest of the Yakima area along the Columbia River are a wonderful series of ancient stone carvings. This site is just north of The Dalles, Oregon. Specifically, the petroglyphs are at Horsethief Lake State Park, 28 miles west of Goldendale, on Route 14. This area was a gathering place for Pacific Coast tribes. They came from miles around to trade, fish, and have a good time.

A little more than 50 miles northwest of Yakima just outside of South Cle Elum comes a report of a field that contains "special power." Supposedly this meadow has such unique energy radiating from it that healers from across the country have journeyed to it to gain extra strength. My source wrote that "New Age people go there to bathe in the aura and to construct their pyramids." Furthermore, she noted, "This would be a good place to be in a nuclear war, because the radiation would have no effect."

Now, how could anyone pass up a report like that? As soon as I could I was

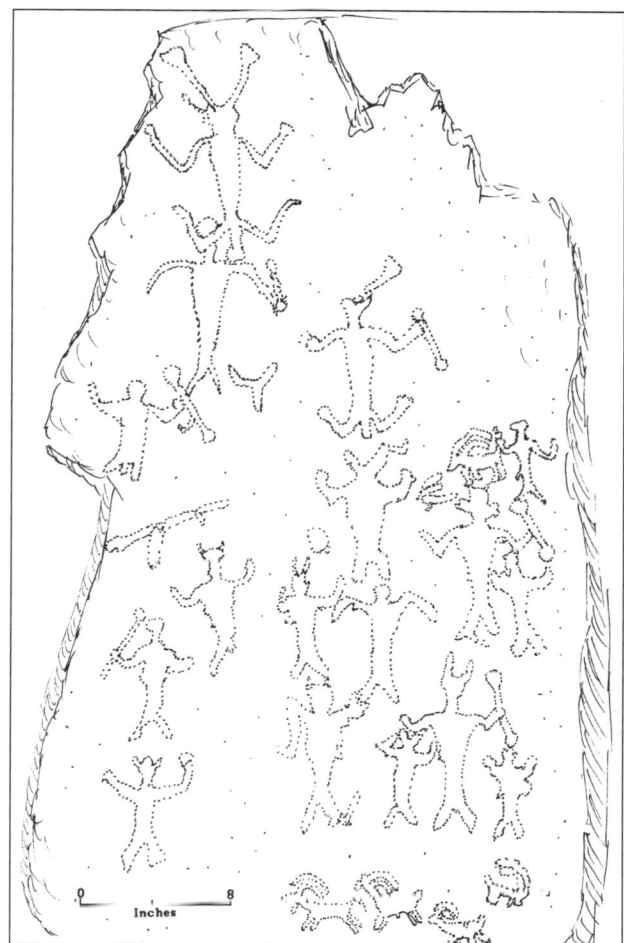

Mysterious images from Buffalo Eddy, on the Snake River south of Clarkston, near Hells Gate Recreation Area in southeastern Washington

there! Unfortunately, I didn't find much. The field in question, a rather nice-looking meadow rolling along the slope of a hill, is now part of the Sky-meadow Community. From the top of the hill, residents command a spectacular view of the surrounding mountains. I stopped by one afternoon and spoke to several members of this community. No one knew what I was talking about, or so they claimed. I then took out my magnetometer and began measuring the field and surrounding land. Nothing. Later in the day at the cute town of Roslyn where the hit television series *Northern Exposure* was filmed, I inquired about the Skymeadow field at a local bookstore. The owner asked why I wanted to know. She then said that there were several "shamans" who lived in South Clc Elum who do indeed draw upon the energy of the meadow.

I felt and saw nothing unusual. Nothing peculiar turned up with the magnetometer; in fact, many times I thought I was the punch line to some big joke. But my intuition tells me that I missed out on something. If you check it out for yourself, do let me know what's there!

Just outside of Clarkston, on a road parallel to the Snake River, are several sacred paintings and mysterious petroglyphs. While some of these images clearly relate to the hunting activities of buffalo, mountain sheep, and the like, others are far more mysterious. Elongated, triangular-shaped humans with antenna-like rods shooting from their heads hold sticks with round balls at either end (called "barbells" in the anthropological literature). No one has a clue as to what these images mean. My first thoughts upon seeing these strange petroglyphs centered on shamans shaking gourd rattles. Perhaps this was once a special place where powerful forces reigned supreme. Unfortunately, the day I saw these powerful icons I had left my magnetometer back at camp. I suspect this site would give off some interesting readings.

These images are tricky to find. They are located in the Hells Gate Recreation Area of southeastern Washington. Specifically, you can find some of the more interesting sites at Buffalo Eddy. To get there travel about five miles south of Clarkston to Asotin. Using Asotin as a reference point, travel twelve miles south. Just after the first cattle guard, around a sharp corner, are a large set of rocks. Across the river are another set of large rocks with a red building nearby. Scattered throughout this area are some of the strangest images in southeastern Washington. Watch out for poison ivy and poison oak!

If you still are having trouble locating these intriguing artifacts, stop by the local Chamber of Commerce back in Clarkston.

Chamber of Commerce
502 Bridge Street
Clarkston, Washington 99403–1933
(509) 758–7712

THREE

Oregon

Between 1840 and 1900, more than 300,000 overland emigrants set course from Independence, Missouri, over a sun-scorched, treacherous ribbon of dirt through wilderness and some 2,000 miles to Oregon. The journey took these intrepid pioneers over six months in a covered wagon. Some never made it: either they died along the way or they turned back. But remarkably, many did make it. Their descendants still live in this abundant state today.

Like Washington, Oregon today is the product of yesterday's volcanic chaos. Millions of years ago the Pacific Ocean plate slammed into and under the existing continental plate, causing obscene folding, twisting, and churning of the rocks. The Cascade Range and ensuing volcanoes erupted continuously, spewing out millions of cubic feet of lava. Cinder cones formed as tectonic tension deep within the earth's crust gave way at the surface, releasing clouds of gas, steam, and molten rock. Eventually the eruption pace lessened, and a seeming calm swept over the land. Today the green and white of the Cascades and the amber hills of the rolling eastern plain are deceptively peaceful. Many of the volcanoes here erupted only a few hundred years ago, and they are still *very* active!

Although geologically simplistic, Oregon can be divided into two major divisions: the western coast and valleys, and the eastern and central high deserts. The difference between these two regions is solely due to the Cascade Range.

In the west, the Pacific Ocean batters the land with waves that have traveled over 6,000 miles. No barrier reefs or islands protect this tortured coastline. Inland, between the coastal mountains and the Cascades, are the Willamette, Umpqua, and Rogue River Valleys. The fertile Willamette Valley was the ultimate destination of the thousands who trekked west.

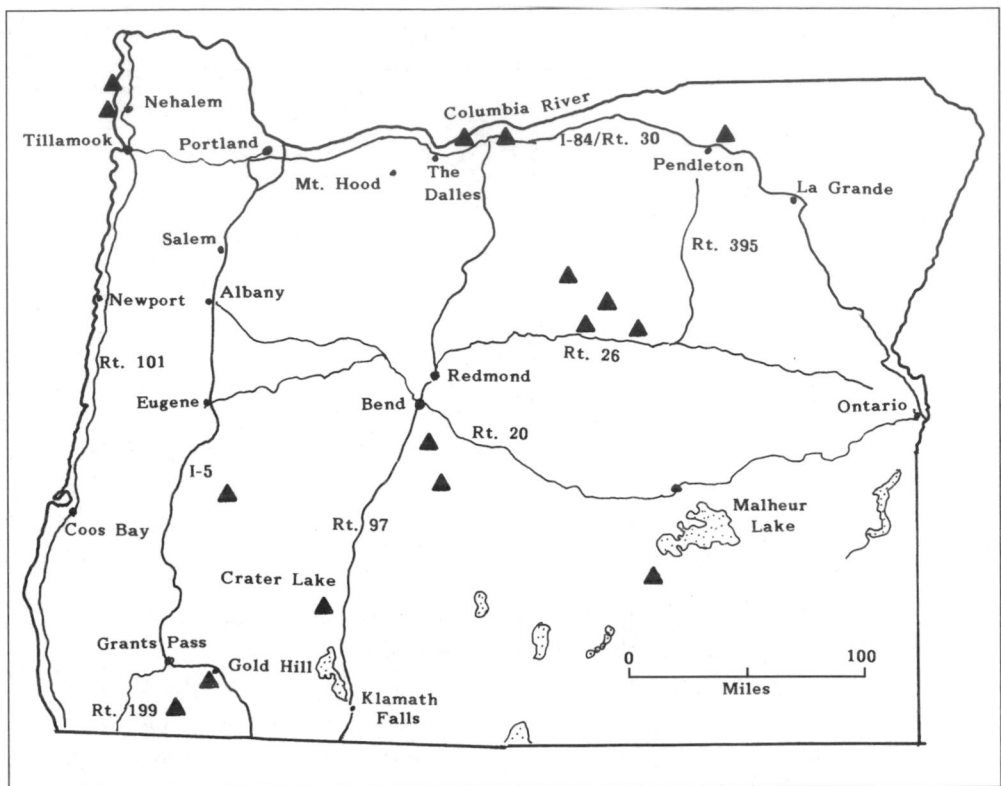

Mysterious sites in Oregon

East of the Cascades the green valleys give way to a high plains desert. This arid landscape held little attraction for the Oregon Trail pioneers. They moved out of this bleak region as soon as they could.

The name Oregon has several possible derivations. The most likely is from the Greek *oregonon* and *orenogonia,* which refer to "mountainous place." Old sailing maps mark the land between California and British Columbia in such a way.[1]

WESTERN OREGON

The western part of Oregon is where 75 percent of the three million people of this state live. It's always been that way. Seafood was abundantly available for the early inhabitants of the region. The wide mud flats held thousands of

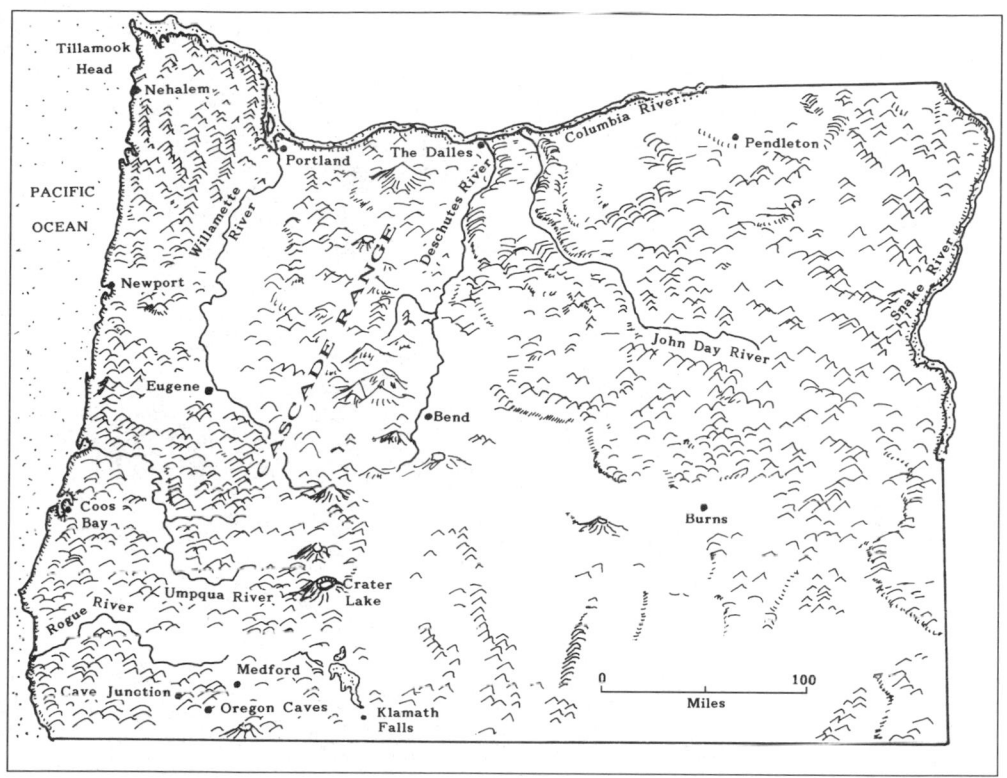

Major landforms of Oregon

clams, oysters, and shellfish. Moist, rich forests lining the coastal range were cut by salmon-filled rivers and tributaries.

White encroachment into the Oregon Territory in the mid-1800s caused an already bad relationship with the natives to get worse. From the Indian point of view, these people with their covered wagons and horses were encroaching upon land their ancestors had lived and hunted on for thousands of years. From a white perspective, Oregon *needed* to be settled by Americans to complete the Manifest Destiny of a united nation, from sea to shining sea.

PIRATE TREASURE
Neahkahnie Beach, Nehalem, Oregon

Site Synopsis
Almost as soon as the first Indian legends spoke of pirate treasure, pioneers lusted after the riches that supposedly still lie buried along a hillside near Neahkahnie Beach.

Location

From Portland take Route 26 west for about 25 miles. Turn west on Route 6. Travel for about 55 miles to Tillamook. From Tillamook drive north along Route 101 for about 25 miles to Nehalem Bay. Continue on to the cute town of Manzanita. Drive through the downtown area to Ocean Road and go north, hugging the coast. Just before Ocean turns into Pacific Road, pull off to the side well away from traffic. The hillside of Neahkahnie Beach is off to your right.

Considerations

Stop in at the Tillamook County Pioneer Museum for an intriguing exhibit on beeswax. Weird inscriptions on stones there may have something to do with the pirate treasure.

Almost all of the treasure holes are on private property. Please contact the respective owners before trespassing.

History/Background

Depending on what level of evidence you personally need to determine truth, the Pacific Northwest has been visited by giant primates half a million years old, by ancient "men" from 200,000 years ago, by Ming dynasty Chinese merchants, by Russian fur traders, English merchants, Spanish treasure ships, and swarthy pirates. While there is intriguing evidence for some of these visitations (the focus of later chapters), here we will examine the swarthy pirate scenario.

Let's start with the legend. By the late 1850s, when white pioneers finally began farming the lush valleys of northwestern Oregon, some took the time to listen to and record the stories of the remaining Clatsop and Tillamook Indians of the region. A tale that kept cropping up among these natives told of a "winged canoe" that sailed near Neahkahnie Mountain a peak 1,795 feet high located on the Oregon coast between the towns of Manzanita and Cannon Beach. The canoe—presumably a large sailing vessel—crashed onto the beach after a storm. Several men then carried a large chest partway up the mountain slope, and placed it and a "black" man inside a deeply dug hole. They covered the hole with dirt, etched symbols on a rock, and left.[2] In variations of this story, the remaining crew sailed either north or south after the treasure pit was dug.

Not much was made of this tale until the early 1890s, when a strangely inscribed stone was found on the slope of Neahkahnie Mountain. An intensive search of the densely covered hillside soon turned up more carved rocks in the undergrowth. And therein began the great treasure hunt.

Old-timers reevaluated the Indian tale. Newcomers saw gold, silver, and gemstones in their future. The hillside was dug, prodded, cut up, turned inside out, and much later developed into a residential housing tract with streets bearing moneyed themes: Pirates Way, Treasure Hunters Street, Treasure Rocks Road, etc.

But the story gets more interesting. All along the nearby coastline, from Neahkahnie Beach to the tip of Nehalem's sand spit to the head of Tillamook Bay, chunks of beeswax—the stuff of beehives, where honey is stored—have been found since the first explorers stumbled into the region. The Tillamook Indians were known to have traded large quantities of the wax in Astoria and Vancouver to the north. Lewis and Clark, sent out by President Thomas Jefferson, even mention the wax in their journals. And where did the natives get the wax? They said it washed up along the shore after the winter storms!

So what's the big deal here? Beeswax was used in candle making. But it was also a common trade item on seventeenth-century Spanish ships sailing the Pacific to the Orient. Spanish captains would trade wax for pearls, gold, jade, and other precious treasures. Laden with exotic wealth, the ships would then cross the ocean and sail south to the Mexican shore. The riches were then carted overland by mule to the Atlantic Coast for eventual shipment to Spain.

A number of years ago large blocks of the wax washed ashore from an unknown shipwreck just off the coast. Through carbon dating researchers at a county museum in Tillamook discovered the wax dated to between 1500 and 1650. Furthermore, pollen present in the wax was identified as being from a species of holly that grows on the northern part of Luzon Island in the Philippines. The Philippine Islands were the last Spanish port of call—where all treasures and commodities were tallied up, accounted for, and packaged before ships embarked on the grueling Pacific Ocean crossing.

Couple this new information with cryptically marked stones on display at the Tillamook County Pioneer Museum and the treasure legend at Neahkahnie Beach takes on a more realistic tone. Let's consider the possibilities. If the story is true, then either an actual Spanish merchant vessel wrecked or a pirate ship wrecked. If the merchant vessel was filled with treasure and was forced onto the treacherous sandbars just off the coast, the logical course would be to hide the treasure, build a small boat, sail to Mexico, and return at some later date with a larger ship able to carry the heavy load. If a pirate ship intercepted the Spanish cargo, then why would pirates bury a treasure?

They wouldn't, unless something happened to their ship as well. Assume a pirate ship captured the treasure and subsequently wrecked off Oregon's northwest coast. Any booty remaining would be a burden to carry off on a small, hastily made ship. Burying the treasure with proper markings and signs insured that it would still be there at a later date.

Which story is more plausible? If a man really was killed and dumped on the treasure chest before it was covered over with dirt, then the pirate theory rings true. Actual accounts from that dangerous period suggest that this in-

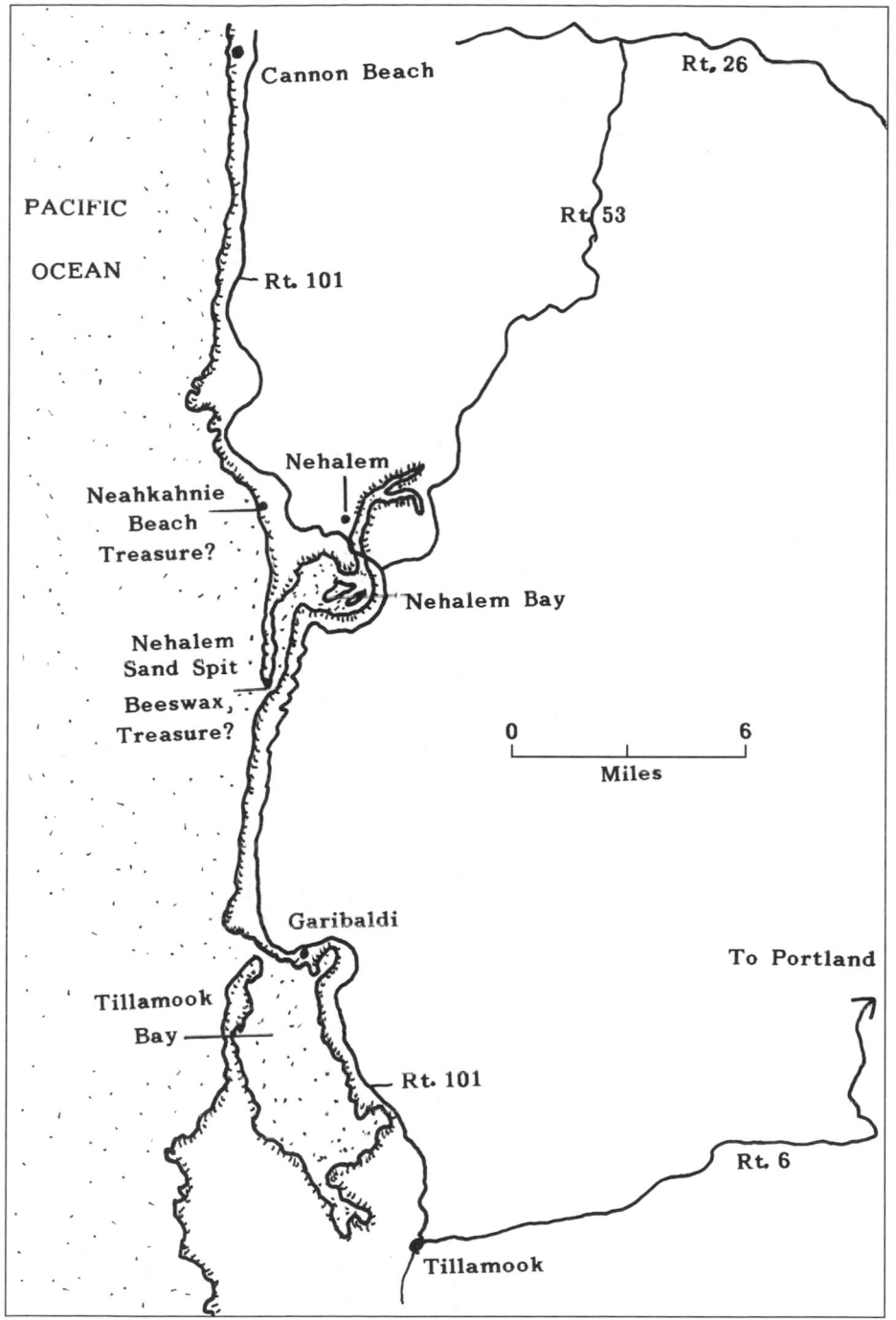

Detail of the coastline around Neahkahnie Beach. The vast amount of beeswax found at the tip of the Nehalem sand spit indicates that a shipwreck is just offshore. Did the treasure of Neahkahnie come from this doomed vessel?

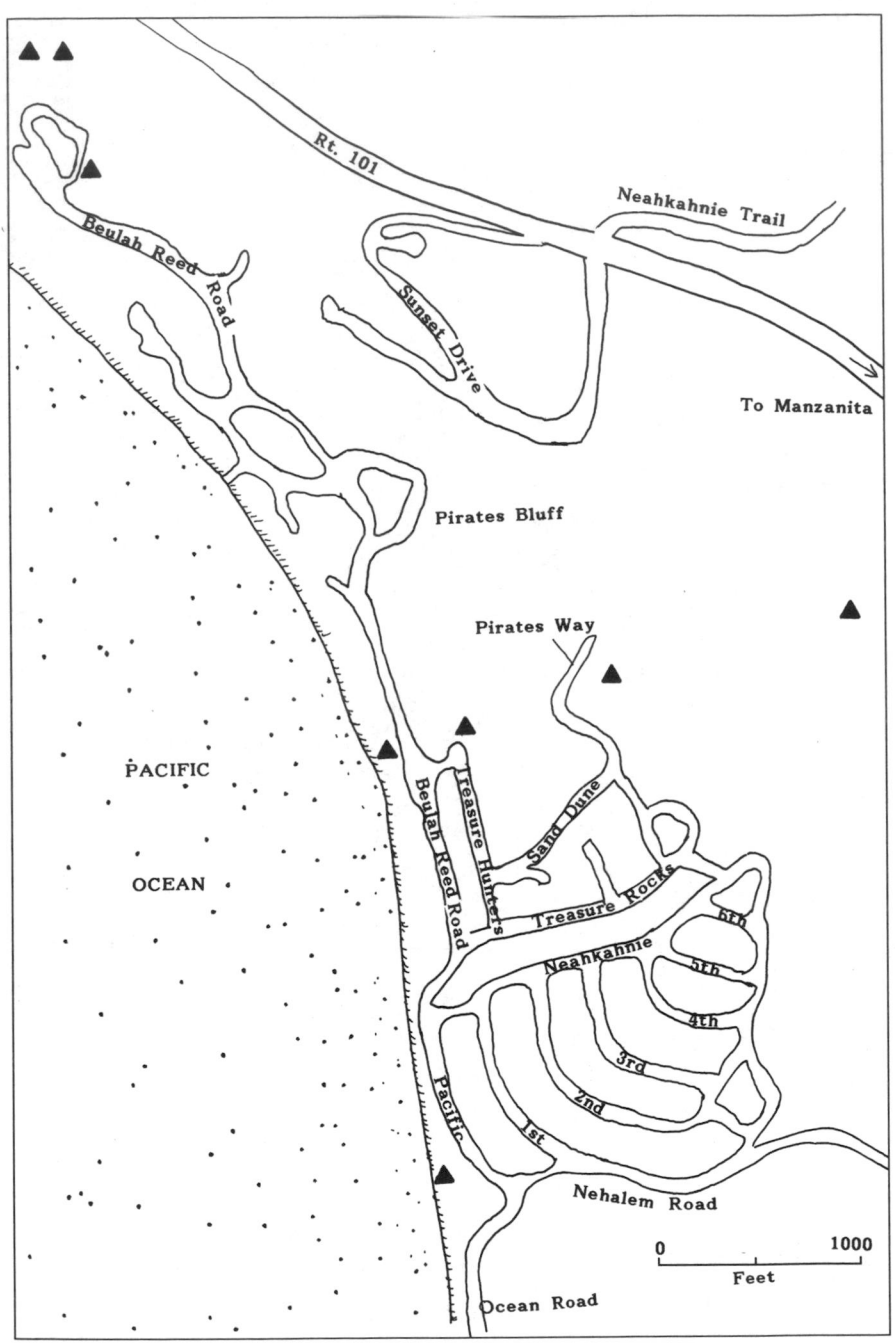

Solid triangles indicate treasure holes dug at Neahkahnie Beach and vicinity. Today, many of these holes are on private property, and some have been filled in to avoid potential injury. The treasure is probably still hidden somewhere on the hillside. (Adapted from Tales of the Neahkahnie Treasure, *Tillamook County Pioneer Museum)*

Piece of beeswax from the Philippines that washed ashore near Neahkahnie Beach, Oregon. This artifact can be seen in the Tillamook County Pioneer Museum.

deed was standard operating procedure for maritime thieves. The hope was that the dead man's ghost would guard the treasure from interlopers. Why else would the Clatsop and Tillamook add this detail to the story? Nothing in their culture comes close to this weird practice. The best bet is that the treasure is still hidden somewhere along the southern hillside slope of Neahkahnie Mountain. Forget the residential area. Unless someone long ago found the treasure and told no one—a highly unlikely possibility, considering the uniqueness and fame attached to the story—that part of the beach has been thoroughly probed. Concentrate on the base of the mountain. And be sure to contact me if you do find something.

Contact Person(s)/Organization
Tillamook County Pioneer Museum
2106 2nd Street
Tillamook, Oregon 97141
(503) 842–4553

Open Mon.–Sat., 8:30 A.M.–5:00 P.M.; Sun., Noon–5:00 P.M. Admission fee.

One of several stones found in the 1890s along the hillside of Neahkahnie Beach. The unusual carvings may be a marker leading to the buried treasure. This stone is now housed in the Tillamook County Pioneer Museum.

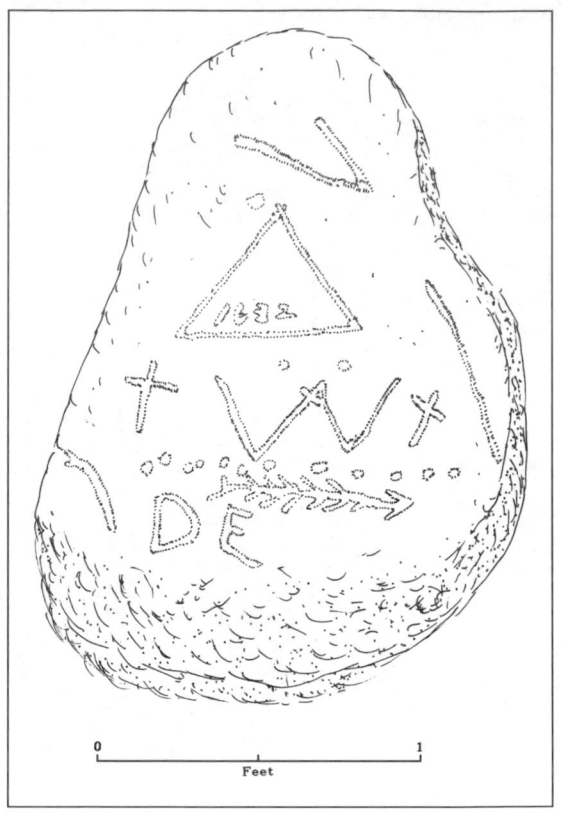

Mysterious characters carved into a 200-pound stone found in the 1890s not far from the shore at Neahkahnie Beach. The letter W with two crosses on either side, the DE, the eight dots, and the arrow are believed by some researchers to hold the key to the treasure. No one has ever successfully deciphered these strange marked rocks.

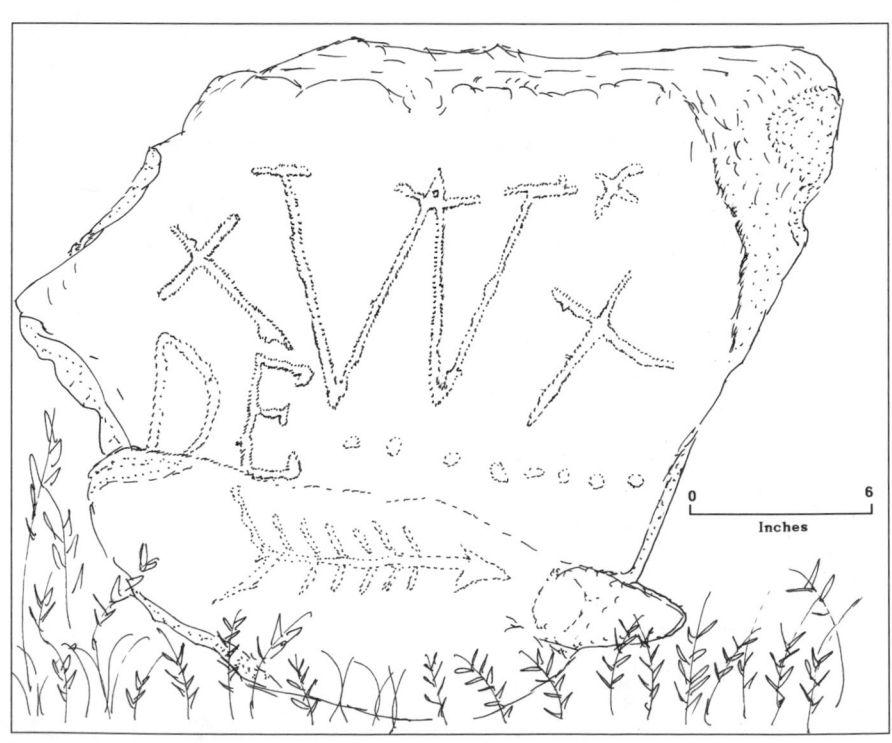

Total Magnetic Field/Inclination Angle
Nothing unusual was recorded here.

Further Investigations in Area
Take the time to visit the Tillamook County Pioneer Museum. There's a wonderful display of beeswax and other artifacts that have been found along the shoreline. This is also an introduction to the type of items that you may find on your own jaunts around the area.

The marked stones that were found at Neahkahnie Beach during the last century are the subject of a lot of controversy. The small boulders are etched with crosses, arrows, dots, and the letters *D* and *E*. Some people claim the cryptic symbols are navigation coordinates; others believe they refer to the location of the treasure. Having worked in pirate country on the Atlantic side of America, I suspect the symbols are a ruse.[3] It was not uncommon for pirates— or for that matter anyone burying valuables during the sixteenth and seventeenth centuries—to leave behind false directions to lead looters off the track. The logic was brilliant: visitors spend months or years searching in a spot with no possibility of success. Eventually everyone gives up and claims the buried treasure was a hoax or the product of overactive imaginations. As I said earlier, concentrate on the base of the mountain.

Before heading out to find the Neahkahnie treasure be sure to walk out to the sandy tip of Nehalem Bay. If you go out after a winter or springtime storm and are lucky, you may find pieces of the beeswax that lends credibility to this story. Be sure to walk around during low tide. Look for tiny chunks of a waxy, tan-brown material. Inspect the sand carefully—the locals claim that shiny things wash up as well.

OREGON CAVES NATIONAL MONUMENT
East of Cave Junction, Oregon

Site Synopsis
A cavern 3.5 miles in length sits atop a high mountain peak in southern Oregon. Many strange geological formations exist here, but so far no one has ever found evidence of ancient people visiting this site.

Location
From Grants Pass in southern Oregon take Route 199 south for 30 miles to Cave Junction. From Cave Junction take Route 46 (Oregon Caves Highway) east for 20 miles to the caves.

Oregon Caves

Considerations

The Oregon Caves Highway (Route 46) is a steep road lined with gigantic Douglas fir trees. The road is not meant for large recreational vehicles, as there are few places to turn off or around. Watch the road carefully—it's a long way down the mountainside!

As with all cave visits, remember to dress warmly, wear good shoes, and carry a *strong* flashlight with extra batteries.

The cave tours are conducted by a private concession and a fee is charged. If you have mobility, breathing, or heart problems, don't go on this tour. A lot of climbing, squatting, and shifting of the body is required.

While not as exciting as a spelunking excursion on your own, the trip up the mountain and the caves are definitely worth it. These caves contain many good features that should prep you for trips to other sites in the country.

The park is open every day of the year except December 25.

History/Background

The strange geology of caves is the focus here. Over 220 million years ago, seashells that accumulated at the bottom of the ocean that once covered this area compacted against each other, recrystallized, and turned into limestone. Over the next 70 million years, the limestone compacted further into marble. When the Siskiyou Mountains pushed up as a result of chaotic collisions of ocean and continental plates colliding and pounding against each other, the conditions were right for cave formation. Millions of years of erosion from seeping rain (which contains carbonic acid) slowly dissolved the marble. Underground streams carved out passages, some eventually 66growing as large as 240 feet long, 50 feet wide, and over 40 feet high.

During the winter of 1874 a hunter inadvertently found the cave after his dog ran down an entranceway. News of the find spread quickly and soon

Cross-section of the Oregon Caves, east of Cave Junction, Oregon

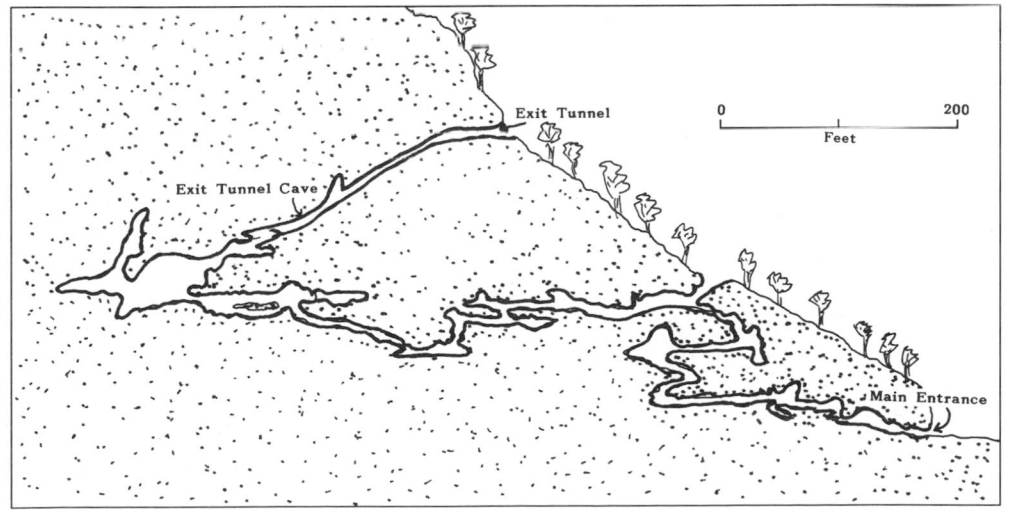

dozens of people were exploring this 3.5-mile cavern of passageways and rooms. The site was proclaimed a national monument in 1909. By the 1930s the National Park Service had taken control of the site.

This is a fascinating cave to visit. It stays a constant 41 degrees all year long, and it is wet and slippery. The tour takes almost an hour and covers a range of differing cave ecosystems. There are endless examples of spel-eotherms: stalactites and stalagmites—rock dripstones. There are also dozens of organisms that live in this dark series of passageways, including Townsend's big-eared bats and Pallid bats. In the fall it is not unusual to see swarms of these creatures entering the cave to breed.

Considering the antiquity of this cave it is a little curious that, as yet, no evidence exists of Native American visitations. These places were natural en-tranceways to the spirit world, and similar caves in other parts of the West were routinely used in vision quests. Perhaps the early restoration work on this cave site destroyed evidence. Perhaps the teams of scientists working there today will one day uncover a new passageway that will reveal more about the prehistoric inhabitants of southern Oregon.

Contact Person(s)/Organization
Superintendent
19000 Caves Highway
Cave Junction, Oregon 97523

Or, contact the concession group:

Oregon Caves Company
P.O. Box 128
Cave Junction, Oregon 97523
(541) 592–3400; Fax: (541) 592–6654

Convenient lodging is available right outside the cave.

Total Magnetic Field/Inclination Angle
Nothing unusual was detected.

Further Investigations in Area
The gold frenzy of the 1850s did not remove all of the precious metal from the mountains of southern Oregon. It is estimated that over 75 percent of the gold is still lying in mountain veins. Every winter severe storms erode part of these mountains, releasing hundreds of trapped gold nuggets and smaller flecks. If you have time, wander around the many rivers and streams,

looking behind boulders and on the sandy river bends. You may come away with the down payment for a house!

While you are looking for those sparkling, dense chunks of gold, keep your wits about you. This is perfect Bigfoot country. (See Northern California section, page 81.) If this large creature actually exists, then the mountains surrounding the Oregon Caves are a perfect habitat.

About 100 miles northeast of Grants Pass is Crater Lake National Park. This amazing lake at the top of a sleeping volcano was formed when the former Mount Mazama erupted in a savagely violent explosion that ripped off the top of the mountain. The eruption released billions of tons of ash and pumice, resulting in a six-mile-wide caldera, or bowl-shaped depression, which slowly filled with water. Today this 1,932-foot-deep blue lake is a prime tourist spot in southern Oregon. There's even a lodge perched on the edge of this location.

Among the many intriguing things associated with this spooky place is the Klamath Native American story of the formation of the lake. It reads almost like an eyewitness account of the explosion. In fact, it is so similar to the geological explanation that some scientists believe an early group of people here actually watched the explosion and lived to pass along the horrific tale through oral legends. It must have been a powerful event, for the eruption took place almost 7,000 years ago. The tale:

A long time ago, the spirits of the earth and sky often came and talked with the people. Sometimes the Chief of the Below-World came up from his home inside the earth and stood on the top of Lao-Yaina—the mountain that used to be. His head would touch the stars near the home of the Chief of the Above-World. There was no lake then, just a hole through which the Chief of the Below-World passed to the outside.

Once, when the Chief of the Below-World was on the outside, he noticed Loha, the daughter of the tribal chief. He told her of his love and promised her eternal life if she would return with him to his lodge beneath the mountain. She refused and the Chief of the Below-World became angry and raged in his Below-World home. In a voice like thunder, he swore that he would take revenge on Loha's people and destroy them with the Curse of Fire. He rushed up through the opening and thundered on top of his mountain.

The mighty Chief of the Above-World descended from the sky and stood on top of Mount Shasta. From their mountaintops, the two chiefs began a furious battle, hurling red-hot rocks at each other, making the earth tremble, causing great landslides. All the spirits of earth and sky took part, and the people were frightened.

The Chief of the Below-World spewed forth an ocean of fire from his mouth. The Curse of Fire devoured forests as it swept toward the homes of the people. They fled in terror and took refuge in the waters of Klamath Lake. Two old medicine men offered to sacrifice themselves and jump into the pit of fire at the entrance to the Below-World. Their bravery moved the Chief of the Above-World. With his ferocious power, he made the mountains shake. The Chief of the Below-World was driven back into his home and the mountaintop fell in upon him.

When the morning sun rose, the mountain that the Chief of the Below-World had called his own was gone. A great hole was in its place.

Rain fell in torrents, filling the hole with clear waters. The Curse of Fire was lifted and peace and quiet covered the earth. Never again has the voice of the Chief of the Below-World frightened the people.[4]

About 100 miles north of the Oregon Caves, along Route 138, known as the Umpqua Highway, ten miles west of Steamboat, are some good examples of vision quest stone piles. A little more than a mile up the trailhead at Susan Creek Falls are carefully laid stone piles. Many tribes in the Pacific Northwest had a tradition of sending young boys into the mountains to find their dream, or vision. They would not drink water or eat any food while they waited for the revelation. A boy would pray for several days and nights. And then, inexplicably, he would pile up a heap of stones. The explanation, as told to early researchers in the area, was to let his people know he had been there.[5]

I suspect more is at work here than one can see. Perhaps this was a place where young boys felt different, due to aberrant geomagnetic fields? This site is high on my list for a detailed set of measurements. Go find it and see if *you* have any visions!

THE HOUSE OF MYSTERY: THE OREGON VORTEX
Gold Hill, Oregon

Site Synopsis
All sorts of weird phenomena are said to take place on the side of a hill in southern Oregon. Balls roll uphill, as does water. People can't stand straight; they lean over. A person's height miraculously seems to change. All of this supposedly is due to a mysterious vortex coming from deep within the earth. Is any of this true?

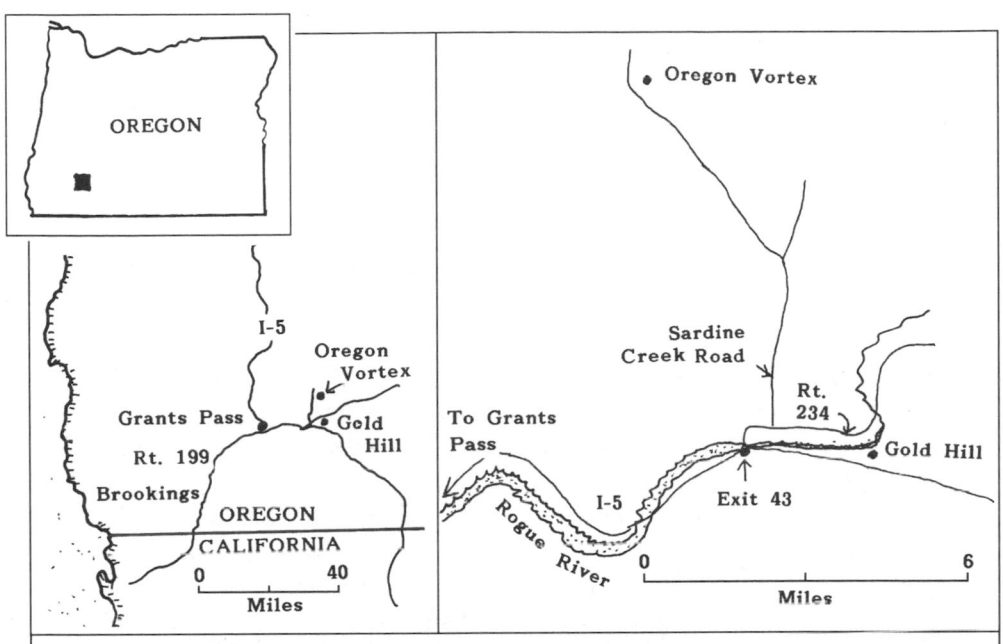

Location

From Grants Pass in southwestern Oregon take Interstate 5 east for 12 miles. Turn off at exit 43 (Gold Hill). Take Route 234 east for one mile before turning left (north) at Sardine Creek Road. Continue on this road, bearing left, for four and a half miles. The site is on your right.

Considerations

Wear a good pair of flat-soled shoes. If boat rides make you queasy, then stay out of this and other places like it (Confusion Hill, Piercy, California; the Mystery Spot, Santa Cruz, California, etc.). The weird angles and sloping floors also make some people queasy.

Apparently a running controversy preoccupies this place. The management is indignant that other sites across the country also claim to have strange things going on. As the Oregon Vortex people put it, the widespread interest in their place and the resulting publicity have caused many to imitate it. They claim that the Mystery Spot in Santa Cruz, California, discovered in 1939 (see California section, page 144), was the first rip-off of their strange site. Others around the country were quick to follow (see the table that follows). They may have a point, although I'm not so sure the Santa Cruz site is all hype. In any case, let the buyer beware.

History/Background

Scattered throughout America are patches of land where people claim gravity doesn't exist, or at least that it works differently there. Sloping shacks where water flows uphill and people are "forced" to stand at strange angles have long amused the visiting public. Most travelers are enticed by an enigmatic sign and goaded by screaming kids. They usually stop, pay a fee, and get treated to a 45- to 60-minute demonstration of events that appear to defy logic. Few have the time to question seriously the validity of what has just occurred. Most leave mildly perplexed yet thankful that their road trip was interrupted by a few hours of entertainment.

The similarities among these "mystery spots" is astonishing. It's as if someone had a quirky idea to make money and scores of people copied, cut, and transported the concept to their own locale. In fact, that's exactly what happened. A sample of these places is listed in the table that follows:

Site	Listed Phenomena	1st Noticed/ 1st Developed as a Tourist Attraction	Explanations Given by Tour Guides
House of Mystery: The Oregon Vortex 4303 Sardine Creek Rd. Gold Hill, OR 97525 (503) 855–1543	Sloping wooden shack built over spherical "vortex," measuring over 165 feet in diameter, skews gravity: optical contradictions, people lean toward vortex center.	1864/1930	Deeply buried iron ore deposit.
The Mystery Spot 1953 Branciforte Dr. Santa Cruz, CA 95063 (408) 423–8897	Sloping wooden shack built over 150 foot "circle" where gravity is defied: optical contradictions, balls roll uphill, weights swing to the southwest, compass needle anomalies, dizzy feeling outside shack.	1939/1941	Deeply buried meteorite, large iron deposit, or excess carbon dioxide gas filtering through soil.
The Wonder Spot Highway 12/Exit 92 Lake Delton, WI 53940 (608) 254–4224	Sloping wooden shack built over a spot 50 feet in diameter where gravity is defied: optical contradictions, water and balls run uphill.	1948	The laws of natural gravity seem to be repealed.
Confusion Hill: Gravity House 75001 N. 101 Hwy. Piercy, CA 95587 (707) 925–6456	Sloping wooden shack: optical contradictions, water runs uphill, weights swing to the north.	1949	Deeply buried meteorite, iron mineral deposit, or lodestone.
Mystery Shack: Calico Ghost Town 36600 Ghost Town Rd. Yermo, CA 92398 (619) 254–2122	Sloping wooden shack where gravity is defied: optical contradictions, water and balls run uphill.	1950 (developed by Knott's Berry Farm)	Optical illusions.
The Cosmos of the Blackhills 3616 W. Main St. Rapid City, SD 57702 (605) 343–7278	Sloping wooden shack where gravity is defied: optical contradictions, water and balls run uphill.	1952	Mysterious forces.
Teton Mystery South Highway 89 Jackson, WY 83001 (307) 733–3316	Sloping wooden shack where gravity is defied: optical contradictions, water and balls run uphill.	Early 1950s	Strange forces under the earth.
Mystery Hill Route 1 Blowing Rock, NC 28605 (704) 264–2792	Sloping wooden shack where gravity is defied: optical contradictions, water and balls run uphill, weights swing to the north.	Early 1950s	Unusual gravity field below shack.
Haunted Shack: Knott's Berry Farm 8039 Beach Blvd. Buena Park, CA 90620 (714) 220–5200	Sloping wooden cabin, supposedly haunted. Ghosts cause optical contradictions, water and balls run uphill.	1954 (developed by Knott's Berry Farm)	Gold miner and his wife's ghost inhabit cabin and influence local gravity.
The Mystery Spot 150 Martin Lake Rd. St. Ignace, MI 49781 (906) 643–8322	Sloping wooden shack built over a spot 300 feet in diameter where gravity is defied: optical contradictions, water and balls run uphill.	Early 1950s/ 1955 (developed by three Californians)	Deeply buried meteorite, or large iron deposit.

The bottom line on these places? Most were built to make a fast tourist buck. All except the Oregon site were "discovered" just before and after World War II, when people had a lot of time to tour the country on extended road trips. During the 1940s and 1950s places like this popped up like dozens of other roadside attractions across America. Manufactured oddities were the order of the day.

The Oregon Vortex is the granddaddy of all these houses of mystery. The story is that Native Americans knew this area as the "Forbidden Ground." The name implies the strange doings there, although if this reference is true it could as easily refer to some type of volcanic action in the region. The first white man who rode through the area in 1864 felt "peculiar." No mention was ever made by a gold-mining company that had an assay office in this particular spot. But since 1914 many local people began to notice strange optical phenomena: people near the assay shack seemed to lean in a particular direction when standing upright. In 1930 the place was opened to the public as a tourist curiosity. The assay office had crept 40 feet downhill by that time.

Soon afterward, amateur investigator John Litster and others began a series of experiments that were to keep them occupied until 1951. Litster and crew believed that the Oregon Vortex is a spherical field of force, half above ground and half below. This "circle"—the perimeter of the sphere—measures a little over 165 feet. Litster wrote a rather interesting booklet on his work where he summarized over 14,000 experiments at this peculiar place.[7] In essence, he found unusual geomagnetic fluctuations at this site. But the fluctuations all conform in a regular pattern, which appears to be spherical. That much is known.

There have been reports of small aircraft compass failures and low-frequency radio problems here.[8] The going theory points to a massive deposit of low-grade iron ore buried somewhere below the ground as the cause.

So what's the deal here? Like all "mystery houses," forget the sloping wooden shack with its angled floors, water troughs, and the like. All of that stuff is an optical illusion caused by the unusual slopes within the structure. The visual "change of height" demonstration is also so much folderol. It's a simple *illusion*, like a magician's card trick.

This is too bad, really, because Litster, who came up with these silly demonstrations, which were soon copied ad infinitum around the country, was on to something very unusual at this place. There *is* an unusual geomagnetic aberration here. But it has nothing to do with balls rolling uphill, changes in height, unusual inclines, and such. If anything, it has to do with the Native American assessment that this was "forbidden ground" and the first white man's "peculiar" feeling in the area. The so-called vortex *does* seem to be in a circle, and it is quite aberrant. Unfortunately, it is difficult for most skeptics who visit this site to come away with anything other than the feeling of being conned by silly misinformation.

At a recent visit to the Vortex site I overheard a guide totally skew Einstein's theory of relativity. The guide was trying to make a connection between light, matter, dimensional space, and the optical weirdness that she claimed we were about to witness. Most of the audience nodded their heads in feigned understanding. The confusion among the masses at a site like this is phenomenal.

"Any questions?" asked the tour guide.

Someone in the audience asked in a very serious, scholarly tone, "What happens if you take a weightless machine and put it inside the vortex? Will the vortex still affect people the same way?"

The guide responded, "Now, that's a very good question! I'm not sure, but I'll look it up right after the tour. I *just* read about those new antigravity machines, too!"

Yeow!

Contact Person(s)/Organization

The House of Mystery: The Oregon Vortex
4303 Sardine Creek Road
Gold Hill, Oregon 97525
(503) 855–1543
June–August: open 9:00 A.M. to 6:00 P.M. The last tour is at 5:15 P.M.
March–May; September–October: open 9:00 A.M. to 5:00 P.M. The last tour is at 4:14 P.M.

Total Magnetic Field/Inclination Angle

I measured some definite aberrations here that seemed to coincide with Litster's original diagram of the vortex; there was a radical change upward in milligauss as one stepped from outside the vortex to inside it. The various "terralines" (whatever those are!) that Litster mentions throughout his booklet appear to be vectors of intense geomagnetic fields. The guy was onto something amazing. Unfortunately, he reduced all of his good field work into a carnival-like setting that blended good experimental data with hocus-pocus optical illusions. His interpretation of this vortex and what it could do to people was, quite simply, incorrect. It is much more subtle—and probably more powerful.

Further Investigations in Area

Litster noted in his booklet that he had found seven vortexes, one of which was at the summit of the Siskiyou Mountains in southern Oregon. It would be extremely interesting to uncover exactly where these other places are and measure their magnetic fluctuations.[9]

EASTERN OREGON

The scorching deserts east of the Cascade Range are in sharp contrast to the rainy rugged coast to the west. Nighttime temperatures drop as the sun sets over the thin air. Horned lizards, kangaroo rats, and snakes coexist with coyotes, bighorn sheep, and Rocky Mountain elk. Hooked ear Kiger mustangs are descendants of the horses left by the Spanish conquistadors in the 1500s.

The ancient peoples who lived east of the Cascades for over 13,000 years led a nomadic existence, following game and the weather. Then in 1848 the U.S. federal government issued territorial status to the provisional government in the region. The California gold rush of 1849 jump-started the great migration into the region. By the 1870s homesteaders were claiming land in the Wallowa Mountain Valley of northeastern Oregon. The formerly easygoing Nez Percé, who had helped the Lewis and Clark expedition and assisted travelers, became angry. Their ancestral lands were in jeopardy. A bloody and violent 11-week conflict between the tribe and the United States broke out. Commanded by Chief Joseph, the Nez Percé finally surrendered on October 5, 1877. The following heartrending comments by Chief Joseph put the events into perspective:

> I am tired of fighting. Our chiefs are killed. Looking-Glass is dead. Too-hoo-hool-suit is dead. The old men are dead. It is the young men who say yes and no. He who led on the young men is dead. It is cold and we have no blankets. The little children are freezing to death. My people, some of them, have run away to the hills . . . no one knows where they are, perhaps freezing to death. I want to have time to look for my children and see how many I can find. Maybe I shall find them among the dead. Hear me, my chiefs. I am tired; my heart is sick and sad. From where the sun stands, I will fight no more.[10]

Two years later this broken warrior spoke to the bureaucrats at the Department of Indian Affairs in Washington, D.C. His words encapsulate the tragedy that befell all Native Americans when East met West:

> I have heard talk and talk, but nothing is done. Good words do not last long unless they amount to something. Words do not pay for my dead people. They do not pay for my country, now overrun by white

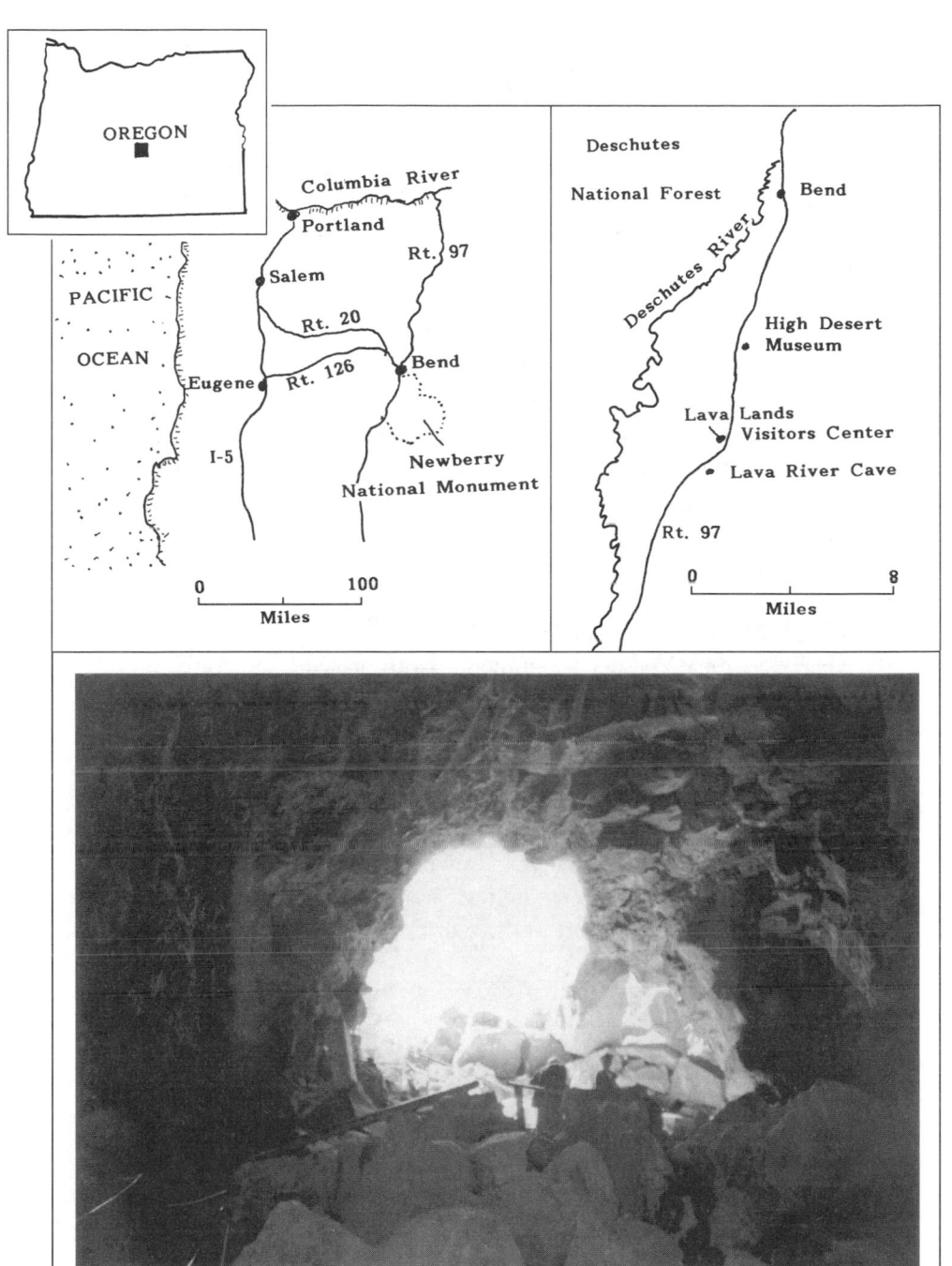

men. They do not protect my father's grave. They do not pay for all my horses and cattle. Good words will not give me back my children. . . . Good words will not give my people good health and stop them from dying. Good words will not get my people a home where they can live in peace and take care of themselves. I am tired of talk that comes to nothing. It makes my heart sick wen I remember all the good words and all the broken promises. . . . Too many misrepresentations have been made, too many misunderstandings have come up between the white men and the Indians. If the white man wants to live in peace with the Indian he can live in peace. There need be no trouble. Treat all men alike. Give them the same law. Give them all an even chance to live and grow. All men were made by the same Great one mother, with one sky above us and one country around us and one government for all. . . . For this time the Indian race are waiting and praying.[11]

Unfortunately, most Native Americans are still waiting and praying.

LAVA TUBE: THE LAVA RIVER CAVE
Newberry National Volcanic Monument, south of Bend, Oregon

Site Synopsis
Large areas of central Oregon are covered by lava flows. Thousands of years ago when the lava cooled, tunnels were formed. No one really knows how many exist beneath the surface of this volcanic area, because their roofs have not collapsed. Mysterious gusts of wind blowing through the snow on Mount Bachelor and elsewhere suggest the region is networked with these tunnels. A good example of one of these undiscovered passageways is the Lava River Cave.

Location
From Bend take Route 97 south for about 12 miles. Exit left (east) into the site.

Considerations
As this site is operated by a tourist concession there is an admission fee. Pay up—this place is definitely worth it!

A constant 40-degree underground temperature means you will need warm clothing, regardless of how hot it is outside. To see in the dim light, either bring along several flashlights (with *new* batteries) or rent a lantern from the main office. At over a mile in length this tunnel takes some time to walk

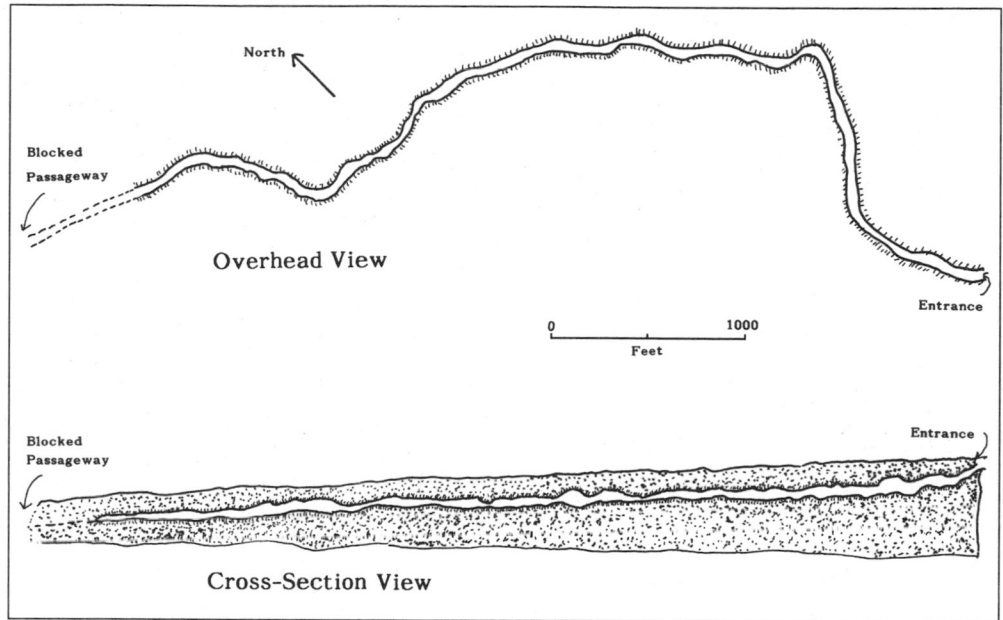

Two views of the Lava River Cave, Newberry National Volcanic Monument, south of Bend, Oregon. The tunnel meanders for a little over a mile before an impasse of sand blocks further travel. (Adapted from Lava River Cave)

through, so wear flat-heeled, comfortable shoes. The ground surface is uneven, so be careful not to twist an ankle.

As in all protected areas, only take photos. Leave all archaeological or geological artifacts, insects, and animals in place. Take out what you bring in. I also recommend that you use the outhouse before heading down into the cave. You've got a hell of a walk ahead of you and there is no place to relieve yourself. Besides, people might be walking by!

History/Background

Central Oregon hides its chaotic origin very well. That is, until one begins to look around closely at the hidden landscape. Beautiful, symmetrical snow-capped mountains in reality are restless volcanoes getting ready to explode. All the soil here is the product of lava flows. A way to better understand this is to trek through lava tubes, the long tunnels formed when hot lava cascades down a slope. The outer portions of the lava stream cools and solidifies rather quickly, while the center continues flowing. Eventually, when the lava stops oozing, a tube remains in its place. While not uncommon around volcanic areas, the tubes are weirdly fascinating places to visit. They put you right in the heart of the volcanic building process. This is frightening territory.

The Lava River Cave (it was once incorrectly thought that a river flowed through this cave, hence the name) was among the first lava tubes to be discovered by white settlers just in from their trek from the East to the good life of Oregon. Over the years the cave was used by settlers as a natural refrigerator for game meat. Many years and several land swap transactions later, the National Forest System oversees the cave.

The main tube of this tunnel is the longest known in the state. It slopes downhill in a northwesterly direction for 5,400 feet. A southeastern extension of the tunnel runs on for 1,560 feet but is closed to the public due to the usual loose rocks associated with caves. It would be a thrill to obtain permission to thoroughly examine this tunnel. The fact that obsidian arrowheads were found near the entranceway to this site suggests that many more ancient items may be within this strange place.

Near the end of the longer tunnel is a large cluster of sand. The tunnel is thought to continue onward, though no one knows how far. Spend time walking through this site. In the hour or two that it takes to go through this tunnel you will be amazed and perhaps frightened at the thought of molten rock coursing through this strange conduit.

Contact Person(s)/Organization
Lava Lands Visitors Center
58201 South Highway 97
Bend, Oregon 97707
(503) 593–2421
The center is 11 miles south of Bend. The cave is open from mid-May to mid-September.

Total Magnetic Field/Inclination Angle
Nothing unusual was detected here.

Further Investigations in Area
Fifty miles south of the Newberry National Monument on Route 97, turn off on Route 31 for Fort Rock Cave, Fort Rock. This ring of hardened volcanic ash formed near the end of the last Ice Age when the region was a vast 40-mile-long lake and a series of rapid eruptions hurled large masses of hot debris into the air. Ancient hunters lived in the caves and cliffs of Fort Rock and other nearby caves. A few years ago in one of these caves sagebrush sandals were found that were carbon-dated to be over 10,000 years old. The early inhabitants of the region moved on as the climate became hotter and the lake dried up. Walk up to the top of Fort Rock and imagine a blue body of

water covering the flatlands in front of you. The mystery here is in the astonishing climate change that has removed all obvious traces of a people who lived, laughed, and loved on the very spot where you are standing.

ANCIENT LIFE
John Day Fossil Beds National Monument, East-Central Oregon

Site Synopsis
In a bleak and somewhat barren part of Oregon are the remnants of ancient life. A close look along meandering trails reveals an abundance of fossil life-forms, some that became extinct and others that developed into creatures we know today. This is a powerful place to witness the interplay between life on earth and a fickle climate.

Location
The John Day Fossil Beds National Monument is divided up into three different locations, or units, as they are called. The most convenient are the Sheep Rock Unit, west of Dayville, and the Painted Hills Unit, west of Mitchell. The third site is the Clarno Unit. Each unit shows a different aspect of evolution.

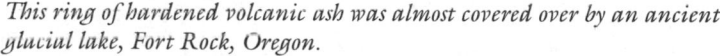

This ring of hardened volcanic ash was almost covered over by an ancient glacial lake, Fort Rock, Oregon.

Research assistant Hayden Hirschfeld stands near the wave-cut base of Fort Rock in Oregon. The ash rock eroded as the glacial lake washed against it.

SHEEP ROCK UNIT

From Bend in central Oregon take Route 97 north to Redmond. Continue on Route 126 for 19 miles to Prineville. Take Route 26 north for almost 80 miles. Turn left (north) on Route 19 and you are there.

PAINTED HILLS UNIT

From Bend in central Oregon take Route 97 north to Redmond. Continue on Route 126 for 19 miles to Prineville. Take Route 26 north for

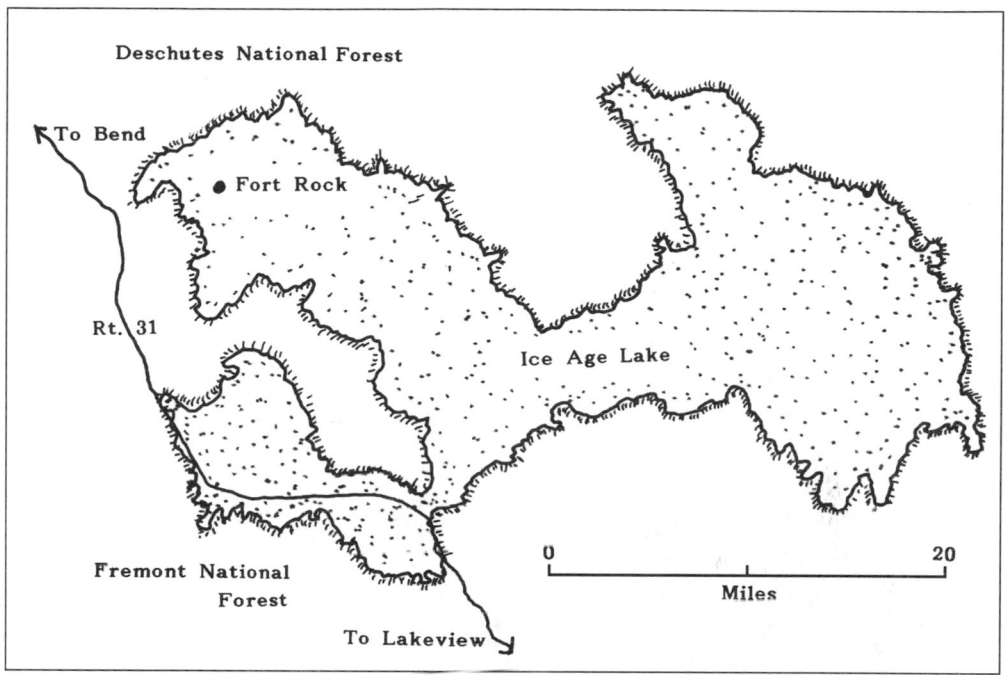

Estimated range of the former Ice Age Fort Rock Lake, circa 11,000 years ago.
The area is now a high plains desert.

43 miles. Just before reaching the lovely town of Mitchell watch for the turnoff sign to the Painted Hills Unit. Turn left (north) on Bridge Creek Road. The monument is a few miles up this road.

CLARNO UNIT

Just west of Mitchell take Route 207 north. In about 20 miles the road will change names on its way to the town of Fossil. At Fossil follow Route 218 west for a little more than 10 miles. The Clarno Unit is north of the road (on your right).

Considerations

The Cant Ranch Visitors Center, headquarters for the National Park Service monument, is located at the Sheep Rock Unit. Start your trip here and spend a few hours at this well-designed center. It's open daily from March through October; from November through February it's closed on weekends and during holidays, but the trails remain open. There are no campgrounds within the monument, but several exist nearby.

Self-guided tour plaques grace a few of the trails throughout the monu-

ment. The trails are open all year. During the summer months bring along plenty of water for your hikes. Comfortable shoes are essential.

This is prime rattlesnake country, so watch carefully for them. Never stick your hands into cracks and crevices. If you see or hear one give it plenty of room to slither away. And finally, leave all fossils in place. Take nothing but photographs!

History/Background

The John Day River Basin contains a *45-million-year* record of ancient plants and animals. Fossil bed sites that are just 5 million years old are rare.

Finding one that is nine times older is amazing. This location in east-central Oregon shows a continuity of life that is, simply put, astonishing. Anyone doubting the science of change through time (evolution) should spend a few days here. It is an overwhelming introduction to extinct habitats and the geological processes that shaped them.

In the 1860s frontier minister and self-taught geologist Thomas Condon first recognized the value of the John Day Basin. He wrote to several prominent East Coast scientists about the abundance of ancient life in the region. Fossil samples sent to Yale, Princeton, and the Smithsonian Institute were eagerly examined by desk-bound paleontologists. Eventually, in 1899, field scientist John C. Merriam began on-site research of the John Day Basin. The work continues to this day.

The entire basin has been likened to an animal and plant Pompeii. Forty-five million years ago this area was a tropical coastal plain. Strange animals like tiny horses, dogs that looked like bears, and saber-toothed tigers roamed the early forest. When the Pacific Oceanic plate pushed against the massive North American continental plate, volcanoes began spewing forth their destructive agents. Ash and mud flows covered up entire life-forms and their habitat. After a period of calm, life returned, only to be buried again and again by clouds of ash from the eruptions far to the west. This cycle continued for millions of years, trapping, as if in a geological time capsule, the evidence of past existence. Eventually the John Day River eroded through the ash, revealing a staggering number of extinct fossils nicely laid down in easy-to-read rock sequences.

More than anything else, these sites put into perspective the changing nature of life on earth. Every major climatological change brought into being newly adapted life-forms. Or, in the terms of population genetics, the tremendous amount of variation in life-forms in each ecosystem allowed those plants and animals that had the ability to survive the resulting ecological chaos to do so. The survivors passed on their genes until the next devastating change. Some species made it through a few million years; others were wiped out of existence. Why? Probably a combination of adaptable traits (genes) and luck. It is not possible to wander through these trails and not think of the human race. Will we be as fortunate as some of the organisms that survived unthinkable volcanic destruction? Or will human skeletons be enmeshed in some rock matrix 45 million years from now as alien forms of intelligence muse about those weird-looking twentieth-century creatures?

To fully understand this site and to begin to comprehend the enormous amount of time represented here, you must intimately experience the trails leading to the fossil beds. Go slowly and savor the moment. Look carefully at all: a simple "rock" may very well be the skull of an early mammal!

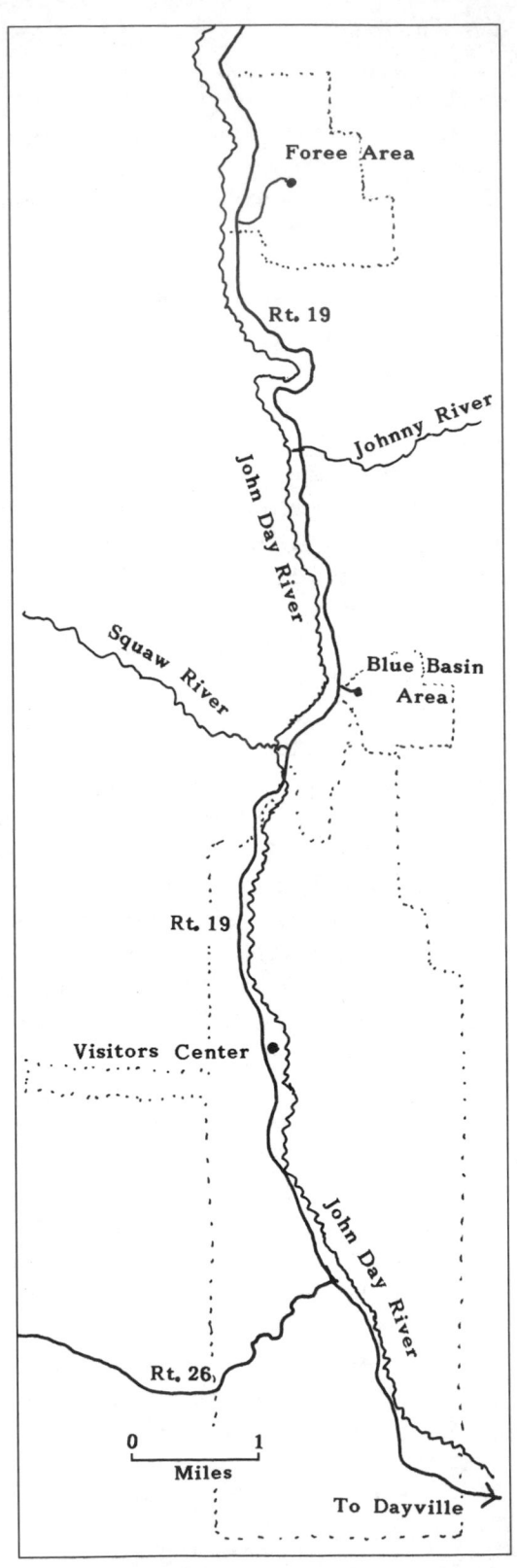

Detail of the Sheep Rock Unit, John Day Fossil Beds National Monument, west of Dayville, Oregon

Foree Area

Rt. 19

Johnny River

John Day River

Squaw River

Blue Basin Area

Rt. 19

Visitors Center

John Day River

Rt. 26

0   1
Miles

To Dayville

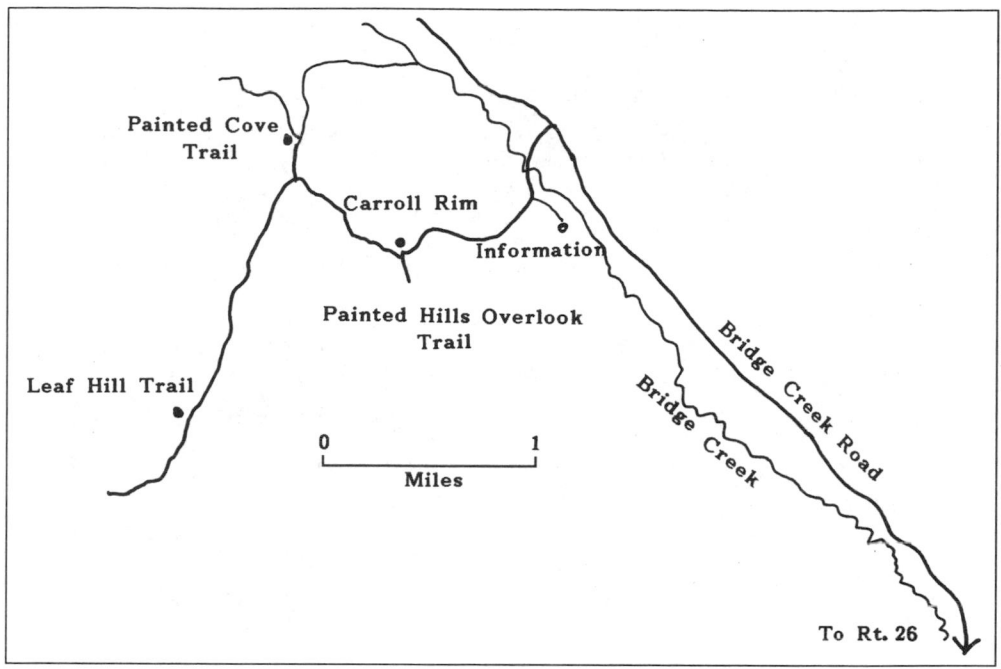

Detail of the Painted Hills Unit, John Day Fossil Beds National Monument, northwest of Mitchell, Oregon

SHEEP ROCK UNIT

This section of the monument has a visitors center that's well worth it. Excellent exhibits, an introductory film, and a fossil laboratory allow the novice to understand why paleontologists get excited here.

Several trails north of the visitors center offer a chance to wander back 25 to 30 million years through blue-green volcanic ash now hardened into a clay-like stone. As you walk farther into the basin, extensive erosion of the clay-stone has exposed thousands of backboned fossils.

PAINTED HILLS UNIT

Hiking the trails throughout this area leads to spectacular views of color. Over millions of years different-colored ash buried the land, hardened, and covered it again. The resulting vivid red, yellow, gold, brown, and black hues allow you to see and understand the action of those long-ago eruptions.

The most intriguing part of this section is Leaf Hill. Almost 34 million years ago a hardwood forest was buried. Over the ensuing millions of years more plant leaves were covered over and preserved. Today a small hill is covered with the debris of these millions of years: fossil acorns, birch leaves,

Thirty-million-year-old fossils are scattered throughout the claystone of the Blue Basin area of the Sheep Rock Unit, John Day Fossil Beds National Monument, west of Dayville, Oregon.

sycamore, elm, and maple abound. Their delicate impressions cover thousands of rock slabs making up this hill. It is illegal to collect fossil leaf impressions at this site, but if you really want a sample, drive 45 miles north to the town of Fossil. On a shale hill behind the high school you'll find more than enough samples. As of this writing, surface collecting is not restricted here.

CLARNO UNIT

This area of the monument is noted for the fossil fruits, nuts, and seeds that were deposited over a period of 40 million years. This is one of the few places in the world where the *complete* plant—stems, leaves, seeds, nuts—is all in one place. Mud flows during these 40 million years covered over successive subtropical forests. Scientists love this place. They can detail the rate of evolutionary change involved with life by systematically dating rocks and forms of plant life associated with that time period. This is one of the few places in the world where such activity is possible.

Contact Person(s)/Organization
Cant Ranch House Visitors Center
John Day Fossil Beds National Monument/Sheep Rock Unit

Reputed circle of stones in a field outside of Pendleton, Oregon

Rt. 19, west of Dayville, Oregon
(503) 987-2333

Superintendent
John Day Fossil Beds National Monument
420 West Main Street
John Day, Oregon 97845
(503) 575-0271

Total Magnetic Field/Inclination Angle
Nothing unusual was recorded here.

Further Investigations in Area
Between Dayville on Route 26 and Sheep Rock there's a gorge cut through over 1,500 feet of lava. Known as Picture Gorge, the cut has several ancient paintings along the walls. Researchers believe these indecipherable symbols may be close to 1,000 years old. Look along the west side of the gorge close to the roadside stone marked 125.

After traveling through the vast desert country in this part of Oregon, south of Burns along Route 395 you'll pass Lake Abert and Abert Rim. Along the western flank of this rock wall are dozens of mysterious petroglyphs.

About 150 miles north of the Sheep Rock Unit (take Route 26 for 32 miles to Mount Vernon; continue north on Route 395), just outside the city of Pendleton, a large stone circle has been reported. The reports are sketchy, but the ring of stone may be a sacred site. It's supposedly in a country field leading out to either the town of Adams (Route 11 north) or Mission. If it is the latter, then it may have something to do with the Umatilla Indians, who have a large reservation out in that direction. Let me know if you find it!

FOUR

California

A t the end of the Ice Age some 15,000 years ago, California was a much different place than it is today. As vast chunks of ice slowly melted, enormous quantities of water filled valleys and ground depressions. For a while, these areas became massive freshwater lakes where Paleo-Indians followed herds of animals to the surrounding shores. Eventually, due to evaporation and water seepage, the lakes dried up, leaving a residue of dusty gypsum in their place.

For centuries the more than 200,000 inhabitants of the Pacific Coast cruised along in a climate that gave them over 3,000 hours of sunshine per year. The living here was easy. Thirty percent of these people living along the coast harvested the abundant sea life. The multitude of cultures found by Spanish conquistadors were hunter-gatherers: days were spent harpooning whales, trapping mountain animals, and gathering grains. Perhaps because of the vast amount of food readily available, California's Native Americans rarely grew their own foods like their brothers in the American Southwest.

The diversity of people in this pre-European environment is demonstrated by their mutually unintelligible languages. Linguists estimate that over 20 language groups—spoken by some 500 separate tribes—existed, and from these over 130 dialects developed. This could have happened only if these groups were isolated for generations. The barriers probably were not physical, such as the mountains or deserts of California, because archaeologists have found trade goods identified with local tribes all over the state. The barriers could have been social—the various tribes apparently kept apart and liked it. No one group dominated the other. While there were indeed battles and hostilities,

Mysterious sites in California

perhaps because of revenge, the general picture painted by modern archaeologists is that peace and tranquillity seemed the order the day.

California began as a dream. It came out of the charming mind of the sixteenth-century Spanish novelist Garci Ordonez de Montalvo. In 1510, Montalvo's romantic novel, *Las Sergias de Esplandian*, was published in Seville. At this time no one in Europe had any idea of what lay beyond the eastern coast of the New World. And yet, Montalvo wrote of a "Mediterranean-like" island in the "West Indies" peopled by black Amazons and ruled by a Queen Calafia. The land was filled with griffins—strange half-lion, half-eagle creatures—and precious jewels and metals of all types. Soldiers read and dreamed about this imaginary place. It probably inspired many to make the month-long sea voyage across the Atlantic to the New World. It definitely was read and remembered by Hernando Cortez, the Spanish explorer and conqueror of the Aztec Empire. For more than 25 years after the novel was published, Cortez explored the land that lay west of Mexico across a sea. He named it California, or the island of Califia. Across the Sea of Cortez (the Gulf of California) Cortez found the peninsula of Baja California in northwest Mexico.

Cortez's misperception of California as an island is easy to understand. Sailing north from the west coast of Mexico, he saw the southern end of the big Baja landform where water exists to the east and west. To conquistadors, flush with the treasures of the Aztecs, this "island" inhabited by gold-dust–covered female warriors must have set many loins afire! As the Spanish continued up the shore of this unknown coast, the entire region became known as California.

California history actually begins in 1542, when the Portuguese navigator Juan Rodriguez Cabrillo, sailing for Spain, tacked north from Mexico to cruise around Monterey. By 1579, the British had sent Sir Francis Drake to explore the same shores. Not much happened for the next 200 years. By the late 1760s Spain had decided to fortify its California real estate. Over the next 50 years Franciscan Padres Junipero Serra and Fermin Francisco de Lasuen built 21 Catholic missionaries and military installations along the coast. Meanwhile, the Russians were in Northern California trading in sea otter fur while the British reappeared in the Pacific Northwest. To further complicate matters, New England sea captains were steering their vessels to these waters in search of California's gray whales.

In 1846, American settlers, increasingly a trading force in California, claimed San Francisco and Monterey for the United States. Mexico did little to resist. And then it happened. On January 28, 1848, gold was found at the

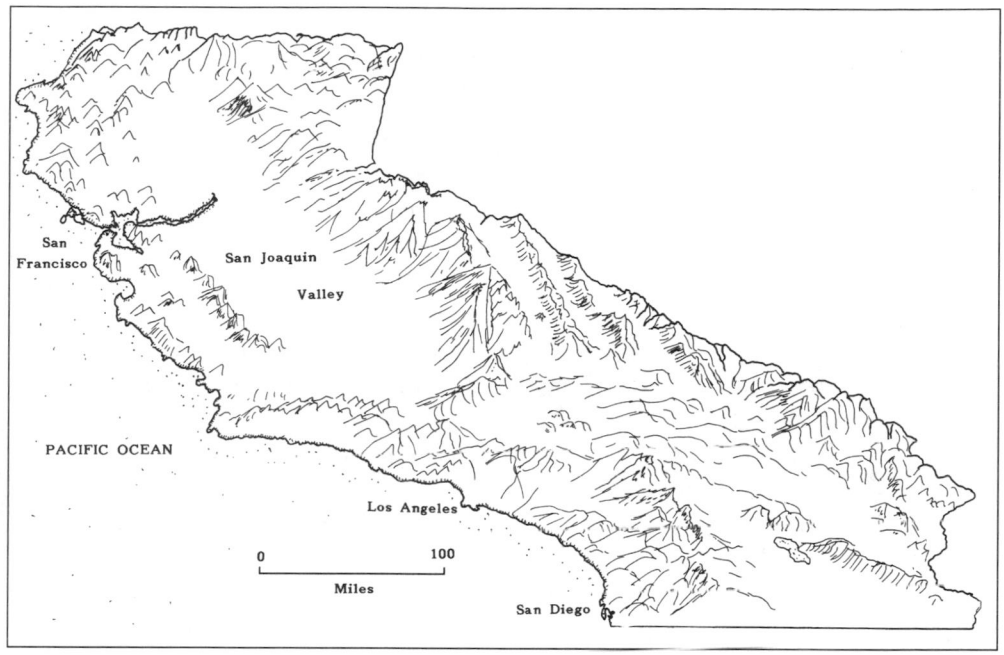

Major landforms of California

base of the Sierra Nevada east of San Francisco. The ensuing gold rush and the developing philosophy of Manifest Destiny brought over 100,000 people into the region. The race to experience the California dream continued up until very recently.

My two-part division of the state includes areas that are not generally thought of as Southern California. Liberties were taken. This was done primarily out of convenience for the explorer of mysterious places.

NORTHERN CALIFORNIA

The northern part of California is a rugged land defined by towering redwoods, volcanic peaks, and warped granite ranges. The Klamath Mountains dominate much of the state's northwestern fringe. South of here and west of the central valley are the coastal ranges that lead into the San Francisco Bay region.

Northern California is where the water is. Moist Pacific Ocean air settles onto the frigid 10,000–14,000-foot peaks and turns to snow. The springtime runoff provides abundant water for this part of the state, an area that has the fewest amount of people. For most of the twentieth century, engineers have faced the daunting task of moving water from the overflowing north to the parched south, where millions of people inhabit a desert terrain.

The northern terrain never had a large population. While blessed with water, food resources, and such, the land is difficult to negotiate. It always has been, even for the early Native Americans, whose population here was never large. Ravines, valleys, limited trailways, and brutal winters allow splendid isolation for the few that live here year-round. Today, the region is used more on a seasonal basis, leaving the difficult weather months to the hardy or to those who want to vanish.

For years strange things were seen throughout Northern California. The east-central region, home to vast tracts of lava, are filled with the mysterious paintings of the ancients. Large tunnel tubes snake through the bedrock, remnants of a once-violent past that could easily happen again. Mount Shasta, a dormant volcano, has evoked legends of weird creatures for centuries. And then there are the stories of gigantic, two-legged beasts.

When miners first ventured into the Klamaths natives told stories of a strange hairy man who lived in the forest. He was known as Crazy Bear (or Sasquatch in British Columbia; Masau-u in Arizona), and tribes inhabiting this productive region often refused to venture far into the mountains where

A common house among the High Sierra California tribes at the time of European contact (DeNadaillac, Prehistoric America)

the best game could be found, preferring instead to spear salmon in foothill streams. According to sources at the time, the natives spoke fearfully of this creature, not reverently, as more often happens in Indian myth. They loathed the beast and it was to be avoided. This is strange, because other potent and dangerous animals, like the rattlesnake, mountain lion, and grizzly bear, for example, became powerful totems. But not Crazy Bear.

Gold miners laughed at such talk, but not for long. As men plunged ever deeper into the northern mountains in search of gold, mid-nineteenth-century records quickly filled up with nervous images of large, hairy creatures who left astonishingly big footprints in the moist dirt. Back in Sacramento and San Francisco, city people chuckled at such talk. Many thought the miners had banged their heads once too often. And thus began the legend of Bigfoot. But *was* it just a tall tale?

BIGFOOT SIGHTINGS
Northwestern California

Site Synopsis
Could a gigantic creature be lurking in the dense forest of the Pacific Northwest? Ancient Indian legends and recent scientific analysis says: Yes!

Location
From Eureka take Route 299 east. The mountain road twists and winds its way toward Willow Creek after some 35 miles. Throughout the years along Route 96 (and in the forest west and east of the highway) north through Hoopa, Weitchpec, Bluff Creek, Orleans, and Happy Camp, an astonishing number of Bigfoot sightings have been made. Hundreds of large footprints have also been found in this region.

Considerations
Newer residents of this part of the state make light of the many sightings. While they tell you in a serious tone, "Yeah, it's a damn big thing up in the woods," they usually wink when they're done. Most of these people who have moved here from somewhere else also own most of the trendy businesses: the galleries, boutiques, bagel/coffee shops. They use the Bigfoot stories to entice more tourists into the area. More people means more money. So everyone's happy, right? Not quite. Old-time residents aren't comfortable with all the change that increasing population density brings. They also know more about these woods than the newer residents care to know.

Before trekking off to Bigfoot Country, I stayed in a little motor court on the coast just north of Eureka. I asked the Bombay-born manager if he ever saw Bigfoot.

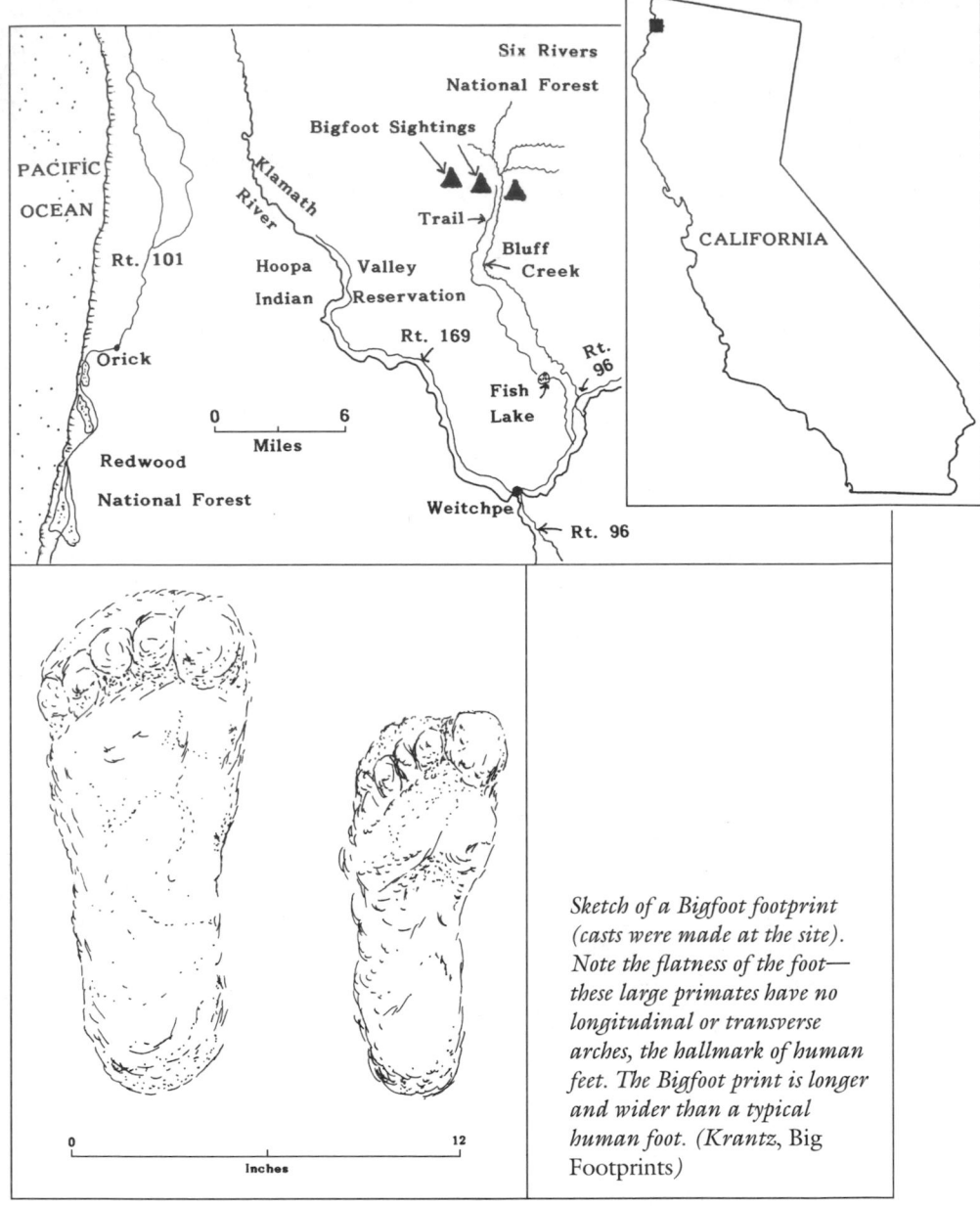

Sketch of a Bigfoot footprint (casts were made at the site). Note the flatness of the foot—these large primates have no longitudinal or transverse arches, the hallmark of human feet. The Bigfoot print is longer and wider than a typical human foot. (Krantz, Big Footprints)

"Oh, no. I have not. But many people say they have."

"Have you ever camped out near the Klamath River?" I asked.

"Good heavens, no. It is dangerous to do so."

I asked a bookstore owner in Eureka what she thought of the Bigfoot legends. She rambled on for a few minutes about alien abductions, genetic experiments, and large, upright hominids stalking the mountains. "Uhhh, thanks," I said.

Forget about interviewing anyone here. Your informant will either laugh (at or with you!) or tell you what you want to hear. Get out to the woods and look for yourself. See the difficult terrain and local conditions before you quickly brand the whole thing a joke. This is rough countryside. It would be easy to disappear out here. The trails are few and access to the deep interior can only be done on foot. If you knew the terrain and chose to, it would be very easy to escape detection.

The longer you spend in this beautiful yet terrifying land of mountain streams, dense forest, and disorienting coastal fog, the closer to reality this Bigfoot story becomes. It becomes less a legend and more a real creature that seemingly has inhabited a very specific ecosystem for a staggering amount of time.

History/Background

The problem with tales of unknown creatures inhabiting a known area is that they sound like typical "fish stories": "I nabbed the biggest salmon ever—almost four hundred pounds—but it got away." A slim possibility that it's true, but more likely it's an exaggeration. You had to be there to really know. Same thing goes with the Bigfoot legend. Some say it's true; others say it's a concocted story, the product of overactive imaginations and a modern desire for the mystery and intrigue of unsettled, unspoiled California. Maybe.

About seven miles north of Willow Creek is Hoopa Valley, the current and ancestral home of the Native American Hupa. The Hupa people have lived in northwestern California for over 10,000 years, as carbon-dating of fire pits in their ancient villages testify. Some of the sites, including sacred ones that go by the names of Tsemeta and Tselundin, are still maintained and used to this day.

More than any other tribe in America, the Hupa have had to share their space with this legendary creature. And it's been difficult. Local lore tells of a huge manlike creature that lived along the Klamath River. Some in the valley believe Bigfoot is a real, flesh-and blood creature that roams the enchanted hills. Others are not so sure. But one thing is certain—the creature, be it real or mythical, is given wide berth. There is a certain nervousness about coming into contact with this entity. There's also a reluctance to say *anything* about it to non-Indians. It's almost as if the real stories about Bigfoot are not to be shared with the general public.

Many cultures of the Pacific Northwest speak of the dangers and rewards of the forest. Two tribes in the region knew a dangerous spirit who stalked their deep woods. Called Bukwus by the Kwakiutl people and Pu'gwis by the Tsimshian, the names mean the "Wild Man of the Woods." Intriguingly, the female counterpart, the Wild Woman of the Woods, was known to the Kwakiutl and the Bella Coola people as Tsonoqua.[1] While these mythical creatures were imbued with a variety of human images and features, enticing details in the stories may refer to Bigfoot.

Despite industrial logging, large sections of northwestern California are still densely covered with giant redwoods. This may be the lair of Bigfoot—when loggers go into such areas they inevitably spot footprints or creatures. (David Brown, Science for All)

An 1840 diary of a Spokane, Washington, missionary mentions a native story about a foul-smelling race of giants who lived to the west.[2] The coastal Salish people spoke of See'atco, which means "One Who Runs and Hides."[3] The Oregon Cascades were home to a large forest monster called Wampus. The Chinookans knew this creature as At'at'ahila, while the Yakima called it Qah-lin-me.[4] The point is that all of the Pacific Northwest Indians before white settlement had an active, fearful tradition of a Bigfoot type of creature.

An early account of this legend comes from Paul Kane, an artist-explorer who in 1847 wrote in his journal:

> When we arrived at the mouth of the Kattlepoutal River twenty-six miles from Fort Vancouver [today known as the city of Vancouver in southern Washington State], I stopped to make a sketch of the volcano, Mount St. Helen's, distant, I suppose, about thirty or forty miles. This mountain has never been visited by either whites or Indians, the latter assert that it is inhabited by a race of beings of a different species . . . and whom they hold in great dread. These superstitions are taken from a statement of a man who, they say, went to the mountain with another and escaped the fate of his companion, who was eaten by the Skookums or evil genie. I offered a considerable bribe to any other Indian who would accompany me in its exploration, but could not find one.5

According to longtime Bigfoot researcher John Green, who has compiled some of the most extensive material on the legend, for over 50 years Mount St. Helens was noted not for its active volcanic status, but for its population of apes![6] Green cites a mid-nineteenth-century story, as told by an early pioneer:

> Grandpa . . . firmly believed the story of the huge apes near St. Helen's Mountain. He went there to hunt once and one of these apemen beckoned to him. He just turned until he reached home.[7]

If ever there were a population of "apemen" living along the slopes of Mount St. Helens, as of May 18, 1980, when half the mountain blew up, they are now buried under billions of tons of mud and debris. But some may have escaped this fiery death.

Back in 1967 the most famous of the Bigfoot stories surfaced. Depending on which "expert" you believe, the only known film/photograph of a Bigfoot is either real or an elaborate hoax. In late October 1967, Roger Patterson and his partner, Robert Gimlin, were riding horseback along the banks of Bluff Creek. Bluff Creek, which feeds into the Klamath River in northwestern California, is about six miles north of Weitchpec along Route 396. The two

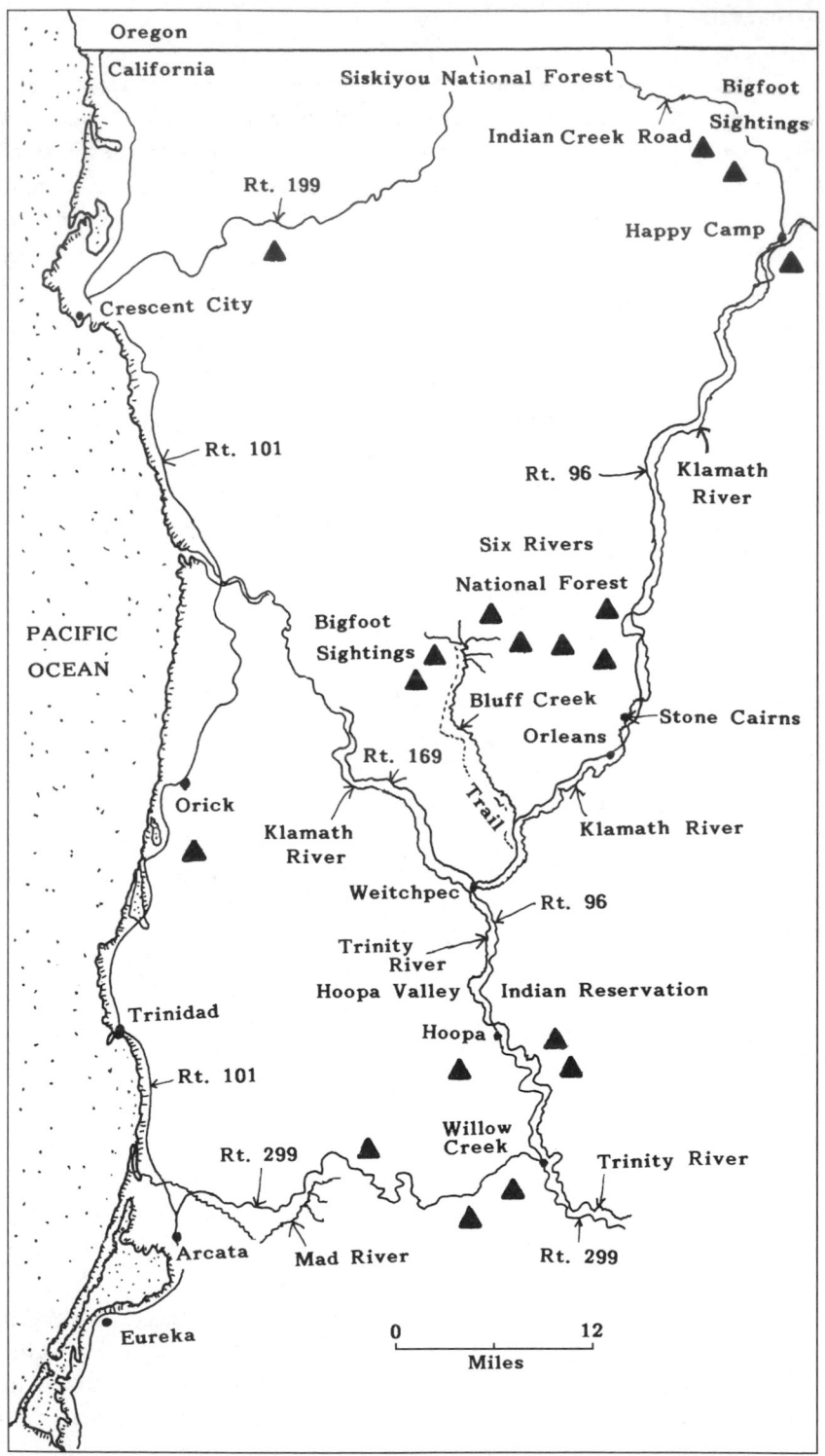

A sampling of Bigfoot sightings along the coastal region of northwestern California

men, who are from Yakima, Washington, went into the woods in search of Bigfoot. Patterson, already an author on the legendary creature, wanted to make a documentary film about his adventures in the wild. A few days into the trip he got his wish. In a clearing about eight yards from the men a large, black-haired thing came ambling out of the woods. Patterson fell off his horse, yanked his 16mm movie camera out of the saddle bag, and got 53 seconds of film that have been scrutinized almost as much as the infamous Zapruder film of President John Kennedy being assassinated that sad day in Dallas.

Several feet of the Patterson film show the disconcerting effects of running and shooting, as he ran toward the quickly departing creature. Eventually Patterson kneeled down to shoot as the elusive creature turned toward the camera and strode into the woods.

Not surprisingly, when the intrepid explorers got back to civilization, most scientists laughed at the film of the "man in the gorilla suit." The scientific community as a whole brushed off the entire episode as a publicity stunt. Bob Timus, a former hunter and tracker, was not so sure. He made his way to the site some nine days after Patterson shot the film and tracked very large footprints well into the woods, making casts of each and meticulously plotting their position on a site map. Timus found that the creature walked up to a

Over the years dozens of Bigfoot sightings have been made along the sandbars of the Klamath River in northwestern California.

ridge and, based on the orientation of the footprints, sat down on a large stone. From the boulder Timus could see the site of the initial confrontation. He concluded that the creature had been observing the men from that spot.

Before their fateful encounter, Patterson and Gimlin agreed that in the unlikely event they came across the creature, they wouldn't shoot it with their rifles. Years later, after being laughed at, ridiculed in the press, and pushed aside as opportunistic cowboys, Gimlin reconsidered. If he had shot the damn thing, he once said, all the criticism would be so much folderol.

Dr. Grover Krantz, professor of anthropology at Washington State University and an authority on cryptozoology (the study of "hidden" or as yet undiscovered animals), has done more work on the Bigfoot controversy than anyone else in academia. His brilliant, frame-by-frame chronological analysis of the Patterson footage, coupled with the sequence mapping of the creature, provides animal behavior insights that others have missed. Krantz meticulously studied hundreds of footprint casts with respect to arches, skin patterns, body posture dynamics, and the like. Years of sophisticated research into all levels of physical Bigfoot evidence led Professor Krantz to conclude that "a large, bipedal [upright, two-footed], wild primate is native to certain parts of North America."[8] In fact, the combination of traits culled from hundreds of sightings allowed Krantz to state:

> What we . . . have here is a perfectly normal species of higher primate that is not especially unusual. . . . In terms of its locomotor adaptations Sasquatch appears to have the basic human design; in most other respects it is essentially an ape; and in some ways it is unique and different from both.[9]

Incredible! An authority on the human species concludes that an unknown animal has been living in our midst for centuries! And what does this "higher primate" look like and do? Based on the collected research material, the creature ranges anywhere from six to eight feet tall and weighs between 500 and 800 pounds. It seems to be a nocturnal species, as most of the sightings occur from midnight until dawn. It has been observed eating berries, roots, pine needles, and hibernating rodents. The ecological niche that the Bigfoot creature supposedly inhabits suggests a solitary, foraging behavior over large areas, similar to that of bears. This suspicion is supported by the accumulated tracks, which appear to be that of solitary individuals. In fact, given their size and sparse food distribution, it's possible the area needed for Bigfoot ranges from 40 to 200 square miles.[10]

If Bigfoot is real, then in what context can we place this hitherto unknown and unrecognized large animal? Surprisingly, some very good fossil evidence

The land between northwestern California and southwestern Oregon is covered with an impressive density of big trees, which is difficult terrain to negotiate during the daytime. If Bigfoot is indeed nocturnal, then the elusiveness of this creature begins to make sense.

points to just such a creature. In the 1930s, in a Chinese cave outside of Peking (now Beijing), scientists found tooth and jawbone evidence of a massive, large-headed, manlike creature. Hundreds of teeth and partial jaws were later found in other parts of southern China and northern Vietnam. Dubbed *Gigantopithecus* (large ape), this giant lived anywhere from 300,000 to one million years ago. Scientists estimate that it weighed up to 900 pounds. All paleontological data suggests that this unusual giant ape eventually became extinct. Perhaps not.

Increasing numbers of researchers believe that descendants of *Gigantopithecus* are the most likely candidates for all of the "large, hairy wildmen" stories scattered across the northern climates from Asia through northwestern Canada to the Pacific states. Over the course of a million years and several ice ages, when the ocean's water was locked up in glaciers, thereby lowering the world's sea level, could this creature have wandered across the resulting land bridges from Asia to North America? Hundreds of other Asian animals found their way into this new world, including mastodons and giant sloths. Much later in time the ancestors of the American Indians discovered the continent in much the same way. Could a gigantic, upright ape really be lurking in the deep woods of the Pacific Northwest? It boggles the late-twentieth-century mind even to consider that possibility. Yet, we must.

As you begin your own search for Bigfoot, I recommend that you start from Eureka. Tucked away in those mountains to the east, somewhere in a valley or mountain slope, there may be creatures that have lived on this land for hundreds of thousands of years. When you get beyond the legend of Bigfoot and consider the actuality of these creatures, the reality of a seven- to eight-foot, upright, fur-covered humanoid weighing anywhere from 500 to 800 pounds, silently watching you from the deep woods, you can't help but feel overwhelmed. Northern California is a magical and mysterious part of America.

A CENTURY OF IMPORTANT BIGFOOT SIGHTINGS AND FOOTPRINTS
Note: A dash (—) sign indicates an incomplete date.

Month	Day	Year	Event
—	—	1886	Miners see a Bigfoot between Happy Camp and the Marble Mountains
—	—	1934	Bigfoot tracks found on Weaver Bally Mountain
—	—	1936	Bigfoot tracks found on Mount Bally
—	—	1947	Two Bigfoot creatures spotted south of Fall River Mills
—	—	1952	Bigfoot spotted on road north of Orleans, near Bear Creek
—	—	1956	Bigfoot spotted running across Interstate 5 north of Mount Shasta
January	18	1958	Several miles of Bigfoot tracks spotted along Bluff Creek Road
August	—	1958	Twenty miles north of Weitchpec, road crews find 18-inch Bigfoot tracks around a tractor
September	—	1958	Same road crew finds more footprints; pieces of heavy equipment moved
September	—	1958	Bigfoot prints seen along Bluff Creek Road
October	1	1958	Bigfoot tracks found along Bluff Creek Road
—	—	1958	Two Bigfoot creatures spotted on hillside above Hoopa Valley
—	—	1958	Bigfoot spotted at night on Route 299 east of Weaverville

(continued)

A CENTURY OF IMPORTANT BIGFOOT SIGHTINGS AND FOOTPRINTS

Note: A dash (—) sign indicates an incomplete date.

Month	Day	Year	Event
October	12	1958	Professional trackers spot a Bigfoot striding across road
October	15	1958	Bigfoot tracks seen on mud flats surrounding Bluff Creek
October	23	1958	Bigfoot tracks seen on Bluff Creek Road
October	28	1958	Several miles of Bigfoot prints documented along Bluff Creek Road
October	30	1958	Bigfoot tracks seen along hillside near Bluff Creek
November	2	1958	Bigfoot tracks seen along Bluff Creek mud flats
August	16	1959	Three hundred yards of Bigfoot tracks found along Bluff Creek
August	30	1959	Bigfoot tracks spotted along Bluff Creek mud flats
—	—	1959	Pilot flying over Bluff Creek sees Bigfoot prints and creature making them
November	1	1959	Bigfoot tracks spotted along Bluff Creek mud flats
November	2	1959	Bigfoot tracks spotted along Bluff Creek Road and down from a canyon leading to the creek
January	30	1960	Bigfoot tracks spotted on Humboldt fir logging road at Bluff Creek and around machinery there
March	—	1960	Bigfoot tracks found near top of Offield Mountain
June	19	1960	Bigfoot tracks spotted on both sides of Klamath River half-mile west of Bluff Creek
August	7	1960	Bigfoot tracks found on a road 9 miles south of Weitchpec
August	14	1960	Bigfoot tracks found on Mill Creek Ridge Road, 8 miles southeast of Hoopa
—	—	1961	Bigfoot tracks found northeast of Covelo
June	—	1962	Bigfoot spotted at home near Fort Bragg
August	10	1962	Bigfoot spotted in lava beds east of McCloud
August	19	1962	Bigfoot tracks spotted along Bluff Creek mud flats
September	26	1962	Bigfoot tracks spotted along Bluff Creek Road and along mud flats
February	28	1963	Bigfoot spotted from plane near Sonora, between Confidence and Cherokee Valley Road
March	—	1963	Bigfoot spotted in mountains near Strawberry

(continued)

A CENTURY OF IMPORTANT BIGFOOT SIGHTINGS AND FOOTPRINTS

Note: A dash (—) sign indicates an incomplete date.

Month	Day	Year	Event
April	—	1963	Bigfoot tracks found near Hyampom
May	—	1963	Bigfoot tracks found near Hyampom
June	13	1963	Bigfoot tracks found crossing Notice Creek near Bluff Creek
June	22	1963	Bigfoot tracks found on Bluff Creek mud flat
June	30	1963	Bigfoot tracks found along Bluff Creek
August	—	1963	Bigfoot tracks found on Bluff Creek Road and at Notice Creek bridge
August	3	1963	Bigfoot spotted leaping over fence near Hoopa
October	—	1963	Bigfoot tracks found near Notice Creek bridge along Bluff Creek mud flats
October	—	1963	Bigfoot tracks found south of Hyampom area
July	—	1964	Bigfoot tracks found at a logging operation west of Bluff Creek; heavy barrels moved
August	—	1964	Bigfoot tracks found on north side of Low Gap in north Yolla Bolla Mountains near Saddle Camp
August	21	1964	Bigfoot tracks with a 52-inch stride found along Laird Meadow Road
September	—	1964	Bigfoot tracks with a 47-inch stride found along Bluff Creek
October	—	1964	Bigfoot tracks found near logging equipment west of Bluff Creek
July	—	1965	Bigfoot sighting/tracks at Blue Lake near Bluff Creek
—	—	1965	Bigfoot tracks spotted along Bluff Creek
October	—	1966	Bigfoot tracks on road near Scorpion Creek, Bluff Creek region
December	—	1966	Bigfoot tracks found 2 miles west of Platina
—	—	1966	Bigfoot sighted north of Weaverville in the Trinity Alps
August	—	1967	Bigfoot tracks found by road crew on Onion Mountain, west of Bluff Creek
August	—	1967	Hundreds of Bigfoot tracks on road near Blue Mountain, west of Bluff Creek
—	—	1967	Bigfoot spotted along Route 299 just west of Willow Creek

(continued)

A CENTURY OF IMPORTANT BIGFOOT SIGHTINGS AND FOOTPRINTS

Note: A dash (—) sign indicates an incomplete date.

Month	Day	Year	Event
October	20	1967	First motion picture of female Bigfoot taken near Notice Creek between Onion and Bee Mountain and Fish Creek Butte
October	25	1967	Bigfoot tracks near Notice Creek, Bluff Creek area
January	—	1968	Bigfoot tracks on Martin's Ferry Hill near Weitchpec
January	6	1968	Bigfoot spotted from plane north of Yosemite Park
April	3	1968	Bigfoot spotted north of Weaverville in Trinity Alps
April	6	1968	Bigfoot spotted wading in South Fork of Salmon River
June	—	1968	Bigfoot tracks between Bluff Creek and Fish Lake
July	11	1968	Bigfoot spotted by Trinity River near Salyer
December	—	1968	Bigfoot tracks north of Orleans
December	2	1968	Three miles of Bigfoot tracks on Bluff Creek Road, East Fork of Bluff Creek to Notice Creek
January	—	1969	Bigfoot tracks spotted from plane between Blue Creek Divide and Nikowitz Road
April	16	1969	Bigfoot spotted on road between Paradise and Stirling City
May	25	1969	Camping seminary students find over 1,000 Bigfoot tracks in Bluff Creek region
June	—	1969	Bigfoot tracks along Klamath River in Siskiyou County
June	—	1969	Bigfoot spotted fighting with dogs at Wildwood Inn
July	—	1969	Bigfoot spotted near Trinity Center in the Trinity Alps
July	—	1969	Bigfoot tracks found near Oroville
July	—	1969	Bigfoot tracks found in Oroville
July	—	1969	Bigfoot spotted at Feather River Highway near Oroville
July	—	1969	Bigfoot spotted on road near Twain
July	—	1969	Bigfoot spotted on road between Twain and Quincy
July	4	1969	Bigfoot spotted north of Wildwood
July	14	1969	Bigfoot tracks found at West Low Gap in Yolla Bolla Mountains near East/South Fork of Trinity River
July	17	1969	Bigfoot female spotted on Cherokee Road south of Oroville
August	—	1969	Bigfoot tracks found in sandbar near Bull Creek in Bluff Creek area

(continued)

A CENTURY OF IMPORTANT BIGFOOT SIGHTINGS AND FOOTPRINTS

Note: A dash (—) sign indicates an incomplete date.

Month	Day	Year	Event
—	—	1969	Bigfoot prints spotted along Bluff Creek
October	—	1969	Bigfoot spotted above Middle Fork of Feather River
October	—	1969	Two Bigfoot creatures spotted turning over rocks in French Creek, near Oroville (rodents?)
October	31	1969	Bigfoot spotted near Oroville
January	—	1970	Bigfoot tracks found near Oroville
April	—	1970	Bigfoot spotted at Manzanita Ranch School, Hyampom
April	16	1970	Bigfoot tracks found near Oroville
May	14	1970	Bigfoot tracks found in Basin Gulch Campground, southeast of Wildwood
June	17	1970	Bigfoot spotted at Stuart Gap, south of Wildwood
July	15	1970	Bigfoot tracks found by a deputy sheriff near a lake north of Mammoth
January	6	1971	Bigfoot tracks found on Fenders Ferry Road, Round Mountain
September	1	1971	Bigfoot spotted southeast of Mammoth
October	8	1972	Bigfoot spotted crossing Clear Creek at the Placer Street Bridge near Redding
January	—	1973	Truck driver hits a Bigfoot on Route 101
July	—	1973	Bigfoot spotted in the Castle Craggie Mountains
September	3	1975	Bigfoot spotted near Oroville
March	23	1976	Two policemen spot Bigfoot near Mill Valley
May	30	1979	Bigfoot spotted running across Route 395 near Bridgeport
June	9	1980	Bigfoot sighting and tracks in Scotts Valley

Contact Person(s)/Organization

If you are interested in the scientific basis for a large, furry primate wandering around the Pacific Northwest, then the place to look is Professor Grover S. Krantz's groundbreaking *Big Footprints* (Boulder, Colorado: Johnson Books, 1992). In this astonishing study Dr. Krantz, an anthropologist from the University of Washington, examines all the data on Bigfoot, from sightings, to footprint casts, to movie clips. Krantz's exhaustive analysis

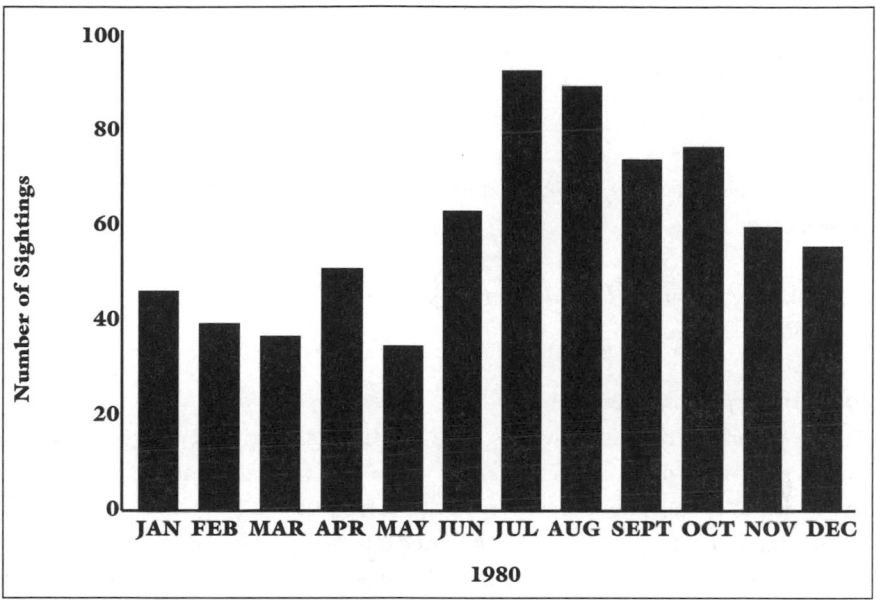

Bigfoot sightings in California, Oregon, Washington, and British Columbia in 1980. The greater number of encounters during the summer is probably due to increased human outdoor activities during those months.[11]

of how two-legged creatures make footprints in mud should be required reading for all critics of the subject of Bigfoot. Krantz paints a picture of this elusive upright primate that makes sense in the ecosystem.

Another fascinating account can be found in Robert Michael Pyle's *Where Bigfoot Walks* (Boston: Houghton Mifflin, 1995). In this splendidly lyrical book, ecologist Pyle, who holds a Ph.D. from Yale, brings the reader into the very heart of Bigfoot country with vivid descriptions of both the terrain and the people living there.

Every September 2–4 the town of Willow Creek celebrates Bigfoot Daze, a tongue-in-cheek tip of the hat to the elusive primate. The celebration is held at Veterans Park. For more information, call: (916) 629–2693.

You must stop in at the Willow Creek–China Flat Museum, a joint venture set up by several community members to keep track of the growing number of Bigfoot reports. The museum has a delightful collection of Bigfoot lore, legend, and original casts of the fur-laden hominid. There are also wonderful displays of American Indian stone tools and artifacts from the local mining, ranching, and logging cultures.

Willow Creek–China Flat Museum
P.O. Box 102
Highway 299
Willow Creek, California 95573
(916) 629–2653
Open Friday, Saturday, Sunday, and holidays, 10:00 A.M.–4:00 P.M., April
28–October 8

Total Magnetic Field/Inclination Angle
   None taken here.

Further Investigations in Area
   Based on increased sightings in the Midwest and elsewhere in North
America, Professor Krantz suggests that the big-footed primate is making a
comeback of sorts. These creatures have been sighted all the way to Ohio!
   An intriguing report regarding a mysterious humanoid animal recently
came out of China, when the Shennongjia national park in the central Humbei
province, a range of densely forested mountains, was opened for the first time
to foreign tourists. Shennongjia is the reputed home of China's fabled "Wild
Man," an elusive six-foot-tall creature that for decades has been sighted there.
The creature is supposed to have red hair and the ability to walk upright. All
attempts to track him down have failed, including one of the most sophisticated. In July of 1995, 30 scientists equipped with the latest satellite tracking
gear, night scopes, portable computers, and other sophisticated electronic sur-
veillance equipment found nothing. The search did, however, publicize the
park and made it a major destination for Chinese tourists.
   The "Wild Man" has all the earmarks of a Bigfoot-like creature.

PETROGLYPH POINT
Lava Beds National Monument, south of Newell, California

Site Synopsis
   Sometime in the dim past ancient people carved over 5,000 mysterious
symbols along a cliff face. The meaning of these strange, geometric patterns
continues to confuse and frustrate all who look upon this largest rock art concentration in America.

Location
   One-half mile south of Newell on Route 139 turn right (west) at the sign
pointing toward Petroglyph Point. Stay on this road (County Road 120) for
about three miles. Pull off the dirt trail into the gravel parking area and pre-
pare to wonder.

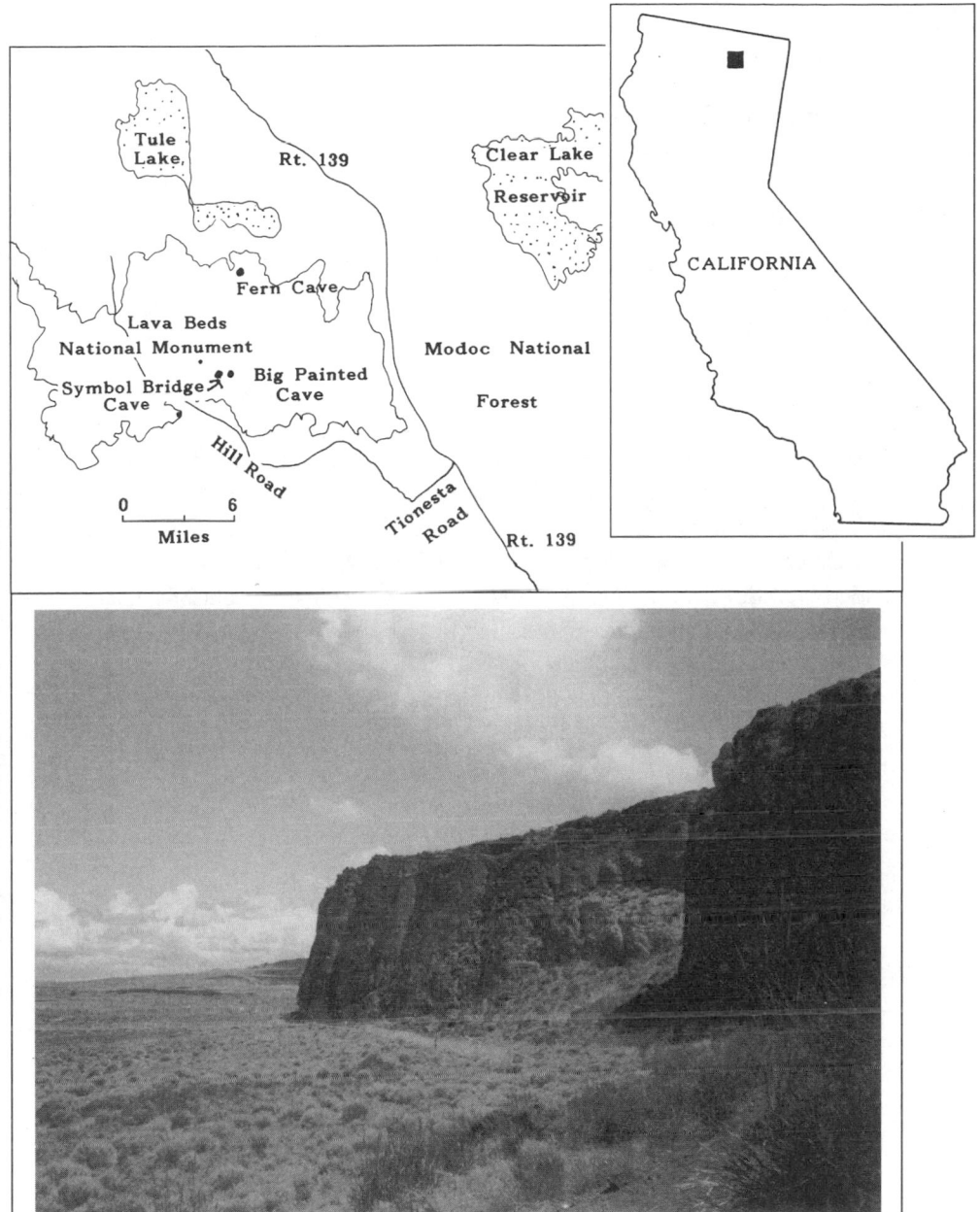

Considerations

The road leading to this site is not paved. Drive carefully after a rainstorm.

A fence protects the ancient glyphs. Please stay behind it! And remember, take only photographs. Leave artifacts of any type in place, on the ground.

A good pair of binoculars will allow you to observe details of the carvings that would otherwise be missed.

If you can arrange it, visit the site during a full moon. The setting becomes much more magical.

History/Background

More than a quarter of a million years ago, violent eruptions scattered volcanic debris over a good part of northeastern California and Oregon. Explosive magma shot up through cracks in the earth's crust, resulting in huge deposits of fiery material. Successive eruptions forced more molten rock and dust clouds to cover the region.

Much later in time, some 11,000 years ago when the last vestiges of the Ice Age trickled to a halt, massive freshwater lakes filled the natural depressions in northeastern California. Glacial meltdown created deep and extensive inland bodies of water that became stopping points for migratory birds, mastodons, and eventually, the first people who followed this game. The Klamath and Tule Lake basins were occupied between 8,000 and 9,000 years ago. Tule Lake provided everything for these people: animal foods, water, and plants. The name Tule refers to a hard-stemmed plant called bulrush (*Scirpus acutus*), which still grows in the marshy areas of the lake. The plant was woven into mats, shelters, baskets, clothing, and sandals by the early inhabitants of the region.

Along the eastern shore of the once extensive Tule Lake is a mound created of successive muddy layers of volcanic tuff, Petroglyph Point. Near its base are thousands of markings incised into the soft stone. The meaning of these petroglyphs—rock carvings—is unknown. Thousands of years ago Petroglyph Point was an island surrounded by the deep waters of Tule Lake. The ancients had to approach the cliff by canoe or some other type of water vessel.

How old are these petroglyphs? Over the years varying climatic conditions caused the lake level to fluctuate. Repeated wave action against the soft tuff created shelflike ridges, or wave cuts. Close examination of the petroglyphs reveal that they were carved within successive wave cuts. Based on this and other climatic data, researchers have determined when each water-eroded cut occurred. The carvings therefore had to have been cut after that part of the cliff face was exposed. The exposed part of Petroglyph Point resulted from a widespread drought that began more than 6,000 years ago, so no petroglyph can be older than that. Scientists who have studied this intriguing spot believe that many of the carvings fall into a period dating from 4,500 to 2,500 years ago. This is remarkable—thousands of generations of people came to this cliff to peck out their mysterious markings over a period of thousands of years. What incentive was there to do this? Why here? What do the symbols mean?

The carvings are unique in that multiple geometric patterns consumed the artists. Elsewhere in the region, animal-style images are the rule; here they are the exception. One of the more striking features of this spot is the vast numbers of patterns carved over older ones. This is odd, considering that there are

Examples of the many mysterious carvings at the base of Petroglyph Point. As with most petroglyph sites, scholars are at a loss to explain their meaning. Wave erosion patterns indicate that the ancient artists had to paddle out to what once was an island to carve these strange symbols.

More strange incisions in the base rock at Petroglyph Point

large stretches of the rock wall that could easily have been used. It wasn't a question of running out of space. Something else was at work here.

Petroglyph Point was a sacred place because the same spot was used repeatedly by people from completely different time periods. Perhaps it was a site to attain power? Was this island cliff face the focal point of spiritual communication? Was there anything tangible that drew the artists to this place? Perhaps.

Since Tule Lake was drained at the beginning of the twentieth century, the markings at Petroglyph Point have shown extensive erosion. The once-moist, damp wind off the lake now carries tons of sand, blasting the cliff face and causing devastating damage to the carvings. There is no known treatment that would lessen the damage to the carvings other than erecting a Plexiglas shell around the glyphs.

As you visit this site keep in mind that it was once an island. Imagine the rituals that must have happened here as the carvers incised, abraded, and drilled to create these bizarre yet engaging designs.

Contact Person(s)/Organization
Lava Beds National Monument
Box 867
Tule Lake, California 96134
(914) 667–2282

Total Magnetic Field/Inclination Angle
Preliminary measurements suggest there's a hidden agenda to this place. I found that the total magnetic field at the northern end of the cliff face was much higher than at the extreme southern end. In fact, field recordings dropped steadily throughout the north-south line. Furthermore, the lowest readings were associated with the *highest concentration of superimposed petroglyphs.* Perhaps the radical fluctuation of the magnetic field at these places along the cliff face somehow influenced the behavior of the ancient artists. Perhaps they experienced a vision at these particular spots. This pattern is consistent with other rock art sites throughout the Pacific Coast states.

Further Investigations in Area
As with most petroglyph sites, there's more here than is immediately obvious. After viewing the extensive array of weird carvings, step back and walk *across* the dirt road. Walk with your eyes fixed on the ground. Within a few moments you will see an array of artifacts. The sandy soil between the clumps of scrub brush are filled with the debris of times past: broken mortar and pestles, chipped arrowheads, and cracked hammerstones. These are the material

remnants of people who visited and carved this peculiar point of rock. But remember, leave all artifacts in place! Take only pictures.

BIG PAINTED, SYMBOL BRIDGE, AND FERN CAVES
Lava Beds National Monument, south of Newell, California

Site Synopsis
Mysterious lava tube caves are scattered over this region. A few were chosen by the ancients as places of special power. These caves are covered with painted symbols and patterns. Why?

Location
There are two ways to get to these intriguing sites: One-half mile south of Newell on Route 139 turn right (west) at the sign pointing toward Petroglyph Point. Continue on this road (County Road 120), driving past Petroglyph Point. About 17 miles along this road will put you at the monument's visitors center.

Alternatively, from Newell continue south on Route 139 for about 17 miles. Watch for Tionesta Road on your right (west). Take Tionesta Road for about 2.5 miles. At that point bear right onto Lava Beds National Monument Road. Continue on this road, which turns into Hill Road, for 17 miles to the Lava Beds National Monument Cave Ranger Station.

About two miles north of the visitors center is the eastern turnoff for Skull Cave. One mile east along this road is the parking area for Big Painted Cave and Symbol Bridge Cave. Walk along the trail for about three quarters of a mile. Big Painted Cave is on your left. Symbol Bridge is straight ahead. You must be accompanied by a ranger to visit Fern Cave (see below).

Considerations
There are over 400 lava tube caves in this national monument. Some are easy to get to, while others are not. The three listed here are *must-sees*, as they are the most accessible and have an abundance of strange swirls, patterns, figures, and other weird symbols.

Big Painted and Symbol Bridge Caves can be visited on your own. You *must* make reservations in advance to see the unusual symbols at Fern Cave. A park ranger takes groups of 10 out to the site only on Saturday mornings (due to staffing problems). On an occasional basis some rangers offer a tour to Fern Cave on Wednesday afternoons. Call well in advance and plan your visit around this reservation. You will be forever grateful that you did!

Walking through any cave is inherently dangerous, and the lava tubes present their own version of danger. The many pathways, turnoffs, uneven floors, low ceilings, cool temperatures, and jagged rocks present some formidable

obstacles. Wear warm clothing and protective headgear. Carry at least three sources of light as backups (flashlights can be checked out free at the visitors center). Never explore a cave alone. Bring along a few friends or join some visiting group. Make sure you also tell the rangers exactly where you are going.

Rattlesnakes live in this environment, so walk with care. Never stick your hand or foot into crevices that you can't see into. Watch out for ground squir-

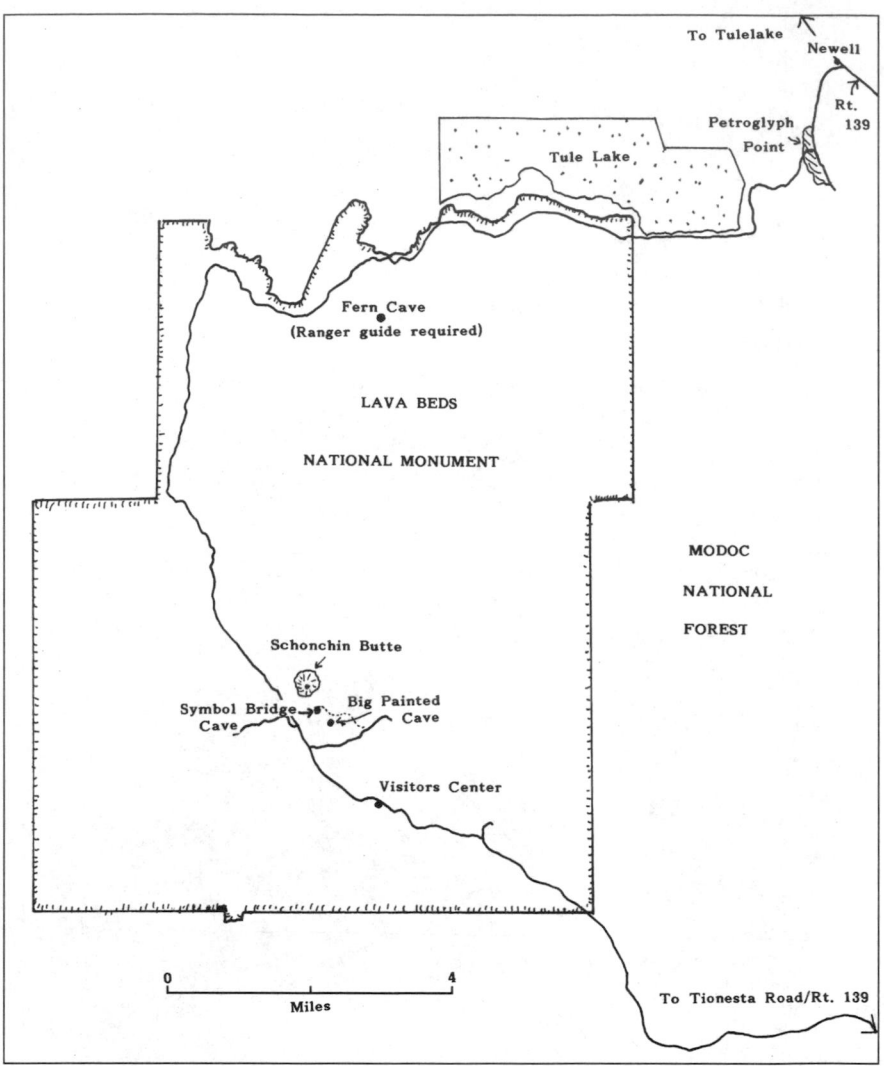

Overview of Big Painted Cave, Symbol Bridge Cave, and Fern Cave, Lava Beds
National Monument, south of Newell, California

rels and other rodents. Don't even think about feeding or petting them. Many
are infested with fleas that carry the bubonic plague bacterium—that's the
Black Death, folks, the one that wiped out three quarters of Europe's population in the thirteenth century!

Bring along plenty of water. Dehydration is always a constant threat in this
dry ecosystem.

History/Background

Lava Beds National Monument rests on a landform known as the Modoc Plateau. This huge moonscape was formed thousands of years ago by the slow oozing of basaltic lava and other types of liquid rock. The terrain is made up of cinder cones, shield volcanoes (the type that slowly oozes lava), and lava tubes. Lava tubes are formed when molten rock flows down a pathway. The cooler sides and top of the molten rock flow harden and form a roof. Hot lava continues moving along inside until it hardens at its source and is blocked. A tube or cave is left in its wake.

Lava tubes are common in areas of active volcanoes. The monument is unusual in the number and size of the tunnels: over 400 have been located and explored, but far fewer have been described. The longest is almost 7,000 feet in length.

Many of these caves were used by the first inhabitants of the region. Selections were based on supplies of fresh water, which often percolated through the porous rock. The reigning native tribe in this area was called the Moadoci by the powerful Klamath Indians of Oregon. This lyrical name eventually was shortened to the more guttural-sounding Modocs. Archaeological studies of the surrounding region suggest that the Modocs have lived in this basin area for well over 9,000 years. It was their ancestral homeland; that is, until they were forced out by the United States Army in a bloody five-month war in 1873. Newly arrived white settlers needed the Indian land to graze their cows. They also feared being so close to the "savages." The army brutally defeated the warriors and in the process destroyed the cultural identity of a people. The remaining Modocs were shipped off to a reservation in Oklahoma.

Before Manifest Destiny brought the East Coast to the Pacific Northwest the Modocs led relatively peaceful lives, aside from the usual skirmishes with marauding tribes (for food, women, and hunting weapons). The land they lived in was unusually bountiful. Tule Lake is a stopping place for huge numbers of migratory birds. Early white explorers noted that at times so many birds filled the air that a sunny day became dark. Excavations in the region confirm that waterfowl were a primary part of the Modoc diet, so the lake provided the perfect place to live. With such an abundant food source available, it gave the Modoc time to contemplate the nature of things. A complex cosmology evolved among these ancient peoples.

Food kept the Modoc people in the region. Not even active volcanic eruptions could force them out; there is ample evidence that lava flowed throughout the Modoc homeland as recently as 500 years ago. Living with such abundance on the one hand, and on the other with the very real danger of being burned alive one sleepy night, must have created a strange dichotomy for these people with respect to their environment. The many caves, weirdly

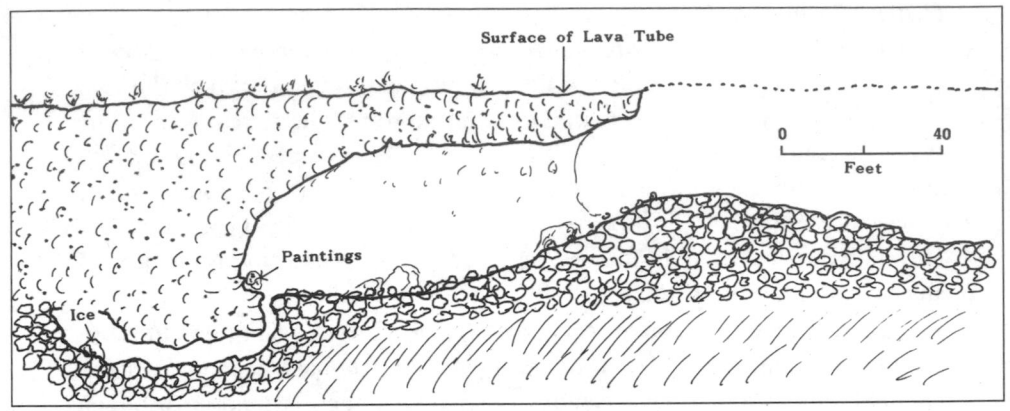

Cross-section of Big Painted Cave and paintings found at the rear of the lava tube, Lava Beds National Monument, south of Newell, California

shaped rocks, and shaking earth had to be a major factor in their outlook on the world. It is known that adolescence was a special time for Modoc youth, as it was for many Native Americans. Youths were required to seek a guardian spirit through a power or vision quest. The idea was to put yourself into a trance state by fasting, exercising, dancing, diving underwater, or hanging out in a dark cave until the spirit revealed itself to you.

The three caves listed in this section may be examples of cave visits for the vision quest. There are a wealth of cave associations in the legends of the Modoc. Modern Modoc tribespeople journey from Oklahoma every year to experience the sacredness of these sites.

Big Painted Cave opens near the base of the Schonchin Butte cinder cone. A tortuous downhill trail brings you to the rear of the cave. At the end of the cave are several faded glyphs. They appear to have a triangular design, which is difficult to detect, so let your eyes adjust to the darkness before scanning the rocks at the rear wall a few feet to the right of the trail end. Most of the paintings are at eye level. It's possible that this cave was used as a water source. In 1917 some local men excavated the opening at the trail's end and discovered a large pond of ice.

Just beyond the turnoff to Big Painted Cave is a wonderful pictograph site. Symbol Bridge is a short lava tube that's open on both ends, hence the "bridge" reference. A steep trail leads down to the opening of the tunnel, where on both sides of the rock face are beautifully colored symbols. Contemporary Modocs who have visited the site recite centuries-old legends that speak of wonderful activities at this cave. It was a place of great spirituality. The symbols must reflect that in some mysterious way, though their meaning has

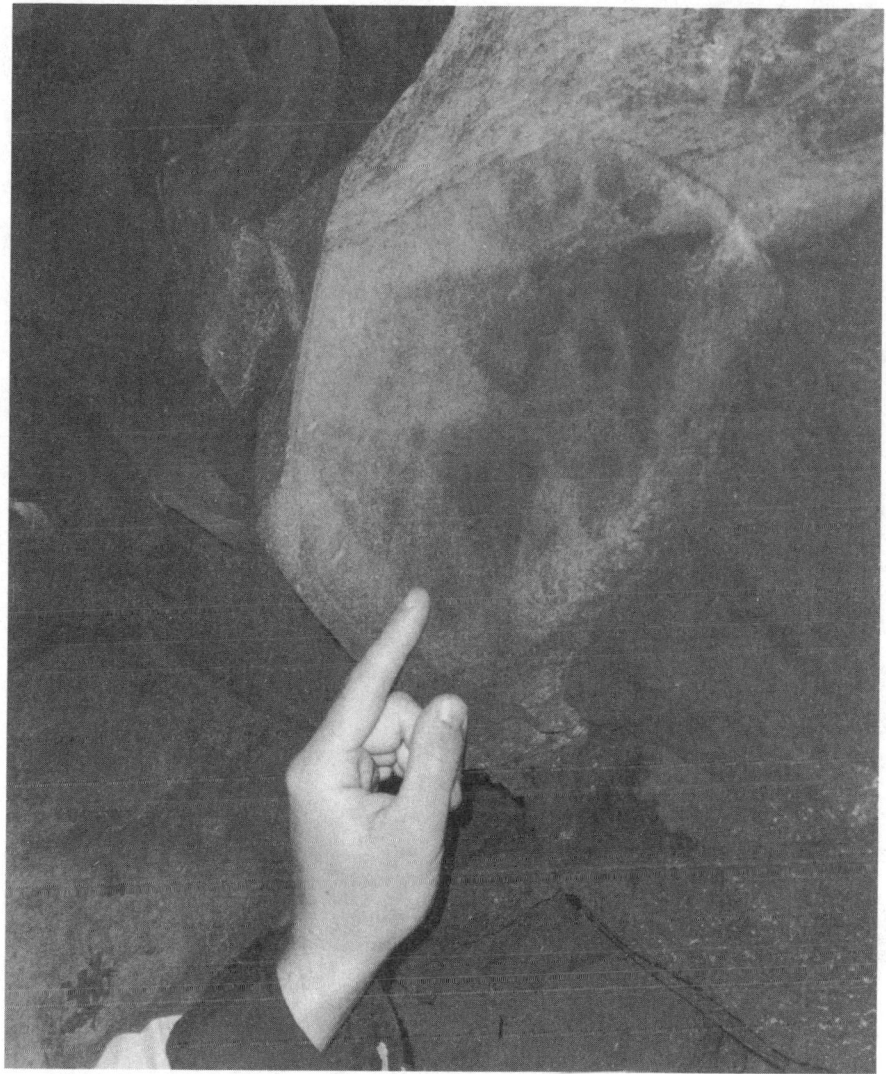

Triangular pattern in paintings along the rear wall of Big Painted Cave

been lost through time. Something special kept happening here—you can feel it as you walk along the rubble scanning the walls for the marks of antiquity.

Fern Cave is spooky. It's located on the northern perimeter of the monument, just south of the present Tule Lake, and a ranger guide must accompany all visitors. Fern Cave is a lava tube with a collapsed ceiling in one small area. This circular opening is the entranceway into the cave. (Before the opening

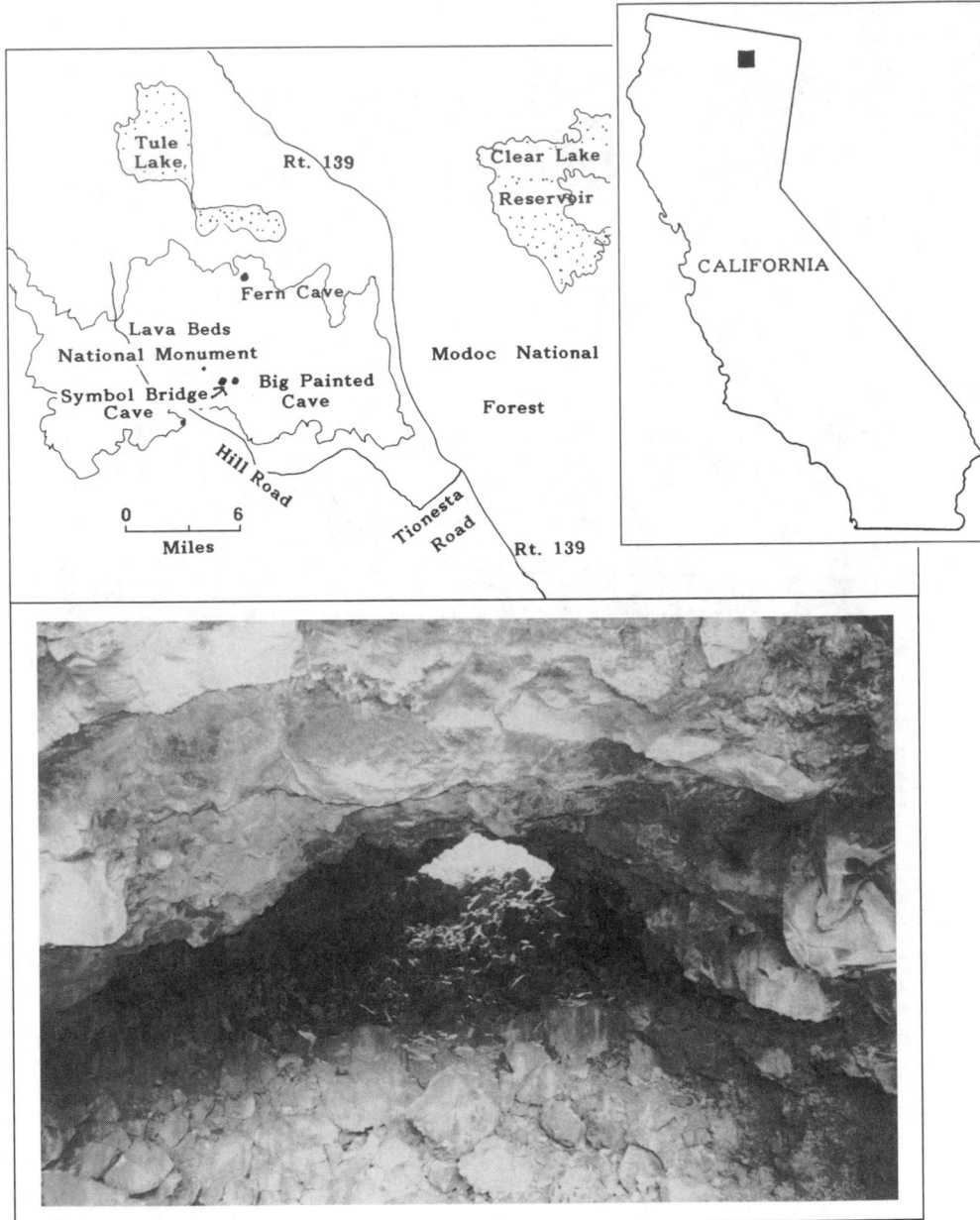

was gated with steel bars in the 1930s disrespectful idiots vandalized some of the interior.) When the gate is unlocked the faithful descend directly to the ground below on a ladder. Some 20 feet below is the floor of the cave. Over the centuries windblown earth and ferns penetrated the ceiling hole, creating an hourglass-shaped mound. Beams of bright sunlight stream into the dark cavern from above. This natural effect is similar to the ocular openings in medieval French cathedrals where a glass-covered roof hole was designed to bathe an altar with brilliant light.

On the east and west wall of this cavern are hundreds of painted images: swirls, circles, rays, white dots, lines, zigzags, animal images, and more. The effect is dazzling. People either sit down in confusion or float off to another dimension. This cave was used for thousands of years by countless numbers of people for something special. If you sit down just south of the mound you'll see that the mound's perimeter is lined with stones. Just above, the world of the profane enters as light. The combination of the contrast of light and dark, the symbols, and, as I discovered, fluctuating magnetic fields cause the most unsettling behavior in even the most stolid, hard-nosed individual.

The stories are many of this cave. Rangers tell of Oklahoma Modocs who come to Fern Cave to recover a part of their past. They come to meditate, to live a dream they had as a child at the cave, even though they had never been to California in their present life. These people speak of the spirits at this place. They claim it is a place of great power. They say they hear the voices of their ancestors here.

Now, I know this probably reads like so much nonsense. Before I visited Fern Cave I had read these stories, I had talked to these people. But nothing prepared me for the overwhelming sensations within this place. No, I didn't hear any voices or see any spirits. But there was a clear, unmistakable feeling of awe, solemnity, and respect, kind of like the feeling you get when visiting a very old, beautiful house of worship for the first time. You can sense that this place was important to a lot of people. Only a blithering idiot would not wonder, why?

Fern Cave is like a gem that should be examined, held up to sunlight, treasured, and then locked away forever in your heart. It is a mysterious, unexpected site that overwhelms almost everyone who visits. It remains in your soul long after you leave.

Contact Person(s)/Organization
Lava Beds National Monument
Box 867
Tule Lake, California 96134
(914) 667–2282
Reservations are necessary.

Two excellent references should be read before a trip to Lava Beds (a complete listing can be found in the bibliography of this book): Carrol B. Howe's *Ancient Modocs of California and Oregon* and Charlie and Jo Larson's *Lava Beds Caves.*

Total Magnetic Field/Inclination Angle

Some unusual patterns were recorded at these cave sites. No doubt the ever-changing active volcanic underground has something to do with this.

Summary

BIG PAINTED CAVE

The total magnetic field started out low upon entering the cave. Midway it shot up over 200 milligauss, then, at the cave's rear wall, only near the paintings, the geomagnetic field dropped down to levels below that at the cave opening. If these readings are correct, then this fluctuation may induce an unusual set of feelings in this place.

It's important to know that while at Lava Beds I took random lava tube geomagnetic readings to see if any similar pattern existed in the nonpainted caves. No lava tube matched the readings I got at the three painted caves.

SYMBOL BRIDGE CAVE

In general the center of the tube, along the east-west axis, had low total magnetic field readings, while the walls with the painted symbols gave exceedingly high geomagnetic readings. The milligauss numbers dropped along the wall sites where there were no symbols. Once again the *placement* or *location* of the painted motifs coincided with a radically changing magnetic field.

FERN CAVE

The center of the mound within Fern Cave had the highest geomagnetic field reading. Areas of the east and west walls, where the paintings were most numerous, most dense, and most superimposed, had radically lower geomag-

Cross-section of Symbol Bridge Cave and paintings found along the inner walls, Lava Beds National Monument, south of Newell, California

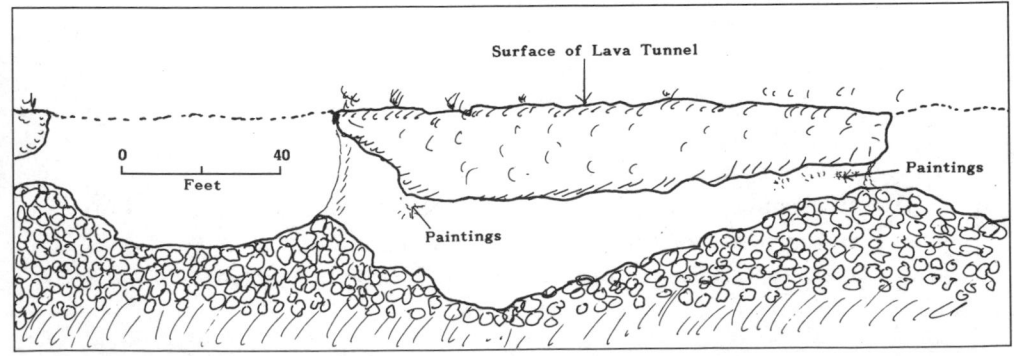

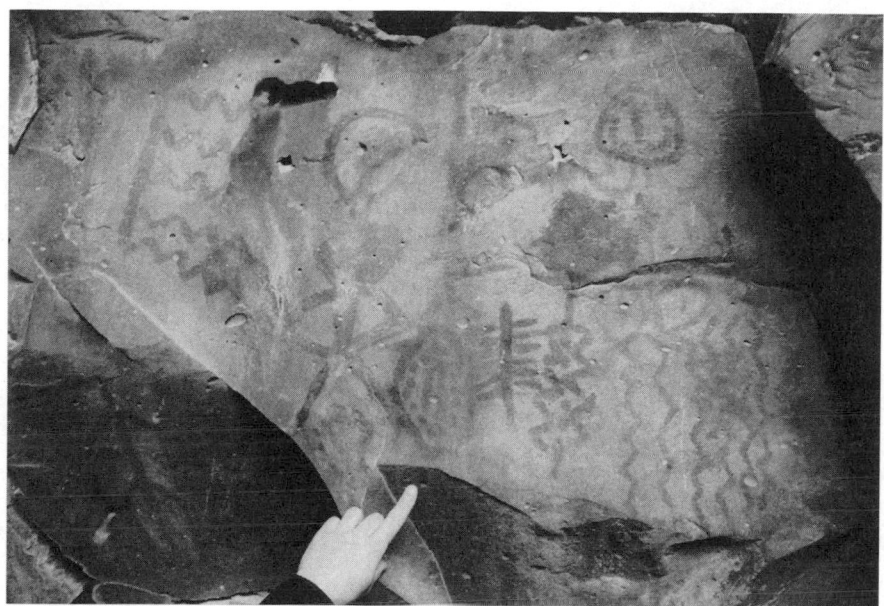

One of the many panels of painted images found in Symbol Bridge Cave

netic fields. This was repeated throughout the cave. The same pattern was observed at Petroglyph Point.

So, what does all of this mean? It is possible that one of the reasons why these particular caves were used had to do with the physiological effects of changing magnetic fields. Perhaps those who painted these motifs felt a particular wall spot was exactly the right spot. Perhaps a vision came to the artist after walking through a cave. As discussed earlier, radically shifting geomagnetic fields can influence an array of brain chemicals that influence perception and behavior. If this idea is even 1 percent correct, then the power of these caves begins to make sense. Of course, it's possible that the caves and the placement of paintings were chosen simply because the Modoc spirits said so. If so, how do we ever measure that? Obviously, we can't. It becomes a non-question and a testament to faith. Now that's truly mysterious!

Further Investigations in Area

Lava Beds National Monument comprises a huge area. In fact, the highest concentration of lava tubes found anywhere are within this park. The Catacombs Tunnel is almost 7,000 feet long—with adjoining passageways and such. Be sure to climb Schonchin Butte on a clear day. You will see the entire layout of the monument, including the former extensive shoreline of Tule

Lake. Plan on spending several days getting to know this place. It will put all of the underground tunnel stories into perspective.

It is impossible to leave this area without brief mention of the Mount Shasta controversy. Mount Shasta is a 14,162-foot dormant volcano that occasionally vents steam but has not erupted in modern times. Legends sur-

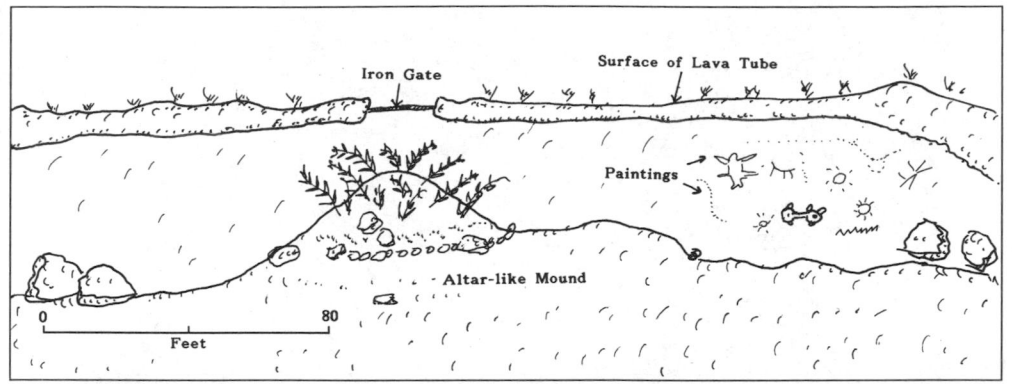

East wall cross-section of Fern Cave, Lava Beds National Monument, south of Newell, California. Mysterious symbols are also painted along the western wall of the cave.

rounding this place are colorful, fanciful, and similar to other stories I've heard over the years.

For years people have talked of strange creatures coming up from the ground below Mount Shasta in north-central California. They have talked of weird underground tunnels snaking through the mountain. The Hopi Indians, for example, mention the lizard people, who built underground tunnels in several Pacific states. Much later, a local author came up with the idea that survivors of the lost continent of Atlantis set up shop underneath Mount Shasta. Well into the twentieth century various cults have formed around the reputed power of the mountain. A host of strange and weird beings were said to be part of the volcano. Various New Age groups swarmed to this major earth "power center" in the summer of 1987 when the so-called Harmonic Convergence of the planets was in order. Variations of that moment continue today at the base of this awesome peak. There are a host of groups that have set up business to tap into the volcano's spiritual power. And much more recently, UFO/government conspiracy groups claim that extensive underground passageways for aliens exist throughout Shasta and the entire United States.

What gives? Why does the icon of underground tunnels and power persist? Do "alien" transport havens truly exist from Mount Shasta to Georgia? If so, what's the price of a ticket?

At the most basic level, this snowcapped, dormant volcano is gorgeous. It rises majestically from the surrounding horizon. The town of Mount Shasta is nestled at its base. Waking up over morning coffee and seeing this incredible peak in front of you *does* cause a shiver. It's a spectacular sight.

Climb partway up the mountain and turn around. The view is heart-stoppingly gorgeous. It's easy to understand the attraction of this place.

The Modoc Indians still regard Fern Cave as one of the most sacred spots in the region. They regularly visit this tunnel to commune with their spirit ancestors. No one really knows what the strange markings mean. Some scholars claim they are vision quest depictions; others say the predominantly geometric renderings represent hidden messages long since forgotten. If you spend time in this cave, especially if you grew up in the 1960s, you may conclude that the ancient shamans were experiencing assorted psychedelic communications.

My suspicion is that the underground cities/tunnel system theme has a specific point of origin, that it can be traced to an actual locale. And that place is northeastern California. Mount Shasta is about 80 miles southwest of the lava tubes of Lava Caves National Monument, the densest concentration in North America. For anyone not living directly on top of these tubes it is difficult to imagine that they exist. But when you consider the trade goods that passed through the country, from the Pacific shores to the northeastern part of California to the deserts of southern Arizona—and archaeological records testify to such trade in shells, precious stones, and so on—it is possible to understand how a story about underground tunnels and cities could have formed. Imagine an Indian explorer from southern Arizona traveling along one of the many trade routes crisscrossing the continent in ancient times. Imagine him wandering through Modoc country. Imagine his incredulity at seeing an almost perfectly round tunnel snaking through the ground. Imagine that image, indelibly etched on his consciousness, as he moved on and spoke of it in other villages trading goods. The story then took on different mean-

Examples of the dozens of dots, lines, stars, slashes, squiggles, and shadow figures that are painted along the walls of the sacred lava tube, Fern Cave, Lava Beds National Monument, northeastern California

Mount Shasta has been the scene of many strange occurrences. Early Native Americans regarded the entire region as sacred, and much earlier in time it was reputedly the location of weird ancient civilizations. It's easy to understand the draw of the place. The dormant volcano looms over the town of Mount Shasta, and on a clear day the view from below is spectacular. (Bryant, Picturesque America)

ings as other Native American groups unfamiliar with these places repeated the tale among themselves. Eventually a myth was formed that stretched into the modern world.

I have no idea if this scenario ever happened, but as a professor of mine at Oxford once said, "If it didn't happen that way, it damn well should have!"

CONFUSION HILL
South of Piercy, California

Site Synopsis
Another sloping wooden shack where the owners claim that gravity has taken a hike. Is it real, or is it a clever copy of the Oregon Vortex?

Location
From Eureka take Route 101 south for about 90 miles. Follow the signs a few miles south of Piercy to the site.

Mount Shasta

Considerations

As with all so-called gravity houses, wear comfortable shoes.

History/Background

In 1949 George Hudson and his wife, Willie, built the Gravity House on a hillside they called Confusion. They constructed a wooden shack on the slope of a redwood covered hill that had all the necessary accoutrements: angled floors, boards laid out for water to flow uphill, places to stand at an angle within the house, perception boards that seem to make people get smaller or taller, and hanging weights that appear to lean toward some unknown force.

Signs at Confusion Hill state that powerful magnetic forces from deep within the earth radiate with such intensity that they will magnetize a metal bar when held vertically against the earth. Oh yes, and when that same bar is held horizontally, it becomes completely demagnetized. Nice story—no, an amazing story. The trouble is it's all pure and simple hype. Nothing mysterious exists here, except maybe the continuing stream of people who pay good money to get duped. There are *no* intense magnetic forces coming from the earth's core at this place. It's all a fabrication!

Confusion Hill is an uneventful imitation of the Oregon Vortex, and the Mystery Spot in Santa Cruz, California. All of the "observed" phenomena are the product of optical illusions. The unusual angles of the shack, as well as the slope of the hill, create the sensation of leaning, balls rolling uphill, and so on. But unlike the Oregon and Santa Cruz sites, there are no geomagnetic aberrations here. So why do I list it in a field guide to mysterious places? Because people continue to visit this site. Perhaps it's a testament to a culture looking for answers that intuitively "feel" right, as opposed to looking for the answers in rational thought. It's easy to see how some may reject science, given all the potentially hazardous problems that go along with it: nuclear bombs, ozone depletion, dependency on computers, etc. People go to places like Confusion Hill for the same reasons that they continue to play lotteries: they want to believe there is something more to existence than what they know or perceive. Ironically, there is, but it's not at Confusion Hill.

Contact Person(s)/Organization
Confusion Hill
75001 North Highway 101
Piercy, California 95587
(707) 925–6456

Total Magnetic Field/Inclination Angle
I spent the better part of an afternoon taking base-line measurements inside this place, a few hundred yards away, a few miles away, and so on. *Nothing* unusual was detected.

Further Investigations in Area
About 20 miles north of Piercy, near Miranda, the Redwood Grove Area "Avenue of the Giants" is made up of ancient, towering redwoods. At one time these trees were the dominant foliage around. Unbroken groves of these coastal trees, the *Sequoia sempervirens*, stood in defiance of disease, fire, and destruction. Scientists estimate that their numbers ranged in the millions, covering vast areas of northern California and southern Oregon. But logging over the past 150 years has decimated the stately giants to isolated clusters. Redwood is resistant to fungus, insects, fire, decay, and water destruction— making it the wood of choice for suburban patio decks, hot tubs, cabins, and wine vats. Sadly, over the next few years, even more of these trees will find their way to the sawmill.

The native population along the northern coast scrupulously avoided wandering through the inner forest—it was said to be the place of ancestral spirits. They stuck to the seacoast. If the traffic is light and the disorienting fog just right, you can still sense the trepidation these native peoples must have felt while walking through such a place of majesty and mystery.

Twenty-five miles north of Miranda is the town of Scotia, one of Cali-

One of the many weird lava tubes at Lava Beds National Monument in northeastern California. The graceful arch of the tube as well as the side "ridges" are all natural—the result of liquid rock cooling. Not all tunnels have been mapped out at this strangely forbidding place.

fornia's last lumber company towns. The Pacific Lumber Company sustained generations of families through its systematic transformation of primeval trees into twentieth-century products. Take the Scotia exit and cross the Eel River going toward the town of Rio Dell. Just over the bridge take a right on Edwards Drive. Continue on this road, which is parallel to the river. Park at the end of the road and walk down the trail to the river. Just across the water along the eastern bank are the Scotia Bluffs. Ensconced within the soft sandstone cliffs are the several-million-year-old remnants of primordial California,

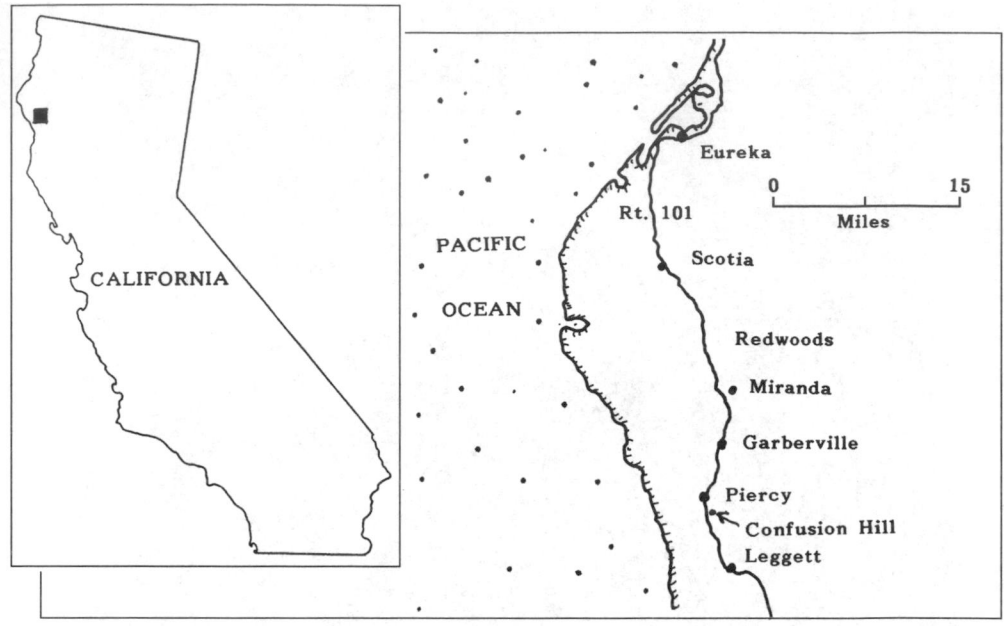

fossil clam shells. All of the rocks along the river are the solidified remains of mud and sand deposited in the ancient shallow sea that once covered vast stretches of this region. Walk along the riverbank (or ford the river) and look for these prehistoric bivalves from another time.

RIDGE-TOP MYSTERY WALLS
Berkeley, Oakland Hills, east of San Francisco Bay, California

Site Synopsis
Ranging along the hills east of San Francisco Bay are long stretches of walls constructed from closely fitted basalt boulders. Some of these boulders weigh more than a ton. In a few places, the walls reach five feet in height and three feet in width. They extend far along the hilltops from Berkeley to Fremont, and beyond to San Jose, some 50 miles to the south.

Location
A short hop from downtown San Francisco are two of the most accessible wall sections.

From San Francisco take the San Francisco–Oakland Bay Bridge (known locally as the Bay Bridge) on Interstate 80. Once across the bridge continue on Interstate 580 for about a mile. Exit northeast on Route 24. In about

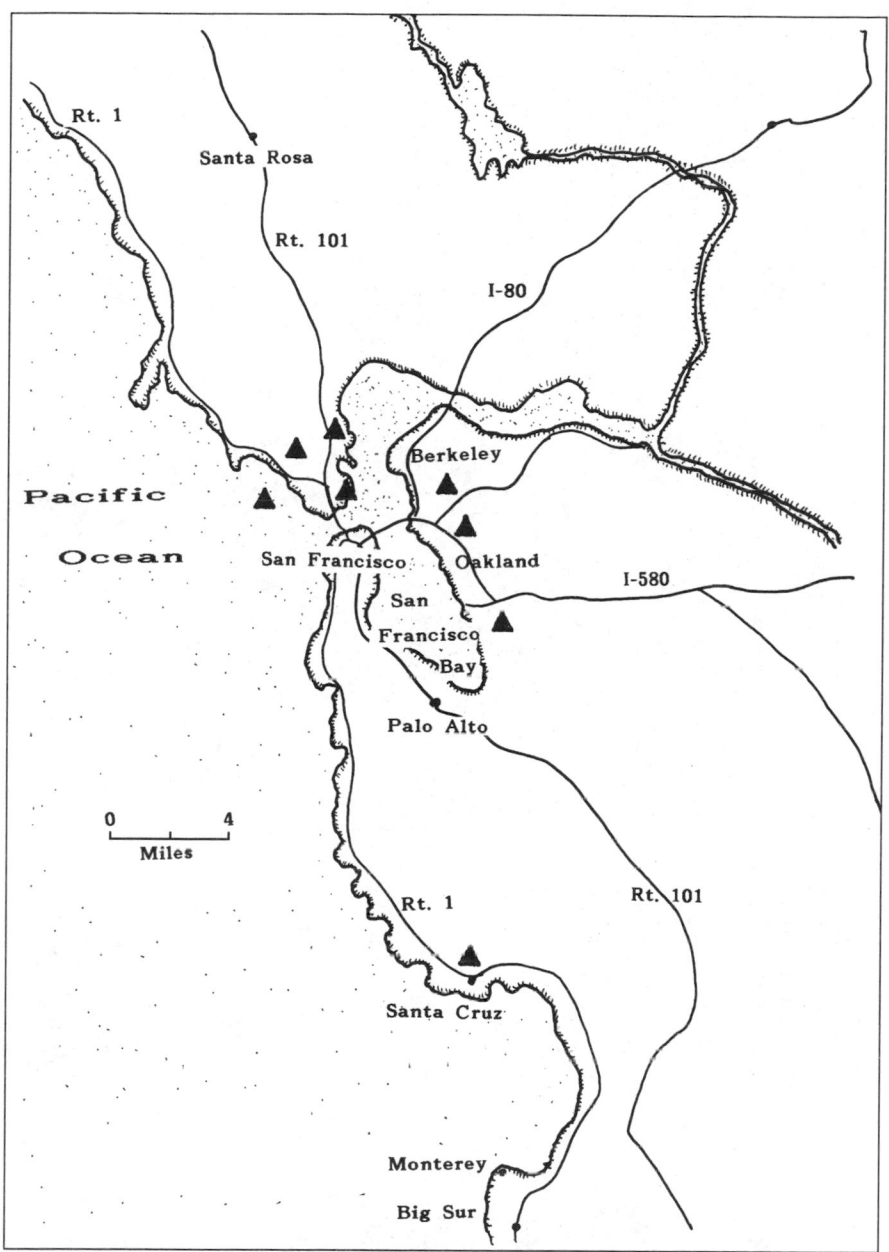

five miles, just after passing through the Caldecott Tunnel, exit north on Fish Branch Road. In three quarters of a mile turn right (east) onto Grizzly Peak Boulevard. The asphalt road winds uphill and affords the most spectacular views of San Francisco and the Bay. Stop and take it all in. The Tilden Regional Park turnoff is a mile up the road. Pull into the upper parking lot, not the lot near the miniature train. Hike up Seaview Trail.

The wall near Berkeley stretches along the crest of the hilltops. Parts of the wall are barely visible.

Continue walking along the trail for about half a mile. Vollmer Peak will be on your left. Almost due north of the peak is a turnoff for a dirt trail. Four hundred feet along this path will bring you to a segment of the ridge-top Mystery Walls.

Another more mysterious section of the wall can be found south of the Berkeley site along the southeastern slope of Round Top Mountain in the Robert Silbley Volcanic Regional Preserve. To get there, exit Tilden Regional Park taking Grizzly Peak Boulevard south. Do not turn off at Fish Branch Road. Continue following Grizzly Peak Boulevard—the road goes over the Caldecott Tunnel and enters the Robert Silbley Volcanic Regional Preserve. About a mile south of the tunnel overpass is a gated entranceway to the pre-serve. Turn left (east) and park. Round Top Mountain is about three quarters of a mile along the trail. Look for the 300-foot expanse of stone wall snaking up from the base of the mountain.

Avid hikers may want to follow the East Bay Skyline National Trail south. Segments of the wall crop up just to the east of this pathway. The most sensa-tional section of this wall can be found about 40 miles to the south near the city of Fremont. Along the northeastern side of Mission Peak in the Mission Peak Regional Reserve east of the city is a massive section of this mystery

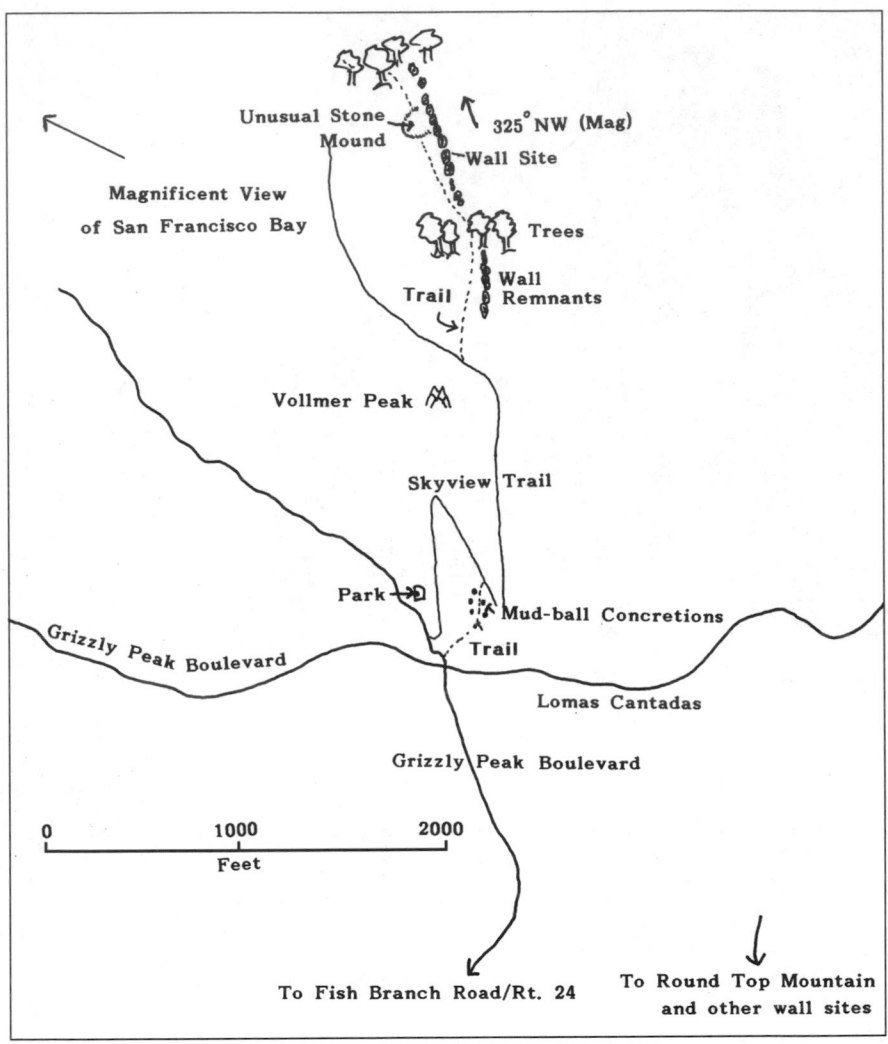

Detail, Oakland Mystery Walls

wall. To get there from Berkeley, take Route 24 east to Walnut Creek. Pick up Interstate 680 south until you reach the intersection of Route 238 (Mission Boulevard). Travel on Mission Boulevard for two tenths of a mile before exiting east (left) onto Mill Creek Road. Travel east on Mill Creek Road for about 1.5 miles. At this distance you will just begin to climb up Mission Peak. Pull off to the side of the road and walk along the eastern flank. Be prepared for an astonishing sight!

Section of the Mystery Walls at Mission Peak, Fremont, California

Considerations

Some of the walls extend onto private property. Follow the directions listed above to avoid problems with landowners.

History/Background

Upon first glance the walls look every bit like property boundaries found throughout New England; in fact, along some stretches landowners have placed wooden and barbed wire fences paralleling the stones. But if you look closely, mysterious details are evident. There are no metal tool marks anywhere on these basalt boulders. Whoever quarried the blocks did so by prying out giant slabs from base rock without drills, levers, and the like. The stones have all the hallmarks of fire-quarrying. Before the advent of metal tools a time-honored technique for shaping stone blocks consisted of laying animal

Sections of the walls are made up of massive blocks of basalt.

fat in a line along a stone and setting fire to it. After a few hours of cold water being thrown on the fire, the rock cracked and, depending on the skill and luck of the quarryman, split into manageable "tidbits." It's much easier to quarry stone with metal drills. The ridge-top wall stretches along the Berkeley and Oakland hills are tangible evidence that someone was messing around with stone without using metal tools. Who could that have been?

Over the years there's been rampant speculation about the wall builders

San Francisco Bay at the Golden Gate in the 1870s. Reports of strange stone walls atop the surrounding mountains have perplexed residents since the first Spanish missionaries. (Bryant, Picturesque America*)*

and their motives. Candidates ranged from a lost tribe to extraterrestrial visitors. A *San Francisco Chronicle* reporter in 1904 asked, "Who built the prehistoric walls topping the Berkeley Hills? Do the miles of mysterious stone barriers, which serve no modern purpose, bespeak a lost civilization of Toltecs or Atlanteans?"[12] The fact that the walls were a complete mystery in the early 1900s, some 50 years after the gold rush rocketed San Francisco into the modern consciousness, is astonishing.

Searches of property records going back to the Spanish missions give no hints of who built the walls or why. Furthermore, the fact that the walls meander up and down hills with no obvious plan probably makes them pre-Spanish in origin. Researchers also rule out the Ohlone Indians, who moved into the region 1,500 years ago. Extensive archaeological excavation of Ohlone sites in and around the Bay Area revealed no stone walls.

Most likely the walls predate the Ohlone. Given enough time, and if more sites can be looked at before they are covered over by townhouses and parking lots, archaeologists probably will find an earlier group of people who settled San Francisco Bay. Perhaps one of these peoples were more in tune with the earth's harmonics than other more "modern" tribes have been. In fact, all wall data collected so far suggest that the walls were constructed well before A.D. 500.

My preliminary work at the Berkeley and Oakland Hills sites suggests that

A vandalized section of the wall reveals its interior construction: wide base with larger stones on the outside and smaller rubble tossed inside. The people who constructed this long wall knew what they were doing. This is a time-honored method of wall construction.

the stones follow natural lines of geomagnetic flux within the earth's crust. (See Total Magnetic Field/Inclination Angle section below.) That would explain the serpentine meandering of some sections of the walls. I suspect the builders laid out the structures to take advantage of the collective field aberrations. The radical changes in magnetic field experienced while walking close to and parallel to the walls probably produced profound swings in behavior and perception. The walls may have been a tangible marker for those in search of a vision quest.

Exactly who were these builders? Unfortunately, we don't know. But it is clear that they were delving into and attempting to control an ancient and powerful natural force. Try walking the walls yourself. Some, but not all of you, will experience the unusual. Most will be challenged by competing forces: the amount of caffeine in your system, your susceptibility to the radiant electromagnetic fields from nearby towers, and other factors. Powerful manmade fields oftentimes mask the subtle clues and signals that trickle from the earth like fresh water bubbling from a mountain spring.

Contact Person(s)/Organization

Back in the mid-1980s the *San Francisco Chronicle* ran a series of stories about these strange wall segments. The articles mention several people who, at the time, were interested in the site. References can be found in the bibliography at the end of this book.

Total Magnetic Field/Inclination Angle

The wall site north of Vollmer Peak yielded some intriguing preliminary results. The total magnetic field along a 100-foot stretch of the wall was quite different from measurements taken 30 feet west and east of the alignment. Furthermore, the wall measurements seemed to fluctuate up and down in a wavelike, or sinelike, pattern: 512, 500, 482, 513, 500, 480, 500 (all magnetic field data are in milligauss units). Data taken 30 feet on both sides of the wall were between 35 and 100 units lower.

One of the many mud-ball concretions found at the base of Vollmer Peak, near the mysterious walls

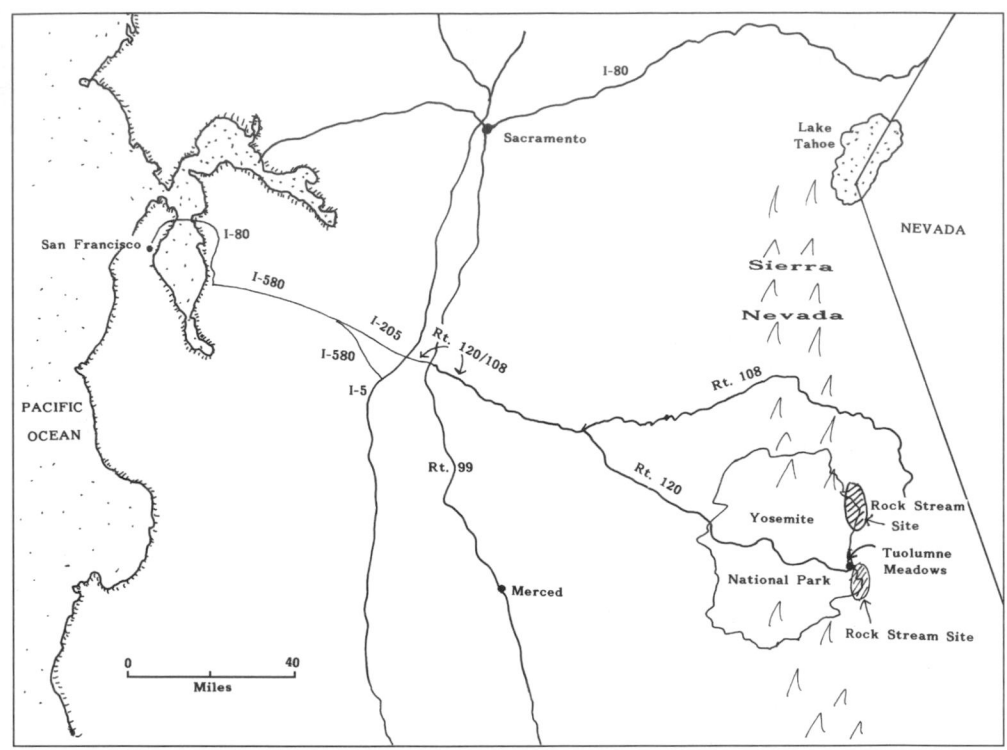

Rock stream sites in the Sierra Nevada of eastern California

Measurements taken at Round Top Mountain and at Mission Peak to the south revealed even more dramatic changes between the wall placement and the region surrounding it. In some cases the difference was over 300 milligauss units! These data suggest that the builders of the wall site took pains to locate them along specific pathways of high geomagnetic fields. Whoever these people were, they no doubt felt different atop the walls. Walking along the wall probably evoked strange sensations and thoughts due to the cascade of neurotransmitters being secreted into the bloodstream. Perhaps one use of these mystery walls was to "map out" the pathway to receiving visions. Could different stretches of walls enhance neural activity?

Further Investigations in Area

A well-planned archaeological excavation at a few of the wall sites would answer some nagging questions, such as: How old are they? Surely the builders dropped remnants of themselves as they were planning, lifting, and placing the basalt stones. Their cast-off debris would provide the necessary

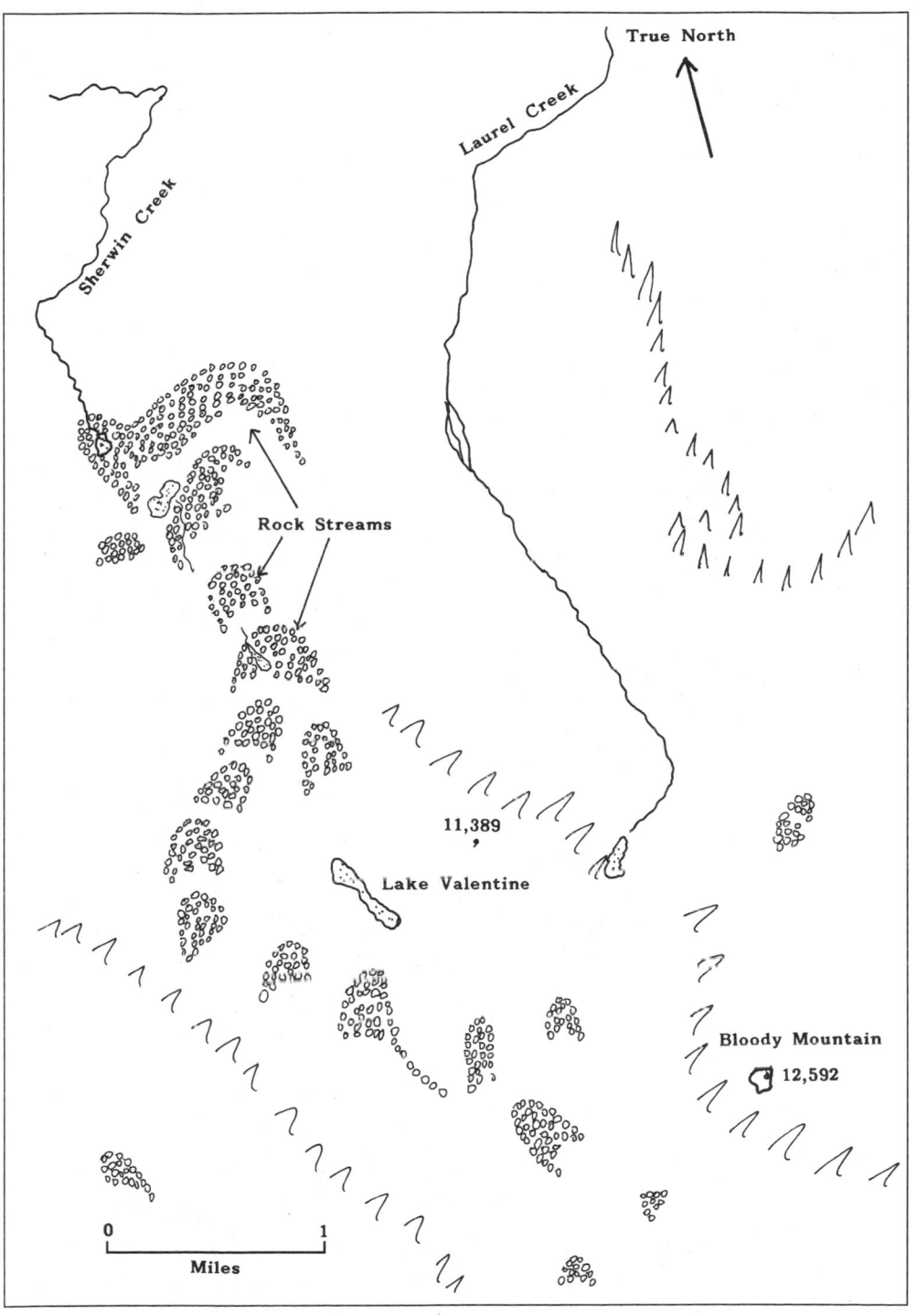

Rock streams in the valleys of Sherwin and Laurel Creeks, Sierra Nevada, eastern California (Adapted from Kesseli)

High up in the Sierra Nevada of eastern California are dozens of mysterious rock streams. Some researchers argue that they're artifacts of the last Ice Age. Others aren't so sure. (Bryant, Picturesque America*)*

clues to their identity. Until then, however, all we are left with are suspicions, innuendos, and possibilities.

As with most mysterious sites, there's more to this area than the main attraction.

On the way up to the most accessible mystery walls are dozens of mud-ball concretions. These strange round clumps of stone are scattered all over the base of Vollmer Peak. If you traverse the switchback trail leading up to the mysterious ridge-top walls, you'll notice hundreds of these layered stones. Geologists are at a loss to explain their origin.[13]

East of Vollmer Peak is Mount Diablo State Park. Many strange tales are centered on the main peak, Mount Diablo. The early Bolgone Indians claimed that a "devil being," or Puy, lived inside this 3,800-foot mountain. Early settlers thought the same, for they often heard strange noises and saw unusual apparitions on its peak. Researchers today maintain that any strange phenomena heard or seen at Mount Diablo can be attributed to the weather. Perhaps.

High up in the Sierra Nevada of California are strange accumulations of tongue-shaped blocks of stone. Some of these "streams" of rock measure less than 200 feet in length; the longest is more than two miles. Some geologists suggest that these bizarre distributions of rock streams originate from melting glaciers. Others speculate they come from creeping landslide deposits. Some of the fringe "researchers" think otherwise. They say they are the handiwork of an ancient civilization. It's difficult to believe the latter, as these are gigantic lengths of stone. Whatever their origin, they are an intriguing phenomenon.

This is a tricky site to get to. From downtown San Francisco take I-80 across the Bay Bridge. Pick up I-580 east. Travel on I-580 for about 50 miles before exiting to I-205 east. In about 15 miles, I-205 will lead into the Route 120 connector. This in turn will lead into Route 120/108. Stay on this combined road for about 45 miles, turning on Route 120 when the highway splits off into Routes 120 or 108.

Continue on Route 120 for about 100 miles into Yosemite National Park (the park road is closed in winter). South of Mount Lyell are the streams depicted on the accompanying map. I recommend that you visit the Sherwin and Laurel Creek rock streams. They can be found on the Mount Morrison U.S. Geological Survey quadrangle topographic map, which can be purchased at most hunting or sporting goods stores. As there are no direct roads, you will need to get park permits (at the ranger station) and hike into the valleys.

I recommend that unless you have a lot of outdoor-camping experience you pass by this site. While intriguing, it takes a good deal of high-altitude hiking to get there. If you do go, however, bring along the usual camp gear: tent, sleeping bag, food, water, butane stove, and the like. Two to three days of wandering about should be adequate to understand the nature of these weird deposits.

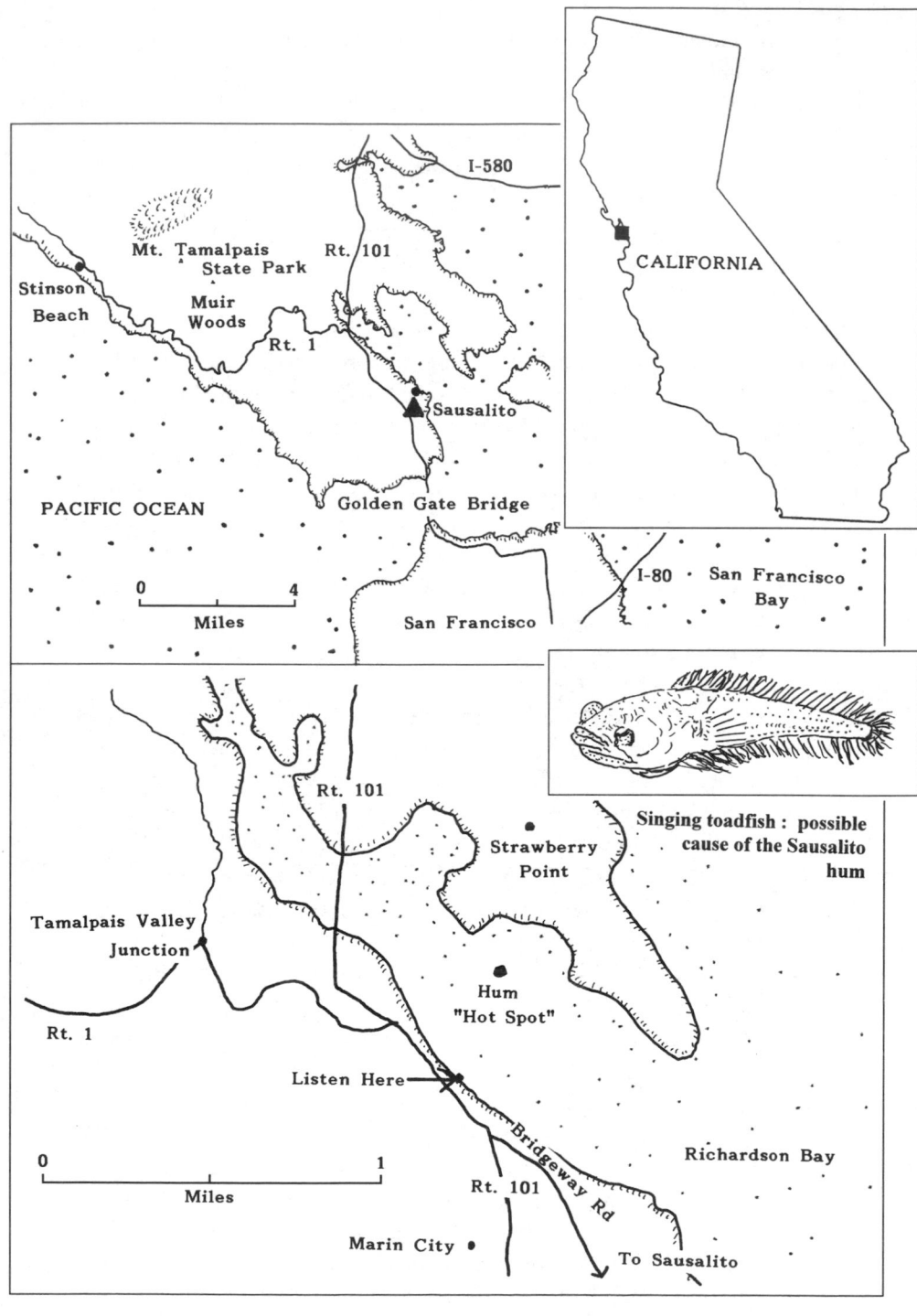

I-580

CALIFORNIA

Mt. Tamalpais
State Park

Rt. 101

Stinson
Beach

Muir
Woods

Rt. 1

Sausalito

PACIFIC OCEAN

Golden Gate Bridge

0   4

Miles

I-80   San Francisco
Bay

San Francisco

Rt. 101

Strawberry
Point

Singing toadfish : possible
cause of the Sausalito
hum

Tamalpais Valley
Junction

Hum
"Hot Spot"

Rt. 1

Listen Here

Bridgeway Rd

Richardson Bay

0   1

Miles

Rt. 101

Marin City

To Sausalito

THE SAUSALITO HUM
Sausalito, California

Site Synopsis

For more than 25 years the exclusive houseboat community of Sausalito has been disturbed during the summer months by a weird humming noise. The buzzing sound starts at around eight in the evening and stops around sunrise. It is silent from the end of September until around mid-April, when it starts up again.

Acoustical engineers from Berkeley could not pinpoint the source of the sound, but biologists believe the noise is made by the plainfin midshipman, which is also known as the singing toadfish. Not everyone agrees.

Location

The sound is best heard in Richardson Bay, a harbor just north of downtown San Francisco, across the Golden Gate Bridge. To get there take Route 101 across the Golden Gate Bridge and exit at Sausalito Lateral. Follow this road to Alexander and drive parallel to the bay, eventually picking up Bridgeway. Stop at Sausalito Point just east of the Village Fair Shopping Center and wait until 8:00 P.M.

The absolute *best* place to hear the hum, however, is about two and a half miles up Route 101, from Sausalito, past Marin City. Just past the junction of Bridgeway Boulevard with 101, park well off the side of the road. Walk down toward the bay. Researchers claim that a humming "hot spot" emanates from the water just south of Strawberry Point, which can be seen in the distance.

Considerations

As the hum can be heard only during the months of April through September, plan on being in Sausalito during those times. It's best to hang out in a restaurant or bar before walking down to the dock area at eight o'clock, as you may be stopped and questioned. This is an exclusive enclave of multi-million-dollar houseboats and the residents understandably are jittery about strangers wandering around.

History/Background

Low- and/or high-frequency acoustical hums are not unique to the San Francisco Bay area. They can be heard worldwide. Some are explainable; others are not. The mysterious, low-frequency hum heard around Taos, New Mexico, for example, has puzzled residents for years. As I detailed in *Field Guide to Mysterious Places of the West*,[14] no one knows what causes it or where it comes from. To further complicate matters, not everyone can hear it!

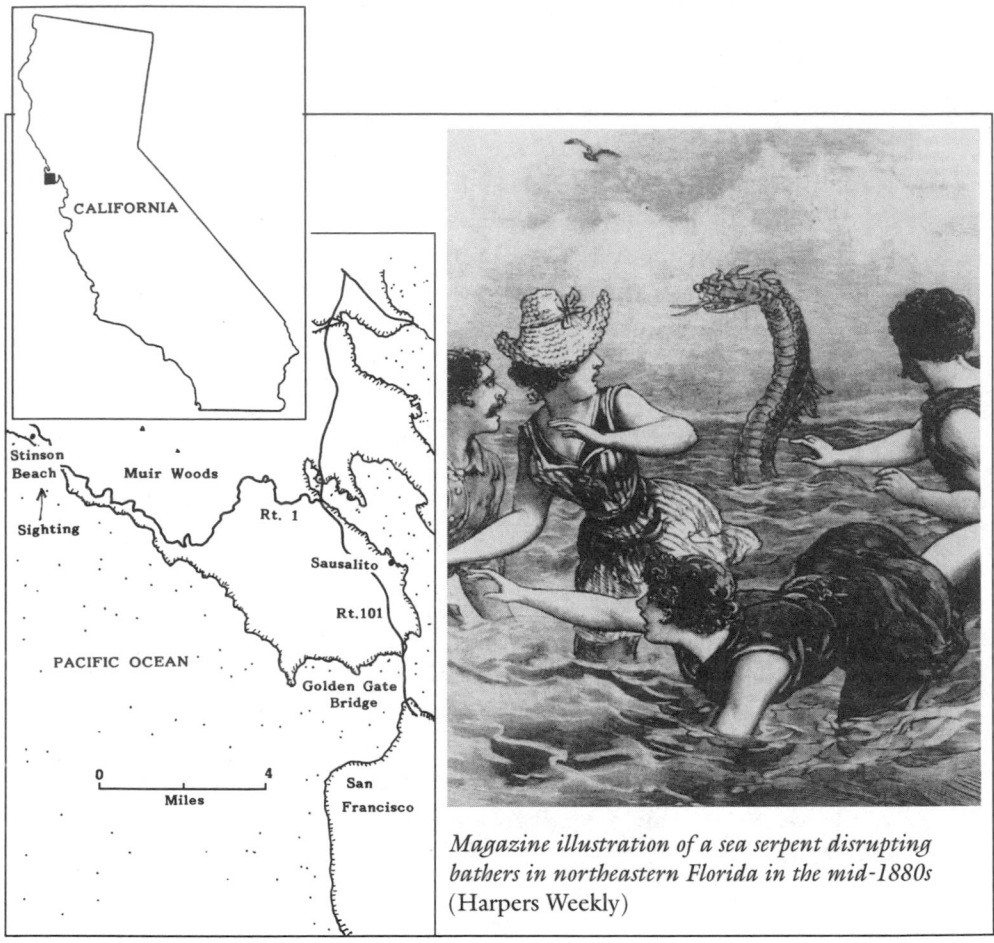

CALIFORNIA

Stinson
Beach
Muir Woods

Rt. 1

Sighting

Sausalito

Rt.101

PACIFIC OCEAN

Golden Gate
Bridge

0   4

Miles

San
Francisco

*Magazine illustration of a sea serpent disrupting
bathers in northeastern Florida in the mid-1880s*
(Harpers Weekly)

The sonic booms periodically heard up and down the eastern shore of the United States are another case of strange auditory phenomena with an unknown origin. On the other hand, the loud noises heard since Colonial days around the southern Connecticut town of Moodus have a credible explanation: shifting geological phenomena deep within the crust.

During the mid-1980s the humming coming from the depths of Richardson Bay, just north of San Francisco, was driving residents crazy. Variously described as everything from a raspy buzz to 10 electric razors running at once, the underwater hum caused great concern among the wealthy houseboat owners who dock in this idyllic locale.

Explanations for the nocturnal sound included secret military devices, alien starships, underwater pumps, and a host of other far-fetched theories.

Acoustic engineers from the University of California at Berkeley spent days recording the sound but could not identify its source. They did run a detailed analysis of the sound waves, comparing it to known phenomena, and determined that the frequency of the hum did not come from any mechanical or electrical device. So much for intergalactic spacecraft and underwater pumps.

With the help of marine biologists the culprit was narrowed down to a small fish known as the plainfin midshipman (*Porichthys notatus*). Old-timers also knew it as the "singing toadfish." The small male emits a series of unusual sounds during its mating season. A recording of the toadfish revealed a perfect match between the frequencies of the sound at Richardson Bay and the recording, so it seemed like a done deal. Not quite. A few months after this "sound match," residents over in San Francisco started hearing *their* version of a hum. No singing toadfish were anywhere to be found! (See Further Investigations in Area below.)

While it is certainly true that the toadfish does let off some unusual sounds, the question is, why were the Sausalito residents the first to notice? People have been mucking about this region since the 1700s, if not before. The fact that no one noticed the cacophony of noise coming from Richardson Bay is strange. Perhaps the fish just "recently" took up residence there? Or maybe the fish isn't the source of the hum.

Contact Person(s)/Organization

Details of this story can be gleaned by contacting the Steinhart Aquarium and the Acoustic Engineering Department at San Francisco State University.

Total Magnetic Field/Inclination Angle

None taken at this site.

Further Investigations in Area

Back in the mid-1980s, over in Pacific Heights and the Marina District of San Francisco Bay just south of the Golden Gate Bridge, a mysterious hum was heard by residents. Some thought the sound came from an earthquake fault, a Navy generator, or a portable CAT-scan machine. It didn't. Biologists discounted the singing toadfish, as the Pacific Heights/Marina District hum began just after the mating season ended. The mystery continues.

SEA SERPENT SIGHTINGS

North of San Francisco

Site Synopsis

During October and November 1983 several sightings of a dark, eel-like creature came from the Northern California coast. Many people, some with

A sixteenth-century woodcut of a sea serpent found off Norway (Olaus Magnus, Historia de Gentibus Septentrionalibus)

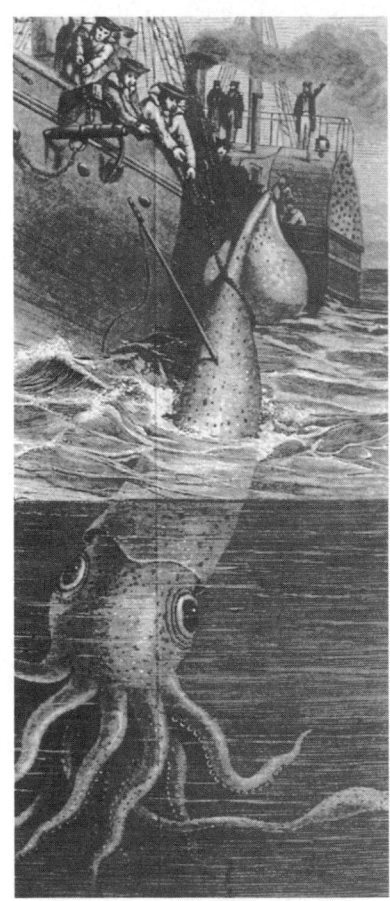

A mid-nineteenth-century French gunboat crew clashes with a giant squid. The sailors encountered the creature in the Atlantic Ocean just off the Canary Islands west of Spain. (Harpers Weekly)

binoculars, reported seeing a small-headed animal followed by a few humps that rose from the surface of the water. At Stinson Beach, north of San Francisco, the sea serpent was followed by a clutch of birds and sea lions. Is this just another "fish story"?

Location

Stinson Beach is just north of San Francisco. From downtown take the Golden Gate Bridge north. Travel north on Route 101, exiting on Route 1 about a mile past Marin City. Stay on Route 1 for about 10 miles as it winds and twists west toward the ocean and the beach.

Considerations

Perch yourself along the sandy shore with a pair of strong binoculars. Bring along a good beach chair and a cooler of drink. There's no guarantee you'll see anything, but if you do, crack open the champagne and toast your good luck. Don't forget to turn on the video camera. Try to shoot the image with something of known size in the frame—like a bird—for perspective. You'll need some proof—*any kind*—to document your findings!

History/Background

Stories of giant sea serpents have been around since people first started sailing. Unidentifiable creatures have been seen by every seagoing culture on every coastline, off every continent. These worldwide sightings by different peoples in different time periods should give us pause. It was the same scenario for the groups who first populated the Pacific Coast. Though the stories vary as seen through the local tribal lens, the gist of the oral traditions quite clearly indicate that unusual things have been spotted by natives up and down the rugged coast.

Just off Canada's British Columbia coast, for example, Indians have for centuries seen a sea serpent cruising through the ocean. Their oral traditions describe a creature with a creepy similarity to the reputed Loch Ness monster in northern Scotland. In fact, in the early 1990s two Canadian scientists pieced together a wealth of data suggesting that the centuries-old Pacific Coast sea serpent sightings were real.

A marine biologist and an oceanographer claimed that since the 1930s six specimens of the mysterious sea creature have been discovered. Their "evidence" included a report of a live baby and a dead specimen found inside a whale's stomach. The whereabouts today, however, of these sample "serpents" is unknown.

Tribes in the Pacific Northwest spoke of a sea creature: the Tlingit called it Gonaquadet; the Haida knew it as Wasgo; while the Tsimshian referred to it as Ginaxcamétk. All of these people said that this monster lived in lakes or in

Mount Tamalpais was a sacred place for the Miwok Indians. From lookouts on the
mountain they watched for hideous sea serpents. (Bryant, Picturesque America)

the sea. Most intriguingly, the Kwakiutl describe a giant double-headed serpent known as Sisiutl. This strange monster could swim in water or travel on
land.[15]

Among the early natives of British Columbia there is the tradition of a
creature called Naitaka. The monster was a water serpent who inhabited Lake
Okanagan and other bodies of water in the region. The creature was loathed
and feared by the natives, for it regularly devoured people who fished or walked
by the lakes. The pre-Columbian rock paintings dotting the cliffs and valleys
throughout the land consistently show the demon side of Naitaka, the lake
serpent. English settlers in the area, in an attempt to mimic the native languages,
referred to this creature variously as Ogopogo, Manipogo, or Igopogo.

So what can we make of all this? Where's the evidence? At present all anyone has are old reports of eyewitness accounts, including an intriguing one
that suggests a full-grown sea serpent could measure over 50 feet in length
and swim at 25 miles per hour—faster than an orca, a killer whale! We also
have a curious topology that connects most of the major serpent-sighting lakes
in British Columbia with deep rivers and the ocean—where the legends of giant sea creatures continue.

Eighty-five million years ago a monstrous sea serpent swam around the
inland sea that is now Kansas. Known as a Mosasaur, this hideously scaled,

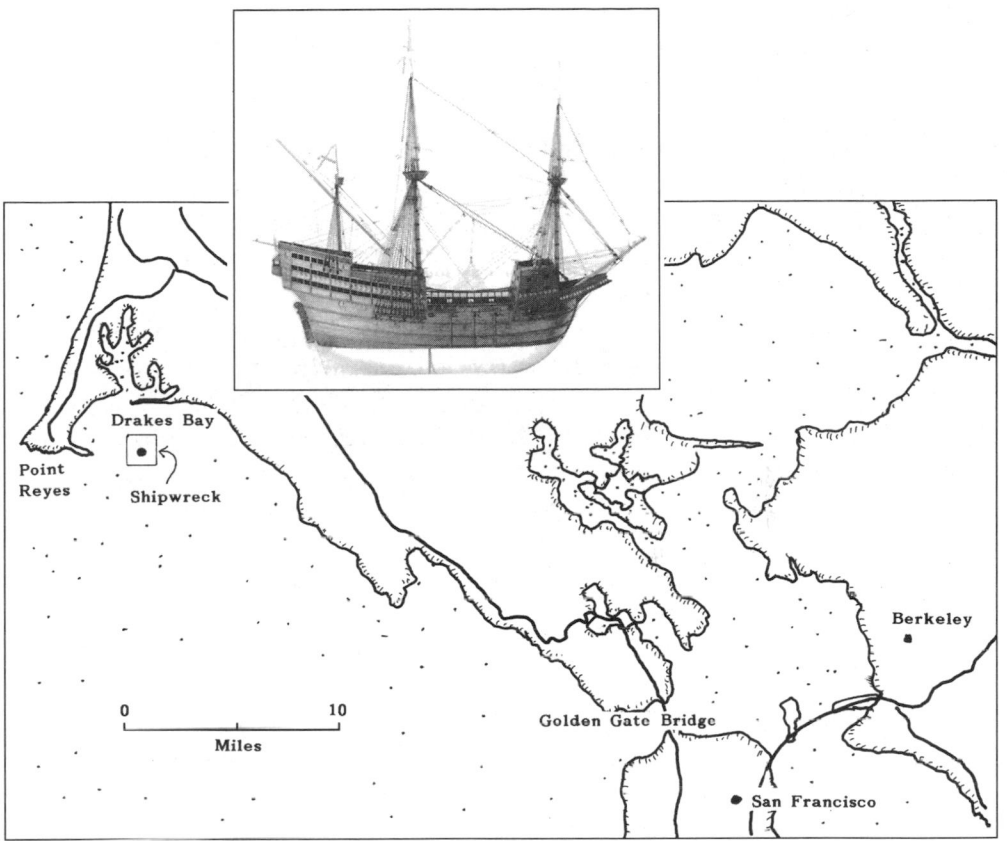

A Spanish treasure galleon that sank in 1595 lies buried in sand near the mouth of Drakes Bay.

30-foot-long reptile dived in deep waters, tearing apart fish with its razor-sharp teeth. This dinosaur-era monster is a good candidate for the West Coast sea serpent sightings. The trouble is this creature supposedly died millions of years ago. Scientists only know about it from the fossil record. Perhaps.

Each time oceanographers probe the depths of the ocean they bring back reports of strange creatures that they never knew existed. While most of these organisms are tiny, some, like the giant squid, are huge. Long thought to be the result of writers with overactive imaginations, the several specimens of giant squid captured from the deep have humbled a lot of researchers. These cousins of the foot-long squid that becomes fried calamari live at depths of over 2,000 feet and can grow to over 60 feet long. We know very little about the creatures that roam freely through an ocean that covers 75 percent of our planet. So keep an open mind about stories of sea serpents. It's probably a good idea to keep a camera handy as well!

Contact Person(s)/Organization

A good article on this subject is "Sea Serpents Seen Off California Coast," in the *ISC Newsletter,* Winter 1983.

Total Magnetic Field/Inclination Angle

Magnetic field information was not taken nor was it necessary at Stinson Beach. But do see the next section!

Further Investigations in Area

The late fall sighting in 1983 could very well indicate a seasonal migration for this elusive creature. It might be wise to scan the coastal waters during October and November.

In *Field Guide to Mysterious Places of the West,* I reported on a nearby stone circle considered sacred by the Miwok Indians.[16] The circle of stones exhibit unusual magnetic properties that possibly were used by shamans to induce visions of Coyote, a spirit that often helped the Miwok through a crisis. Legend has it that a giant sea creature regularly would crawl up from the ocean searching for Miwok children to eat. This went on for years and understandably caused fear among the people, as they had no means to kill the creature. It also slithered into villages at night when everyone was asleep. But one day—the legend isn't too explicit here—Coyote appeared and got rid of the beast.

Now, why would the Miwok have a legend about a *sea creature* causing havoc? Why not some land-based thug, like a Bigfoot? The Miwoks were quite skilled in securing food from the sea. They knew their environment: where the best fish were swimming, where delectable clams were burrowing. They looked toward the sea for survival. The sea was not strange; on the contrary, it was a familiar place. That is, until the creature appeared. The Stinson Beach sightings take on added significance in light of this legend.

In 1595, a century after Columbus landed in the New World, the 200-foot Spanish galleon *San Agustin* sank in 50 feet of water in Drakes Bay, a calm haven some 24 miles north of modern San Francisco. For over 400 years this massive cargo ship, laden with Ming dynasty porcelain, gold, silver, ivory, ebony, and jade, lay covered by the sandy bottom.

The specific type of ship sunk in Drakes Bay is called a Manila galleon. This was a huge cargo vessel built to withstand the torturous Pacific Ocean crossing between Mexico and the Philippines. Ships in the Spanish-owned Philippine port of Manila transported the treasures of the Orient to the New World, where they were then shipped overland to the Atlantic side of Mexico for eventual transport to Spain.

For hundreds of years broken bits of fine porcelain pottery have washed ashore near Drakes Bay. Native Americans in the vicinity used the pottery pieces as beads and as hide scrapers and other sharp tools. Archaeologists

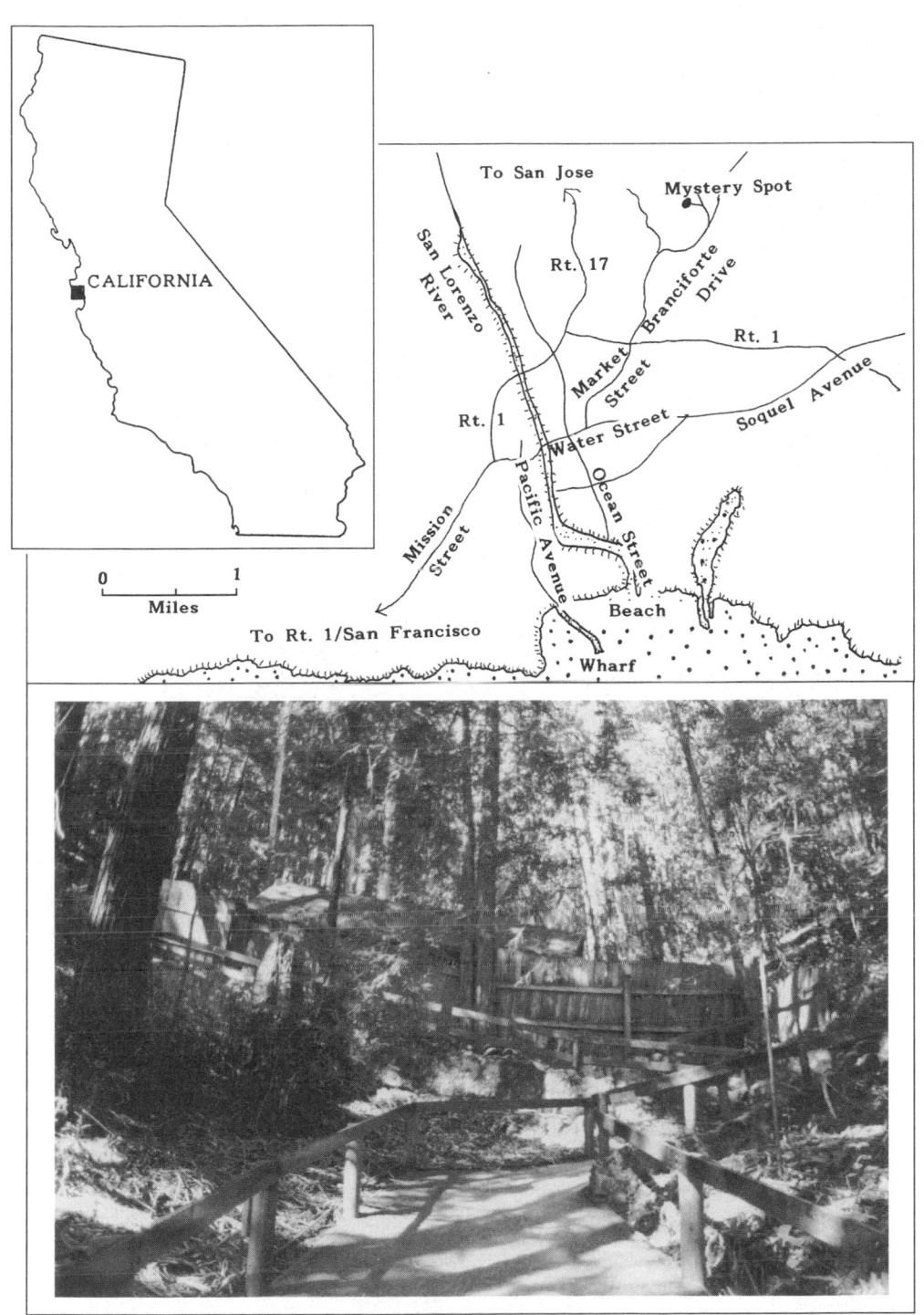

The Mystery Spot shack. Compare this structure with the Oregon Vortex site.

know a staggering amount of treasure is out there. But exactly where, no one knows for sure to this day.

MYSTERY SPOT
Santa Cruz, California

Site Synopsis

About three miles north of the coastal town of Santa Cruz is a hilly redwood slope. Brochures and road signs scattered around town describe a strange "energy" that "pulls" at all who go there. Guided tours take tourists on a 30-minute walk up a steep incline to an abandoned cabin that is creeping down the hillside. Much is made of an underground "force" that pushes golf balls uphill and causes one's perspective to fade. It this all carnival hype, or is this place truly mysterious?

Location

From downtown Santa Cruz take Ocean Street north. Turn east on Water Street. Turn left (north) on Market Street. In about half a mile the road leads into Branciforte Drive. Continue on this road for about a mile. The Mystery Spot entranceway is on the left.

Considerations

The walk up to the cabin is steep. Wear shoes with rubber soles. I don't recommend leather soles or high heels.

There is a small admission fee and a mandatory tour. Hang around the entrance to the sloping house. While everyone is marveling about the weird angles and such, stand near the doorway, then move down toward the east fence. You'll probably feel nausea.

History/Background

Santa Cruz is a party town. It's a tourist-oriented city situated on the northern end of Monterey Bay where surfers have been riding waves for decades. It's also a place where aging hippies hang out. Many of them were the first students in 1965 at the new University of California at Santa Cruz. They were seduced by the region and stayed. Now they are middle-aged, but still having fun. It's easy to see why. The coastal scenery is gorgeous, as are the massive redwoods that dominate the sky just north of town. Up on the hilly slopes are little alcoves of cabins, shacks, and nice homes. This is a wonderful place to hang out.

The Mystery Spot shack. The style of this building appears to be a direct copy of the Oregon Vortex site.

More than 8,000 years ago the Ohlone Indians settled the region and led a peaceful existence with the herds of deer, giant grizzly bears, and flocks of birds resting in the coastal marshes. Not much happened here until 1769, when a Spanish exploratory team camped out near the San Lorenzo River, which now runs through the town. Priests from Mexico stopped by 22 years later and founded Mission La Exaltacion de la Santa Cruz (Holy Cross Mission). The gold rush pushed California toward statehood by 1850 as Americans from around the country swarmed into the region.

The late nineteenth century ushered in a new class of people: those with disposable incomes to spend on vacations. Thus, many cities dotting the California coast became quaint seaside resorts for the newly emerging middle class, Santa Cruz one of them. The early 1900s saw the establishment of an oceanfront casino and, later, an amusement park. The city has been attracting people for many years.

In 1939, a visitor wanted to purchase some redwood property north of town. In his words:

Originally we wanted to get the level ground below here for a summer home or mountain cabin. But the gentleman we were buying from would not sell the level ground unless we purchased the strip across the entire south end of his property including this hillside. Finally we bought the entire piece, mainly to get the level ground, and as we were helping the surveyor along the north line we noted the compass to vary a small amount on the transit and spoke to him about it at that time. He said we might get that variation along a barbed wire fence or some mineral in the ground and let it pass at that. On thinking it over later, there was no barbed wire fence near where we were at the time and as far as we knew no excess mineral in this ground. So we took our own small hand compass and went up over the north line to try and check on it. The variation there was not great enough that we could tell anything about it with nothing to compare it with, as you would have with a surveying instrument or transit. But it is quite rough going up over the point of the hill thru the brush. On returning we came down the little canyon or draw above here. In so doing felt very light-headed or top-heavy, felt like something trying to force us right off the hill. We sat down for a while to try and overcome that feeling. While sitting there we happened to look at the compass again. There the compass had varied enough that we needed nothing to compare it with to tell that it was not correct. We began to check from that and the more we checked the more we found we had this spot of ground here about one hundred fifty feet in diameter, that so far we have not found any instrument absolutely correct over it.[17]

Places like this exist all across the country. And usually they're at the end of some pitted road that assaults your senses with billboard signs like SEE THE TWO-HEADED COW or MARVEL AT THE ICE-MAN. Most of the time the only mystery at the site is why you don't feel your money leaving your wallet. These places make you hunger for the real thing.

Most residents in Santa Cruz quietly scoff at the Mystery Spot. While good for drawing tourists into town, few believe anything is special up in this redwood grove—even though the site's been publicized for years on television, in newspapers, and in magazines such as *Life* and *Fantastic Adventure*. The general attitude of local skeptics can be summed up by a fellow I met in a donut shop: "Darn good way to make a buck, but it ain't worth sheeeet!" Or is it? I've spent a good amount of time in Santa Cruz poking around the hillsides, valleys, and beach recording measurements on a variety of instruments and have found, to my astonishment, that something *is* going on at this place. And it alters perception.

Forget the tour guide's display of Ping-Pong balls rolling uphill (they *don't*) or people walking at funny angles inside the cabin. When you are taken up to the cabin the guide lays out a flat board through a window and places a

Ping-Pong ball on one end. The board appears to slope downward into the structure. The ball *seems* to be rolling *up* the board, away from the downward slant! The effect is pretty persuasive. But it's all perspective: the ball's rolling is a function of a severely sloping redwood-framed house creeping down a steep incline. Strange angles and an upward incline creates the illusion of weirdness. I measured the slope of the hillside against the angle of the board with a carpenter's level. The board is actually sloping downward *outside* the cabin, so gravity still works! But it's a shame that the people here focus on such carnival stuff, for there are real mysteries at the Mystery Spot.

Listen to your gut here. Near the cabin entranceway, well before entering into a room filled with severely sloping floors and walls, most people will feel sick. They should. This spot has one of the most radical geomagnetic fluctuations I've ever measured—and all within a six-foot area! The tour guide should focus on *that* peculiarity! (See Total Magnetic Field section below.)

Contact Person(s)/Organization
Mystery Spot
Mystery Spot Road
Santa Cruz, California 95060
(408) 423-8897
Open 365 days a year. Summer hours: 9.00 A.M.–8:30 P.M.
Winter hours: 9:00 A.M.–4:30 P.M.

Total Magnetic Field/Inclination Angle
The northwestern corner of the cabin's entranceway contains a variety of bizarre total magnetic field and angle of inclination fluctuations. The general TMF/IA in the vicinity of Santa Cruz is around 480 milligauss and 50 degrees. The northwestern corner of the entranceway platform gave a reading of 4570 milligauss (!) and 59 degrees angle of inclination. I took this measurement several times for accuracy. As far as I could see there was no visible metal or wire anywhere in the vicinity. As I moved south toward the cabin, the TMF dropped to 1055, 979, and then, right before I entered the doorway, it dropped to 460 milligauss. Scattered throughout the rest of the entranceway the units were 441/68, 438/60, 501/57, 562/41, 604/38, 667/31. This is the only Mysterious Place along the Pacific coast where such a radical change in magnetic field and angle occurred. Some of the measurements were within two feet of each other! The southern end of the cabin, for example, had no such deviations. Lingering at the northern end and then walking into the sloping cabin may make some people lose a sense of balance and coordination. Some even feel like vomiting. I suspect it's the combined effect of a pineal gland neurotransmitter cascade, as influenced by the changing magnetic field, along with the visual oddity of the angled cabin.

What could be causing such a deviation? There are several possibilities. Local lore has it that a metal-lode meteorite smashed into the hillside sometime B.C. A major fault line in the earth's crust could also explain the weird magnetometer readings, though it's difficult to imagine a change in such a small area. Perhaps this is a function of not having enough data on the Santa Cruz area. Perhaps a detailed scan of the region would reveal other sites as peculiar as this. There may be some relationship with the fault-line hypothesis, as Santa Cruz was near the epicenter of a 1989 earthquake that struck the region.

Of course, there is another explanation. Years ago someone could have dropped or buried something big and metallic right at the cabin spot. For years Santa Cruz lumbered many of its redwoods for a burgeoning market. Could a large ax or saw be the source of the deviation? Those tools *would* cause deviations in a magnetometer. And a big horseshoe magnet would easily create weird readings. But even these possibilities would hardly explain the years of people complaining of feeling sick at this very spot!

Whatever the reason, do be careful at this place. *Something* is causing instrument needles and people's perceptions to wander.

Further Investigations in Area

How many other magnetic deviations are out there in the Santa Cruz or Monterey Bay area? We just don't know. But there *must* be more hot spots in the region. So, to all you backpackers and day-trippers: Keep your compasses close to the ground and let me know if you find any deviations in the needle!

Bird's-eye view of Southern California's geography (U.S. Geological Survey)

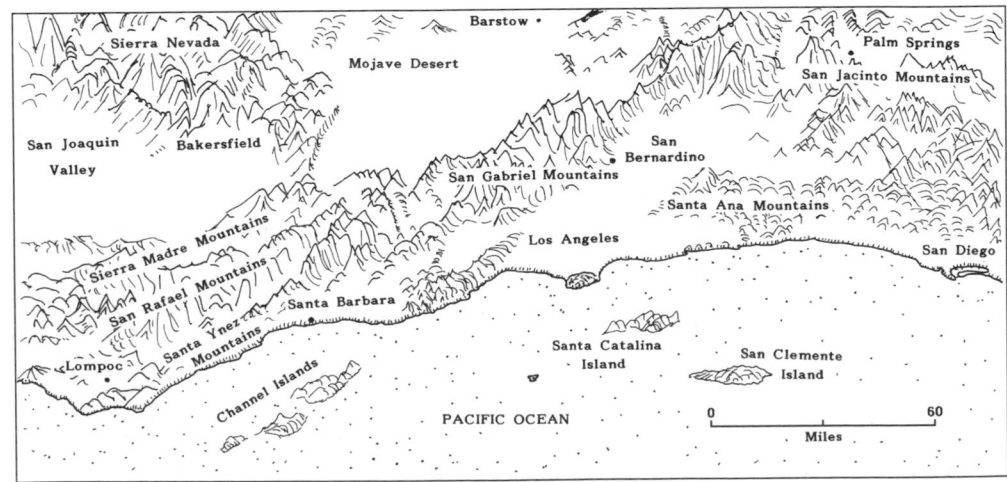

SOUTHERN CALIFORNIA

The Southern Californian lifestyle is unlike any found elsewhere. For years after the mid-nineteenth-century gold rush, people moved to Southern California to get rich, to farm the land, or to escape East Coast sensibilities. Here was a place to start fresh. Here was a land where one could reinvent the self. To some extent, it's still like that today. A balmy Mediterranean climate makes you slow down and appreciate the outdoors. Unfortunately, so many people have moved here over the last 50 years that many are now leaving the state to escape the high population density and the usual problems of crime and pollution that accompany such trends.

South of Monterey Bay the land and climate change: the mountains get smaller and the temperature gets hotter. High desert conditions exist throughout much of the region. In fact, Los Angeles and cities scattered throughout the southern part of the state are living on borrowed time. If not for the redirection of water from the north to the south, from the Colorado River to Southern California, the region would still be patches of orange groves. If it stops snowing for just three or four years, there will be no water available for the millions of people living in the Los Angeles–San Diego corridor, let alone the towns east of these megalopolises. It's scary to visualize the urban chaos that would occur with such a change in climate.

Unfortunately, this scenario is not a question of *if* it happens, but rather a question of *when* it happens. Archaeological excavations throughout the deserts in Southern California and throughout the southwestern region of the United States have shown conclusively that prehistoric civilizations that flourished in the area experienced high population densities and then drought. It's a cycle that seems to repeat itself with frightening regularity. And then there's always the threat of earthquakes.

Thousands of years ago, when there was more and frequent rainfall in Southern California, the indigenous population led a peaceful and bountiful existence. Food and water was readily available. When an ecosystem allows a people to spend a minimum amount of time obtaining food, interesting things happen to the culture. Leisure time allows for relaxed contemplation. The indigenous peoples of Southern California sought out and left their mark on thousands of caves in the region.

HALLUCINOGENIC CAVE
Partington Cove, Big Sur, California

Site Synopsis

A tiny cave, reported to be some 20 to 40 feet above a rock overhang, looks out over the ocean. The Esselen Indians performed shamanistic rituals

in this sacred space. What spirit visions did they conjure up and why did they choose this cave?

Location

The turnoff for Partington Canyon and Cove is 10 miles south of Big Sur along Route 1. Watch your odometer, starting at the restaurant Nepenthe. There are no signs for any of the canyons and creeks here so drive slowly and look around. The road makes a sharp curve around the canyon. Just before the curve you'll see a wide access trail on the west side of the road. Park well off the road and start the hike down to the cove.

Cross the creek and go through the tunnel, which was cut in the 1880s. On the other side you'll see the wooden remains of an old ship-loading hoist. Here's where it gets tricky. Depending on weather conditions there *may* be a dirt trail that snakes along the northern perimeter of this cove. If accessible—that means there aren't any signs prohibiting entry—walk up the trail to the stone outcroppings. The ridge rises steeply on your right. The cave opening is hidden from view, but it's supposedly an easy 20-foot scramble up. Go find it!

Considerations

Be careful when climbing around these cliffs. It's easy to slip and fall. Don't even *think* about swimming or wading here. The surf is totally unpredictable and powerful underwater currents prevail. Stay on land. And remember, *never* turn your back to the ocean!

History/Background

Route 1 straddles the base of the Santa Lucia Mountains. Well before the first Spanish explorers looked out upon this range, thousands of Native Americans called this rugged terrain home. Exactly how long the original inhabitants were in the Big Sur region is the cause of great speculation and debate among archaeologists. It is known, however, that a small tribe called the Esselens lived there and greeted the Spanish padres in the 1700s. In the early 1970s the Monterey County Archaeological Society excavated the skeletal remains of an Esselen woman who was buried over 3,000 years ago. Found on the Post Ranch in Big Sur, the skeleton was laid out in ritualistic fashion: in the fetal position, surrounded by specially made stone spear points.[18]

There are only two ways to get to the Big Sur region, by Route 1 or by boat. The latter method is a tad difficult as there are few safe harbors south of Monterey and north of San Luis Obispo. Coming in from the east is quite difficult due to the high, rugged mountains that block off the valley. These geological conditions contributed to the region's isolation over the years. While the Spanish explored Big Sur, none settled there. By the 1850s, the first homesteaders began setting up modest sites. By the turn of the century,

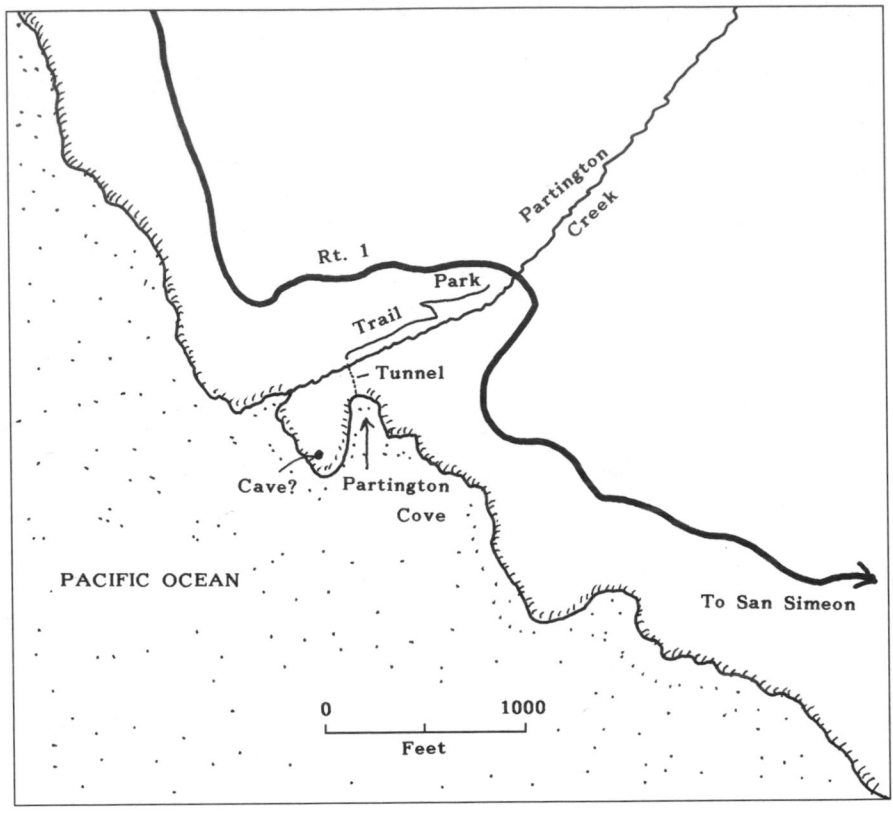

Possible location of Partington Cove's Hallucinogenic Cave

tourism and the canning industry made their way into Big Sur. By the early 1940s and 1950s, artists, writers, and poets "discovered" the sublime beauty of the coast. A colony of creative, individualistic-thinking people emerged.

There are hundreds of painted caves scattered throughout this region. Unfortunately, most are somewhat inaccessible, requiring a two-day hike into the Ventana Wilderness.

A few years ago a friend told me of a cave she was taken to 20 years earlier by a local poet. She said that once inside the seaside opening she was overwhelmed with fear and disturbing images. She felt that she was hallucinating. Her guide told her that this cave was a special place where the Esselens went to experience the divine.

How could I pass this up? I spent the next several days climbing on rocks sprayed by the ocean. One afternoon, someone called out to me: "Hey, man, what are you doing up there?"

Six sunbathers emerged from behind a rock. I told them the story. They

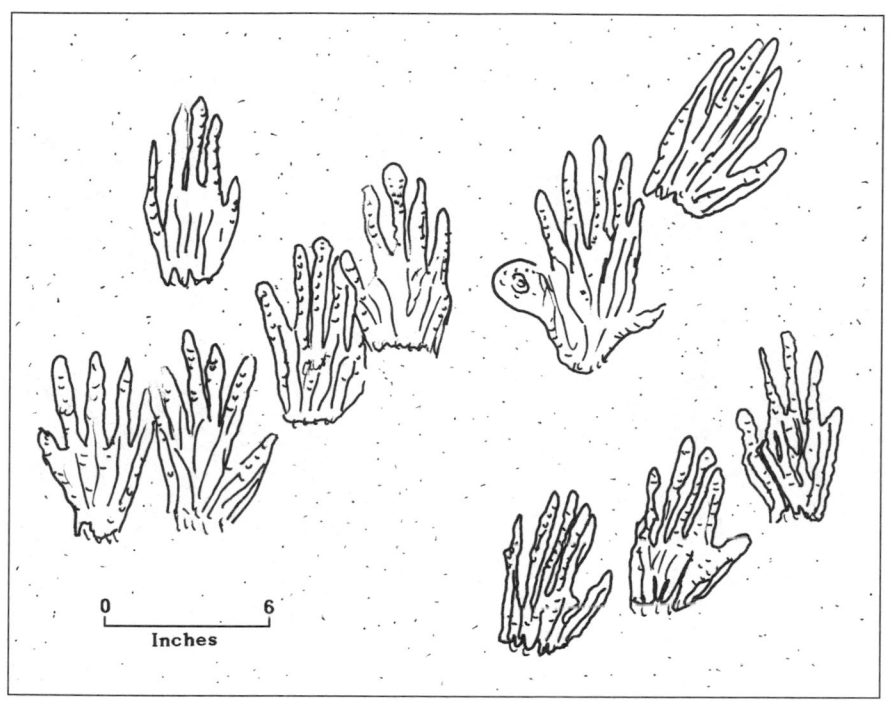

Hand images along a smoke-blackened wall in a cave near Church Creek, northwest of Tassajara Hot Springs, Los Padres National Forest, east of the Santa Lucia Mountains, California

had heard it before but never bothered to look. We spent the next four hours scampering about on those dangerous cliffs looking for the cave. We never found it, but we came close. At the base of a rock overhang I noticed several basalt grinding stones, other hand tools, and broken spearpoints wedged in between a small crevice. I left them in place—as everyone should do when faced with antiquity in the field. The cave had to be in the general vicinity, but unfortunately, I had no time left for further exploration.

Some longtime residents said that the last earth tremor ripped apart several cliffs in the region. It's possible that the cave was partially blocked by falling debris. If so, then it must still be intact, waiting to perform its magic on the unsuspecting.

I spent the night with my new companions in a house overlooking the ocean. The sunset was astonishing. We watched a comet from the deck. Big Sur overwhelms the soul. There are enclaves of people out here who love and live life to its fullest. And all in sight of a primeval world that puts everything into perspective. I found much more at this place than I anticipated. You will, too.

The treacherous Pacific coastline south of Big Sur. East of here, in the mysterious Santa Lucia Mountains, elusive shadow figures reportedly stand high atop the hills, looking out at the ocean. Hundreds of caves painted by Chumash Indians are scattered throughout this astonishing region.

Contact Person (s)/Organization

There is no general reference for this site. But a superb introduction to the Big Sur region can be found in Tomi Kay Lussier's *Big Sur: A Complete History and Guide.*

Total Magnetic Field/Inclination Angle

Measurements taken at the top of the canyon and down near the putative cave site varied greatly. As I walked down toward the splash zone, the total magnetic field dropped precipitously by 400 units. Near the stone tools I was getting readings of 45, 50, and 35 milligauss units. I suspect that the cave site is above an unusually aberrant magnetic field. This could explain my friend's uncomfortable feelings there.

Further Investigations in Area

Although it's very difficult to do—some of the paths skirt private property—try to walk along the coastal splash zone, where the sea meets the sand

Chumash polychrome cave painting found at the southern end of the Santa Lucia Mountains (Adapted from Grant, Rock Art of the American Indian*)*

or rock. Reports tell of dozens of sea caves that were used by the ancient inhabitants of the region.

Well into the Los Padres National Forest, northwest of Tassajara Hot Springs along Church Creek, is a smoke-blackened cave filled with human hand images. The meaning of these highly personal markings is unknown.

Around the Santa Lucia Mountains east of Route 1 there are persistent stories of mysterious shadow figures seen against the tops of the 3,000-foot peaks. Supposedly these dark, humanoid figures stand on the peaks looking out over the land. No one knows who or what they were or are. If these stories are true—and several writers and poets, like John Steinbeck and Robinson Jeffers, have referred to them—several things come to mind. For one to see and be able to recognize a humanoid figure from the coastline below, the figure or thing has to be massive. Looking up from Route 1, some 500 feet above the coastline, toward the Santa Lucia peaks, even cows look tiny. The Ventana Wilderness area, east of the mountains, is so isolated that several unique plant species were found there a number of years ago. The limiting effect of high peaks east and west apparently has kept out a lot of plants and animals. Perhaps it has kept something *in* as well.

There are many cave paintings in the Santa Lucia Mountains. Unfortunately, many are deep within the interior, far away from the usual trails. Nonetheless, as the late painter and naturalist Campbell Grant noted many years ago, the best paintings are found in unusual locations—and, I might add, are probably still not yet identified by whites. Keep looking, but remember, these are sacred sites that must be respected. If you find some cave art, take only pictures, preferably without the flash.

MASS EXTINCTIONS
Sea Cove, west of Lompoc, California

Site Synopsis

In a little bay on the north side of the Santa Ynez River, a mile and a half above the present town of Lompoc, are the fossil remains of untold numbers of a specific species of fish. Known as *Xyne grex*, this fish was similar to the modern

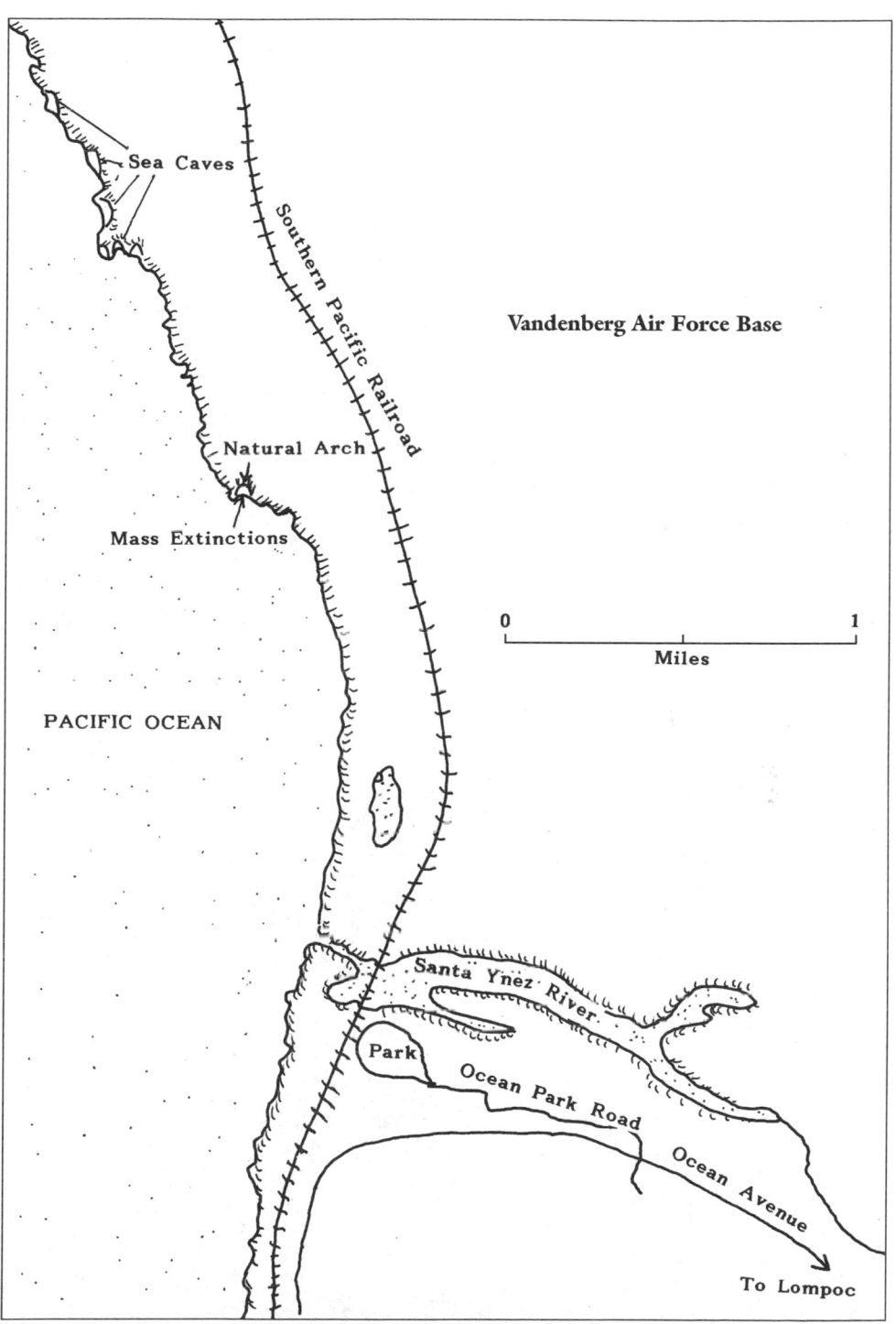

Location of sea cove of mass extinctions, west of Lompoc, California

herring, except that its surface bones were covered with enamel. Measuring six to eight inches long, 25 million years ago these ancient fish, during spawning season, clustered in the bay and died. More than 20 million years later, 350 feet of plankton has settled on, solidified, and preserved the stone remains of these creatures. Why was this bay crowded with a billion *Xyne* to the exclusion of all other fish? Why did they die instantly, quietly, with no sign of distress, and how were they suddenly sealed before going to pieces in decay?

Location

Lompoc is an hour ride northwest of Santa Barbara. From Santa Barbara take Route 101 north for 26 miles. Exit on Route 1. In about 20 miles you'll enter Lompoc. Turn west (left) on Ocean Avenue. Stay on Ocean Avenue for about 8 miles and watch for the Ocean Park Road exit on your right. Turn into Ocean Park Road and park at the end. There's a rest room and phone available.

Walk due west—toward the ocean—crossing the railroad tracks. Walk north to the mouth of the Santa Ynez River. You'll need to wade across—it's shallow, usually about a foot deep, with undulating sandbars. The first cove is about a mile north along the beach. A whitish outcrop, containing good examples of this strange mass extinction, is about 25 yards from the first nat-

The sea cove rocks west of Lompoc, California, are saturated with fossils of herringlike fish known as Xyne grex. *No one knows what killed billions of these ancient fish all at once, 25 million years ago.*

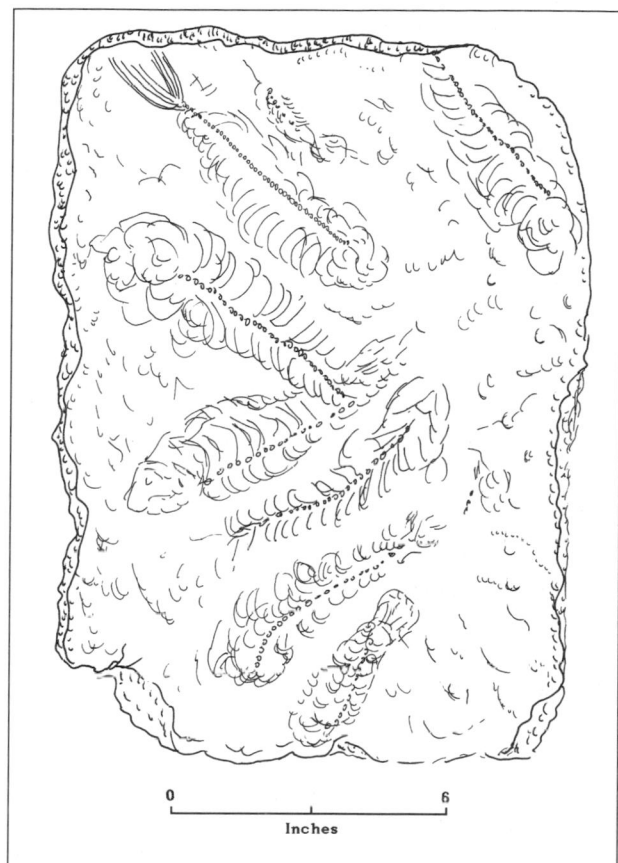

Some of the strange fossils—Xyne grex— that mysteriously died

0 6
Inches

ural sea arch in the cove. Look for tiny polygon patterns in the rock matrix.

If you're feeling energetic and inspired walk farther along the beach to explore the other marvelous sea caves. There are billions of remains here from an ancient time.

Considerations

Time your coastal walk carefully. Walk out to the sea caves at low tide. At high tide you'll be cut off from the access path back to the river.

Also, do be careful of the waves. While they're wonderful to look at, don't get too close. The undercurrent is ferocious and you could easily be swept out to sea.

History/Background

Around 25 million years ago, during a geological time period known as the Miocene, the great continental plates were pushing up against each other, creating huge mountain ranges. The western part of North America was inundated by major faults and volcanic eruptions. Large sections of Oregon and Washington were covered over in unbelievably large lava flows. Things were pretty rocky.

During this time billions of herringlike fish swam into the area now above sea level. At the time, the bay was nonexistent—everything was underwater. Generally fish gather in specific places during mating season; many examples of such behavior has been observed for years. But why did all of these particular creatures die at the same time? Given all the volcanic activity in the vicinity, they most likely were overcome by poisonous gases that filtered through the shallow water. Perhaps their huge numbers precluded other fish from swimming around that spot. We will never know the full answers to these questions, but mass extinction of any type brings forth wider speculation on the nature of existence on planet Earth.

This fossil outcropping is but one example of the mysterious ways of our earth. All life on our planet shares one common feature: locked deeply within the cytoplasm of the cell is deoxyribonucleic acid, or DNA. The sequence of the chemicals making up this macromolecule (which is in the shape of a twisted ladder—a double helix) is the chemical "software" that instructs cells to become elephants or humans or clams. Splice some "new" genetic code into a chain of DNA and you might get a new form of life.

The more you study ancient life from the fossil record the more you'll notice an unsettling concept: close to 99 percent of all the species that ever lived are extinct, be they *Xyne grex* or dinosaurs. The earth tries out new combinations of life every few million years—it keeps spewing them out. The sequence and arrangement possibilities are astronomical. But most life dies off. The survivors adapt to changing environmental conditions; that is, until their offspring lose the ability (or genetic makeup) to carry on because the environment changes. When they die, the crap shoot continues. Survivors carry the game for a while, but eventually they lose. Like in a casino when the only winner is the house, in this case, it's the planet. Some life-forms win, some lose, but the earth continues unscathed. Seen from space the earth must seem like a gigantic, life-generating machine. How strangely wonderful.

Stroll along the beach at Lompoc, look at the evidence of extinction, sit down by the shore, and think about the next set of winners 20 million years from now. It's a humbling experience.

Contact Person(s)/Organization

The best reference on this peculiar site can be found in a 1920 issue of *Natural History*, in David Starr Jordan's article entitled, "A Miocene Catastrophe."

Total Magnetic Field/Inclination Angle
None taken at this site.

Further Investigations in Area
A few miles east of the fish extinction site was the old Lompoc Ranchero. The ranch was part of an old Spanish land grant. In 1833, Mexico, realizing it needed to defend its California territory from the encroaching Russians, British, and Americans, outfitted ranches up and down the coast as military encampments. It was then that soldiers made a peculiar discovery.

Excavating a pit to store gunpowder on a hill overlooking the Santa Ynez River, they came across a human skeleton. But not just any collection of bones. The skeleton was over 12 feet tall, and the upper and lower jaw of its gigantic skull had *double rows of teeth*! Natives of the area freaked out, claiming it was a portent of something evil. From somewhere in their mythology they remembered stories of heinous giants their ancestors had to fight off. No way did they want the spirits of the evil ones around. Military officials quickly reburied the bones and the gunpowder pit was dug elsewhere.

Today a modern correctional facility occupies the land where the ranch used to be. No one involved in its construction ever came across the bones. Or so they said. How apropos that a jail, of all things, was built on top of this spiritually evil place!

The giant with a skull having a double row of teeth is a staple in early archaeological literature. Many creatures of this type have been found throughout North America. Unfortunately, most were uncovered when preservation of such genetic deformities was not the best. All we have are the written description of these oddities. The bones have been lost in time.

ANCIENT CAVE PAINTINGS
Chumash Painted Cave State Historical Park, northwest of Santa Barbara, California

Site Synopsis
Generations ago the enigmatic Chumash Indians selected this cave and with various pigments painted a series of symbols, signs, and inscriptions known only to them. What do they mean and why was this cave selected?

Location
There are two ways to get to this cave. The first is preferable—it's the shorter route and takes very little time. The second route takes twice as long. But get up there regardless of the route. You will be thrilled and amazed!

From Santa Barbara take Route 101 west to Route 154 going north. In

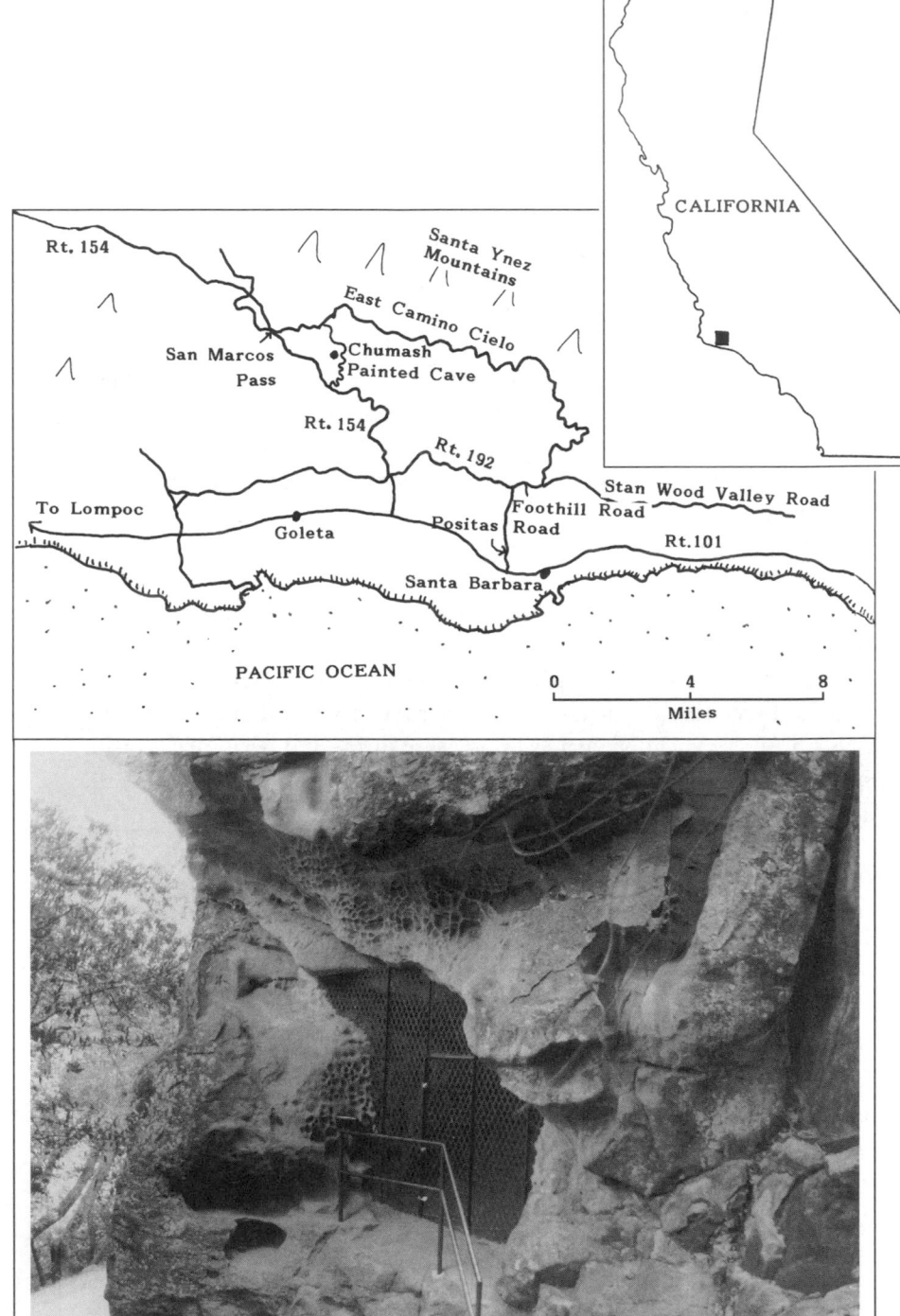

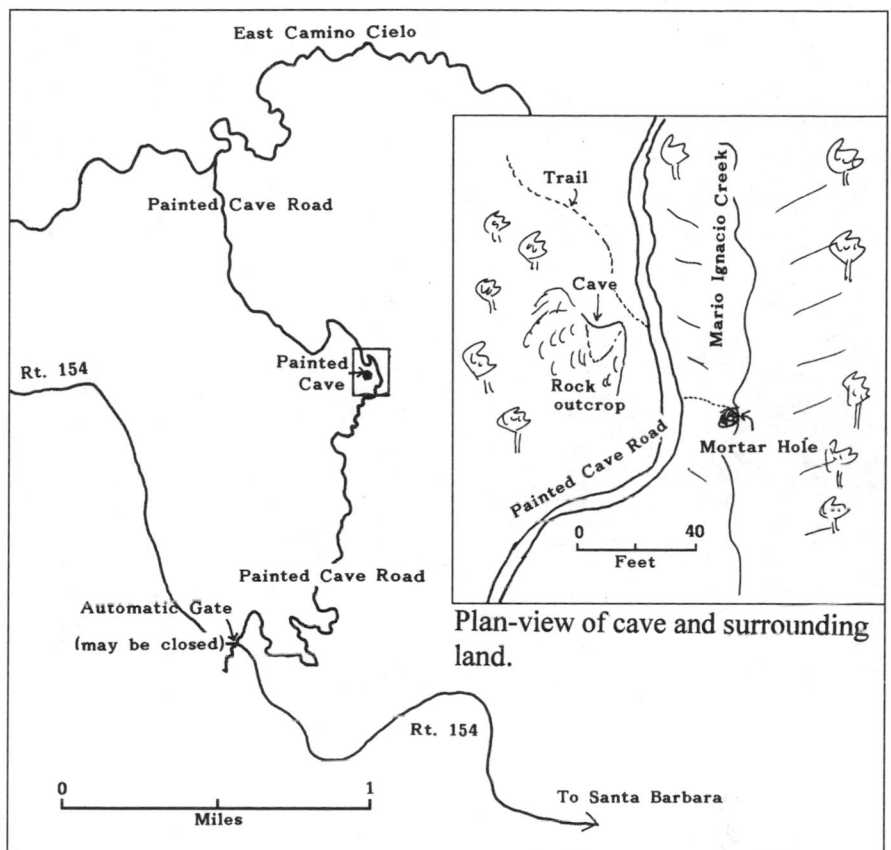

Map and bird's-eye view of Chumash Painted Cave

about four miles exit right on Painted Cave Road, which at one time was an ancient trail leading up to the site. Here's where it gets tricky. There's a solar-powered automatic gate at the entrance to the road. If it's open it's your lucky day. Travel very slowly up this twisting, single-lane road. In about two miles you'll see a tiny sign on your left. The sandstone cave is a few feet off the road.

If the automatic gate is closed the only other way to see this marvelous cave is to take East Camino Cielo. From Santa Barbara take Route 101 west to Positas Road. Travel north for a few miles taking Route 192 (Foothill Road) east. In about four miles exit north on East Camino Cielo. Stay on this road for a little over 13 miles until you spot Painted Cave Road on your left. Turn left (south) on Painted Cave Road. Within two miles the cave site will be on your right.

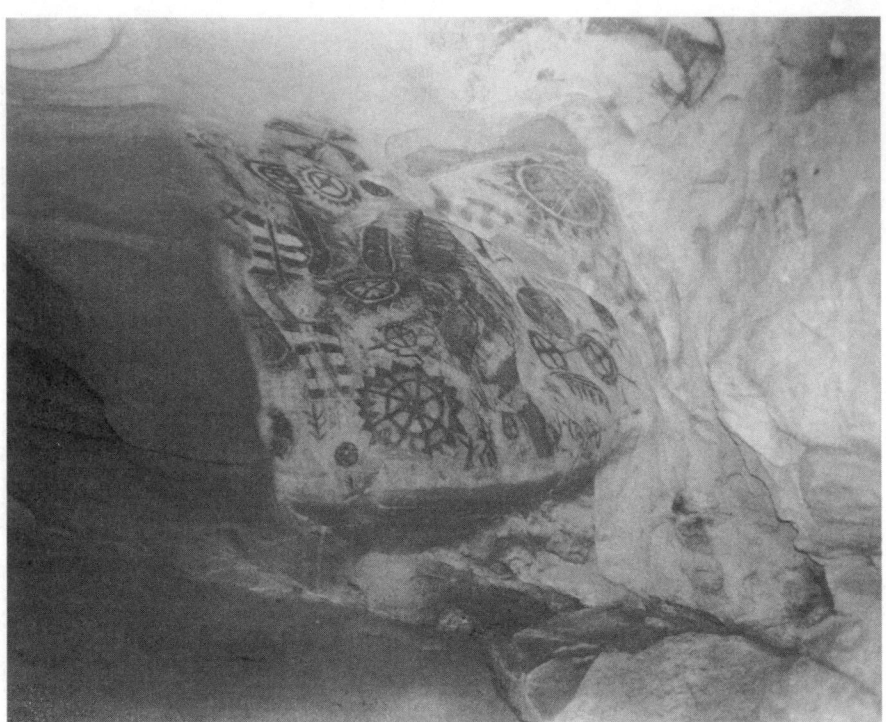

The wall of the protected Chumash Painted Cave north of Santa Barbara is filled with a staggering array of red and black "spoke-wheel" images. It is believed this enclosure was used by shamans to view alternative realities.

Considerations

This is California's most accessible and best-protected painted cave site. Many years ago a thick iron gate was placed at the entranceway to protect the delicate red and black designs. Nonetheless some vandals have managed to carve their initials onto the soft stone near the entranceway.

Because the cave points almost due north and is between two high, tree-covered ridges the lighting makes it difficult to see the polychrome paintings. Visiting the site during the summer at midday, when the sun is directly over-head, allows for a little more light to enter the cave. Bring along a strong, wide-beam flashlight and some low-power (7 x 35 for example) binoculars. These will allow you to study the designs in detail.

Photographing the paintings is easy, provided you have a strong flash and a camera with a lens that's able to fit through openings in the iron gate. Portable, optical flash units are useful here. These hand-held devices (known in the field as "slaves") are set off by your camera's initial flash. If you have a few of these inexpensive units you can light up an entire cavern. They're great at this site.

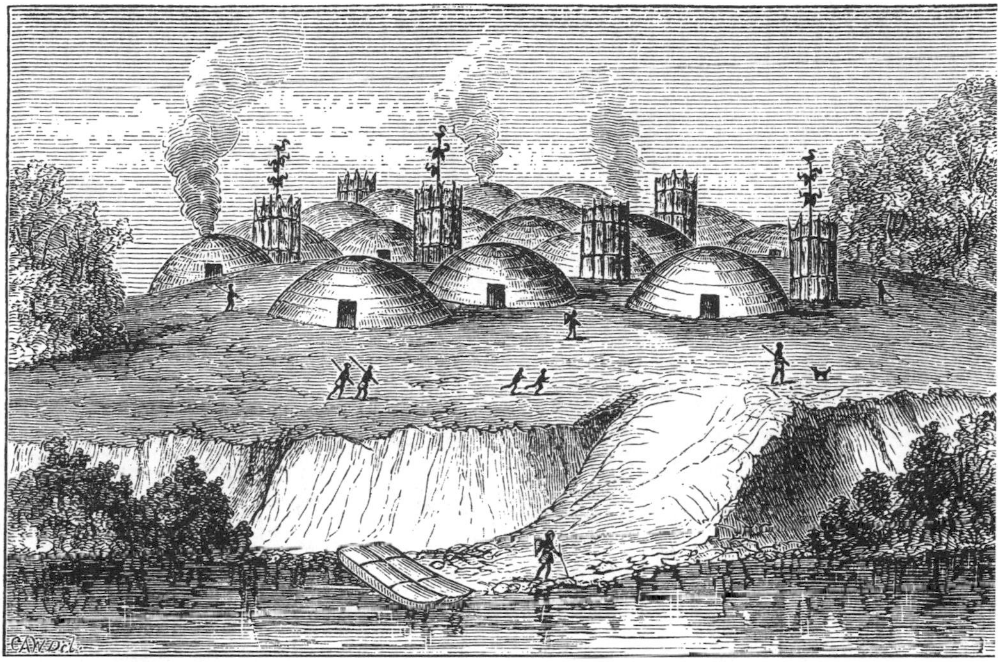

Chumash grass-covered houses along the California coast (Chever, The Indians of California)

Chumash Indians transporting grass seeds for baking in the early 1800s (Schoolcraft, Henry Rowe, History of the Indian Tribes of the United States)

History/Background

The Chumash occupied the coastal and mountain lands between San Luis Obispo and the region north of Los Angeles. Early accounts of these people are filled with admiration. They built 25-foot boats to sail to the offshore islands in search of soapstone and fish. They built massive dome-shaped reed houses and seemed to live life to its fullest. Given their abundant, readily available food supply, the Chumash had plenty of time to think about the cosmos. We know this is so because of the dozens of painted caves found in the Santa Ynez Mountains above Santa Barbara.

Most of the caves are eroded holes within yellow sandstone. Against this background are swirls and patterns of red, yellow, white, and black paintings. The majority of these caves are known only to Chumash elders, state archaeologists, and backcountry hikers. There is one cave that can be visited today.

The Painted Cave, situated just west of Mario Ignacio Creek, is intriguing. It's been called one of the most remarkable examples of Indian rock art in this country—perhaps because of the weird-looking animals, the striped humanoid creatures, the crosses, and the circles of "wheels." The place is eerie.

Archaeologists aren't sure what the symbols mean, and the remaining Chumash either don't know or they won't say. I suspect the latter is true. Nonetheless, noble attempts at interpretation have been made. Some white researchers think some of the symbols honor the moon and the cosmic sun. The four cardinal directions (North, South, East, West) have also been "seen" here. These images evoke another plane of perception, or, perhaps, existence. It's suspected that this cave, as well as others in the region, was used by tribal shamans for reasons that we can only guess.

According to some scholars, the style of the rock paintings suggests they could be anywhere from 200 to 1,000 years old. I'm always amused at such relative dating, for there is nothing of substance to base this estimate on. Carbon-dating pigment on stone is a practice filled with problems. Fact is, we haven't a clue when the cave was painted or for what reason. But we can hazard an educated guess as to *why* this particular cave site was chosen (see Total Magnetic Field below).

Contact Person(s)/Organization

Campbell Grant was a professional artist with a keen interest in Native American symbols. In the early 1960s he began a lifelong quest to document all known rock art sites in California. His work became the source that scholars looked to when they became interested in the subject. Campbell's definitive work on the Chumash rock art sites was republished in 1993 by the Santa Barbara Museum of Natural History. I recommend *The Rock Paintings of the Chumash* by Campbell Grant to anyone with an interest in these mysterious designs.

Total Magnetic Field/Inclination Angle

The many measurements I collected at this site have shed some small light on why this particular cave was painted.

Base-line total magnetic field measurements taken 100 feet from the cave were in the 460 milligauss/60 degree range. Going 30 feet in front of the cave led to readings of 493/54. As I got closer to the north-facing opening, the readings rose to over 700 milligauss and 34 degrees for the angle of inclination. At first I suspected the metal gate was skewing my instrument. But at a few other sites that I was taken to I got similar readings—there are no metal gates on these smaller painted caves.

In summary, it appears that this painted cave—as well as the others I measured—was chosen because of the unusual feeling it no doubt provoked in an occupant. While the Chumash had no way of knowing the actual reason *why* such a place caused visions and perceptual changes, they nonetheless used the cave, perhaps as an enhancer of strange sightings. Remember, a radical change in geomagnetic field can cause significant mood swings in most people. Most likely, the shamans that utilized these caves where more susceptible to such changes.

Further Investigations in Area

As stated earlier, dozens of painted caves can be found in the mountains above Santa Barbara. Unfortunately, you will need permission and a guide to get to these strange sites, for many are on private property or on reservation land.

A Chumash polychrome painting on the sandstone walls of a cave above Santa Barbara. The meaning of these images is unknown.

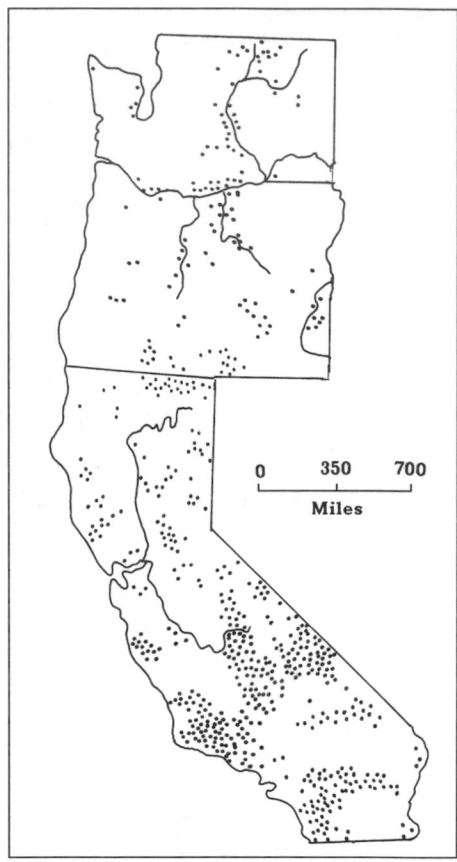

Rock art sites along the Pacific Coast
(Adapted from Campbell Grant)

One can, however, walk along the nearby Mario Ignacio Creek and look for signs of times past. On such an outing I noticed a large boulder with a depressed "cup-mark" carved into its side. These depressions are thought to be mortar holes, places where nuts were placed and ground into meal.

SAN JOAQUIN VALLEY MOUNDS
Near Visalia, California

Site Synopsis
In the Lindcove district of California, about 13 miles east of Visalia, are some of the finest specimens of surface mounds in the state. Hundreds of pimplelike mounds dot this fine valley. Their origin, as with other such mound structures, is unknown.

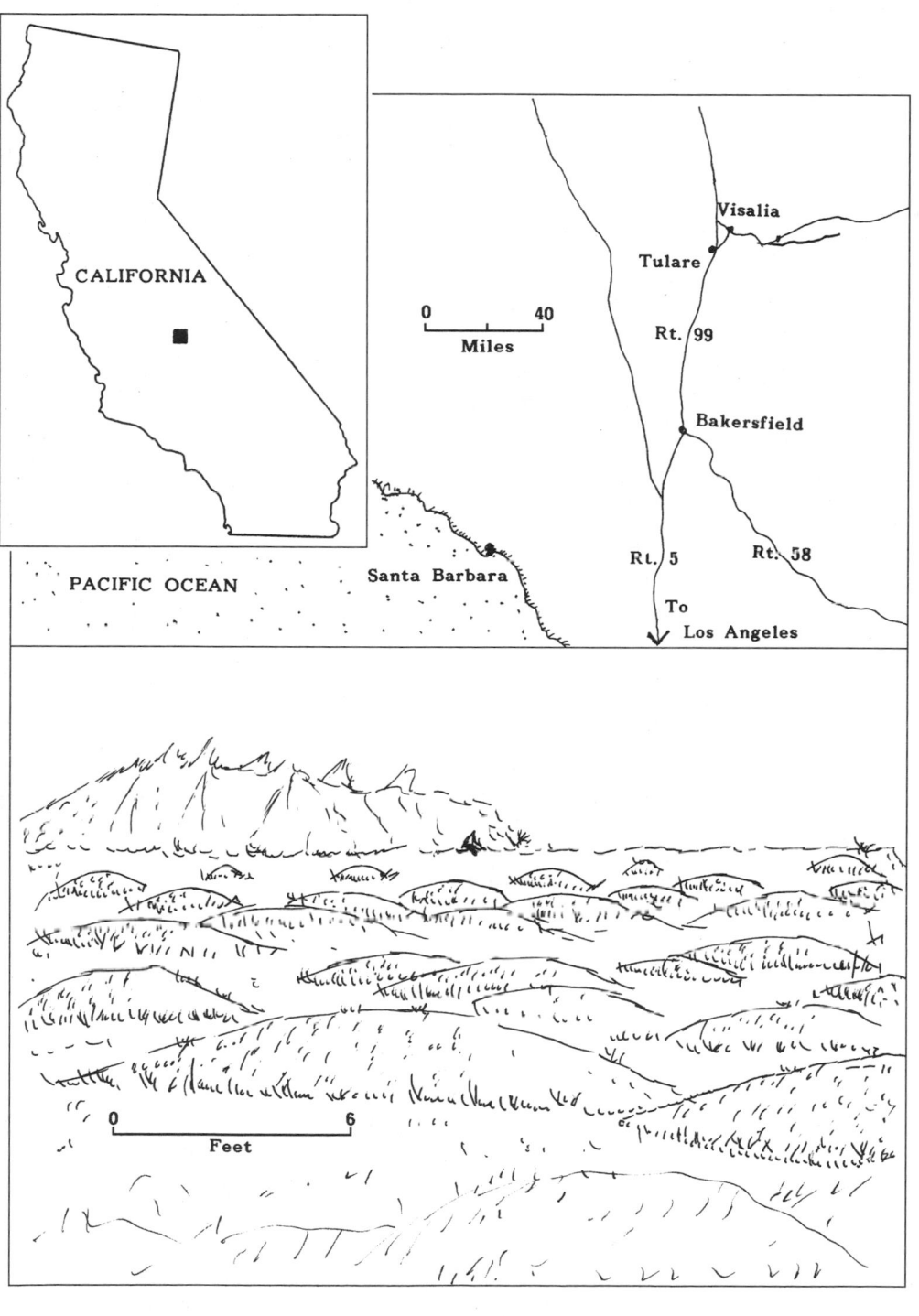

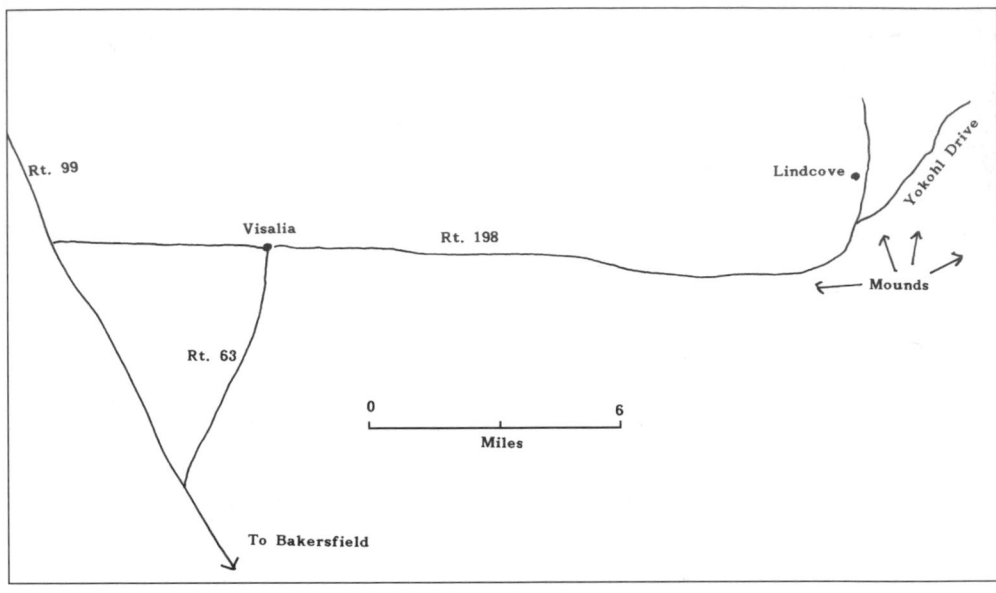

Location of the Mima mounds near Visalia, California

Location

From Bakersfield take Route 99 north for about 65 miles to Visalia (via Route 63). Travel east on Route 198 for about 20 miles toward Lindcove. Just off Yokohl Drive in a field to your right (south) you'll see the strange mounds.

Considerations

All of the mounds are on private property, so please ask permission before walking among these weird bumps.

The best perspective, however, is from the air. There are several private air-fields nearby. It's pretty easy to negotiate a fee to have someone take you up in a plane to look.

History/Background

Small mounds found on vast stretches of land throughout the country have a long and crazy history. The first mounds to come to anyone's attention were those along the Mima Prairie southeast of Olympia, Washington. Called the Mima mounds, these ground surface features have long been a source of controversy as scholars have tried to explain them. Over the years serious consideration has been given to their being Indian burial mounds, giant plant-root bumps, surface erosion remains, giant gopher domiciles, or the result of frost/thaw action. The hundreds of mounds dotting the Mima plain were poked, prodded, cut into, and excavated. Most of the above explanations have

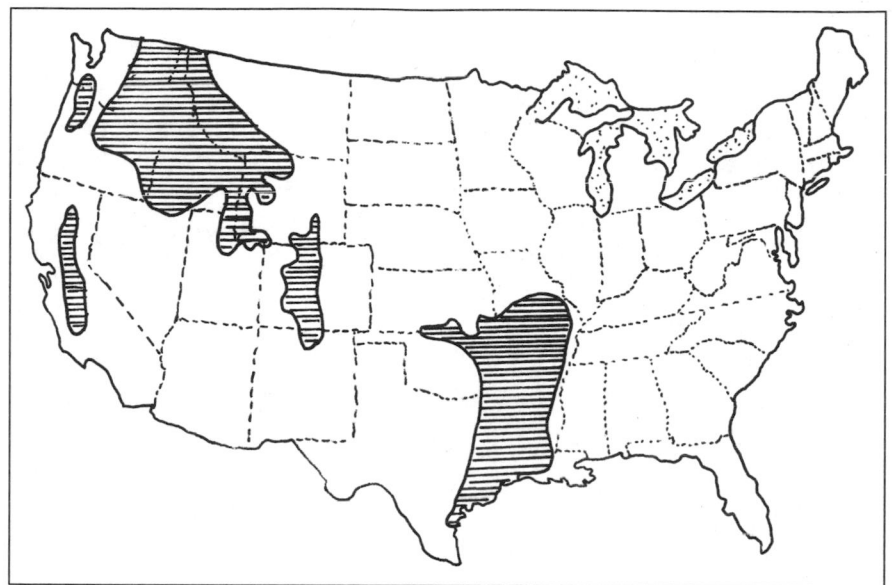

Regions of the United States where unexplained pimple-shaped mounds occur (Adapted from Berg)

been thrown out. Up until recently, scientists merely shrugged, saying "Well, *something* caused them," and left it at that.

Mima mounds have been found elsewhere. In the San Joaquin Valley of central California are some of the best examples ever. The mounds are smooth and round, almost like half-buried spheres. Some are over 6 feet high and 30 feet across. The typical mound is a mix of black silt and small pebbles.

The most interesting hypothesis for the mounds comes from a U.S. Bureau of Mines field operation scientist, Andrew Berg. In 1990 he tackled the century-old mystery in a novel fashion. Berg reproduced small-scale Mima mounds in the laboratory. He took a dirt-covered plywood board and hit it several times. The vibrations created mounds nearly identical to those found on the Mima plateau! Berg concluded that these mounds may be "fossil" evidence of former seismic activity in the area, the soil is fine, unconsolidated, and resting on a ridged base.[19] Intriguing!

Contact Person(s)/Organization

The reference to Berg's article can be found in the bibliography. Details to the Mima mounds can be found in my first book of mysterious sites, *Field Guide to Mysterious Places of the West.*

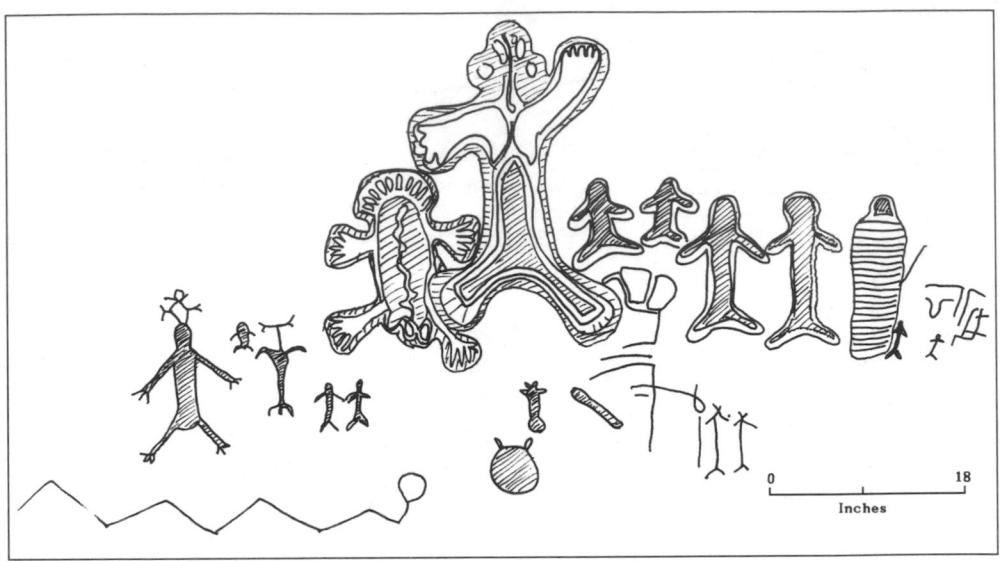

Painting at Rocky Hill, east of Exeter, near the Visalia Mounds (Adapted from Campbell Grant, Rock Art of the American Indian*)*

Total Magnetic Field/Inclination Angle
None taken here.

Further Investigations in Area
About two miles east of Exeter, along the slope of Rocky Hill is a large polychrome painting of strange, sacred-looking figures. The images appear almost "transparent," giving the entire panel the impression of great power.

UNUSUAL MUD-BALLS
Camarillo, California

Site Synopsis
After a rather devastating flood in March 1938, researchers reported tens of thousands of mud-balls near Highway 101. They are still there. The physics of spherical concretion formation is unknown.

Location
Forty miles southeast of Santa Barbara along Route 101 brings one to Camarillo. About a mile and a half west of Camarillo take Las Posas Road south. This road eventually leads to coastal Route 1. Half a mile south along Las Posas Road there's a field on your right (west). Scattered throughout the ditches here and south are the remains of mud-balls, between 3 and 10 inches in diameter.

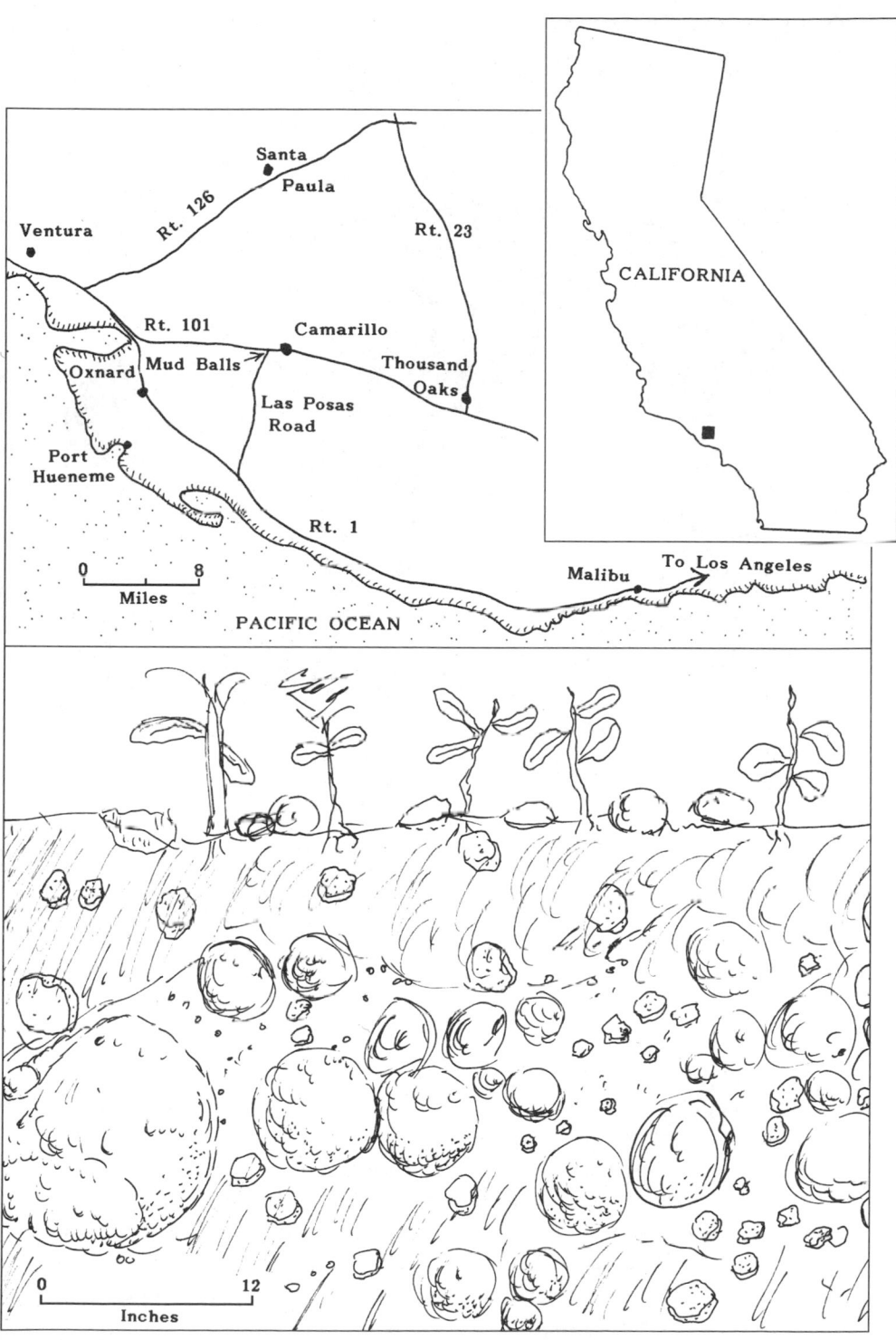

PACIFIC OCEAN

CALIFORNIA

Santa Paula
Ventura
Rt. 126
Rt. 23
Rt. 101
Camarillo
Oxnard
Mud Balls
Thousand Oaks
Las Posas Road
Port Hueneme
Rt. 1
Malibu
To Los Angeles

Miles
0   8

Inches
0   12

The geological process that formed stone spheres is unknown. Examples have been found throughout the United States, like these from Noble, Missouri.
(Spheres courtesy of Ray Fraser)

Considerations

If you can't get local permission to walk the fields, then take along a good pair of field binoculars. You can scan the fields from the road and be amazed at the bizarre spherical concretions.

History/Background

Spherical concretions have been found on every continent. They usually take the form of small, round balls. Sometimes the balls are over three feet in diameter—like that at Cannonball River in North Dakota.[20]

No one really understands why rocks form stone spheres. For example, sample spheres collected just outside the town of Noble, Missouri, are perplexing. Known locally as "stone eggs," these one-to-three-inch spheres are hard, crystalline limestone. Cutting them in half provides no clue on their formation. Mud-balls, on the other hand, are easier to understand. They've been found along beach cliffs of clay and where riverbanks are steep and narrow.

The mud-balls of Camarillo have an origin that's easy to understand. The upper part of Las Posas barranca is filled with clay and stream debris. After a heavy rain, water comes swishing down the channel, pushing along tiny bits of particles and clay. After a few miles the sticky clay takes on a rounded, spherical shape. When the water dries up it leaves the balls stranded along the barranca and in surrounding fields, depending on the force of the flooding.

Contact Person(s)/Organization

The definitive article on mud-balls and this site was written over 50 years ago, by Hugh Stevens Bell. Titled "Armored Mud Balls: Their Origin, Properties, and Role in Sedimentation," it can be found in the *Journal of Geology* (1940, pp. 1–31).

Total Magnetic Field/Inclination Angle

None taken here.

Further Investigations in Area

A walk around the region may reveal other intriguing bits of stone sphere geology.

About 30 miles northeast of Camarillo in the Burro Flats region of the Simi Hills, northwest of Los Angeles, is a small cave with ancient Chumash markings. During late December on the shortest day of the year, light illuminates a maze of polychrome paintings there. Details on this site can be found in my first book in this series.[21]

SUBTERRANEAN SOUNDS
Commerce, California

Site Synopsis

In the late 1980s residents in Commerce, a city east of Los Angeles, began hearing strange underground explosions. The source of these booms has never been uncovered.

Location

The muffled explosions were felt between Gage and Zindell Avenues in Commerce. To drive to this area from downtown Los Angeles, take the Santa Ana Freeway east. Just past Commerce, take the East Gage Avenue exit. In two tenths of a mile you'll see Zindell Avenue on your left. A little farther is 7163 East Gage Avenue, the "epicenter" of these noises.

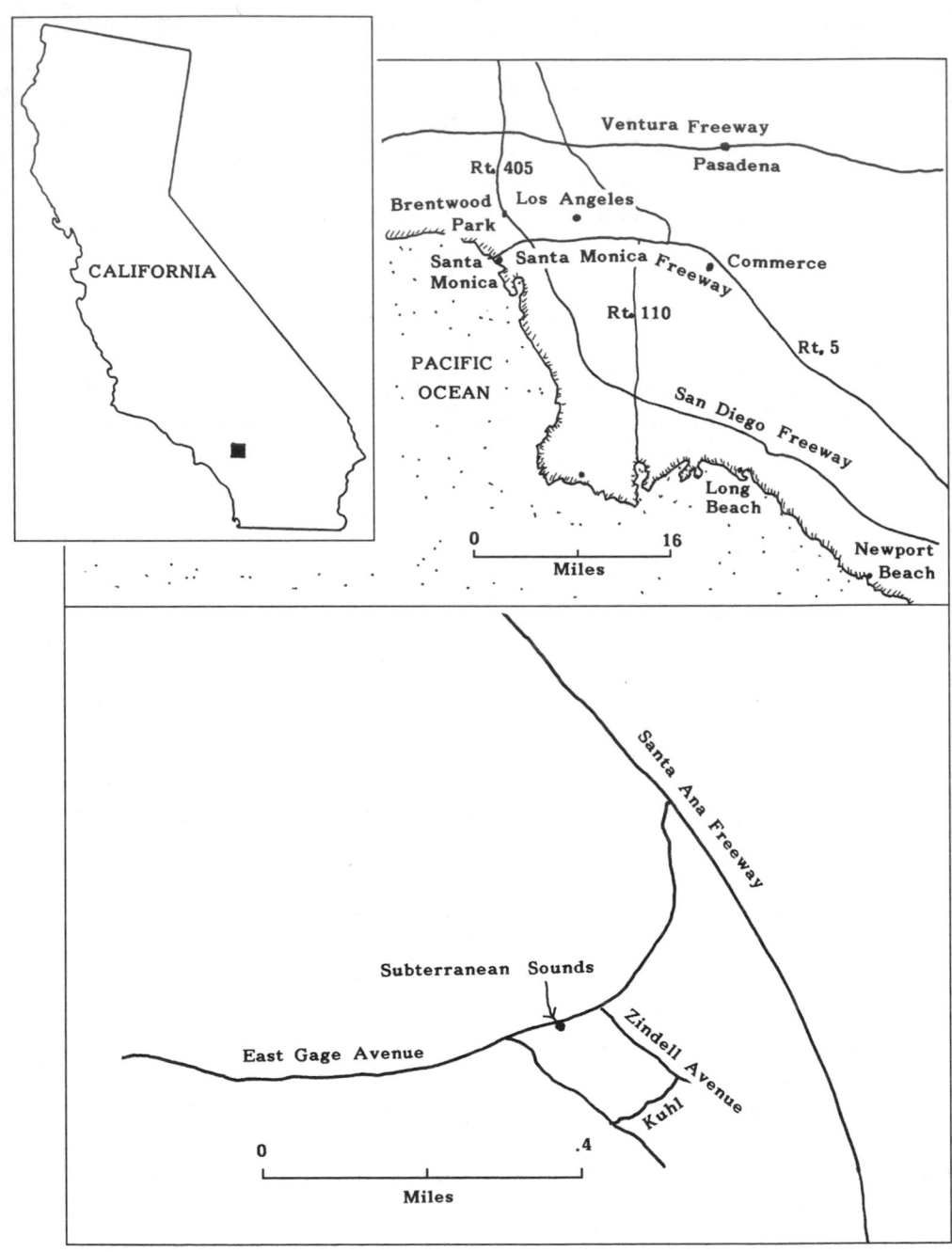

Considerations

Ask permission before you go tromping through some property owner's backyard in search of the perfect sound bite.

Things have quieted down over the last 10 years in Commerce, so there's no guarantee that you'll hear *anything*.

History/Background

Strange sounds coming from the ground have a long, mysterious history. Depending on what part of the country you live in, the sounds either go *boom* or *bam* or *hum*. For generations people have been hearing inexplicable noises. Early white settlers to the Moodus, Connecticut, area spoke of the rumbling sounds coming from the ground. Local Indians attributed this to the spirits within the earth. The sounds continue to this day. Although scientists still aren't sure what causes these sounds, they suspect it may be related to a deep fault in the earth's crust.

In the late 1970s residents along the East Coast of the United States were inundated by astonishingly loud sounds. These offshore "booms" rocked many houses with their power. Yet a thorough study of supersonic jet travel, earthquake logs, and manmade explosions revealed that none of those things were responsible. Several government agencies and scientists explored the phenomena and came to no conclusion. The booms remain unexplained.

So it is not surprising that scientists still don't know what caused the underground booms near Zindell and East Gage Avenue in Commerce back in the late 1980s. Residents at the time complained that it shook their spines. They supposedly boomed every 10 to 20 minutes and seemingly during the early morning hours of 3:00 to 4:00 A.M.

You would think that the regularity of the sounds, coupled with the latest scientific acoustic instruments, would have cleared up the mystery within days. But a thorough study of the area showed no manmade explosions were responsible. Scientists today are still baffled by the mysterious sounds that shook residents of the city and then, just as mysteriously, stopped.

A review of seismic maps of the Los Angeles basin reveals several major and minor faults beneath the city. One runs almost directly beneath the city of Commerce. Could the booms have been the results of rocks sliding against each other? Unfortunately, a check of the seismic logs for the period when this was happening show no such association. What caused the booms? We just don't know.

Contact Person(s)/Organization

Unfortunately, very few people are actively exploring strange sounds, this one included.

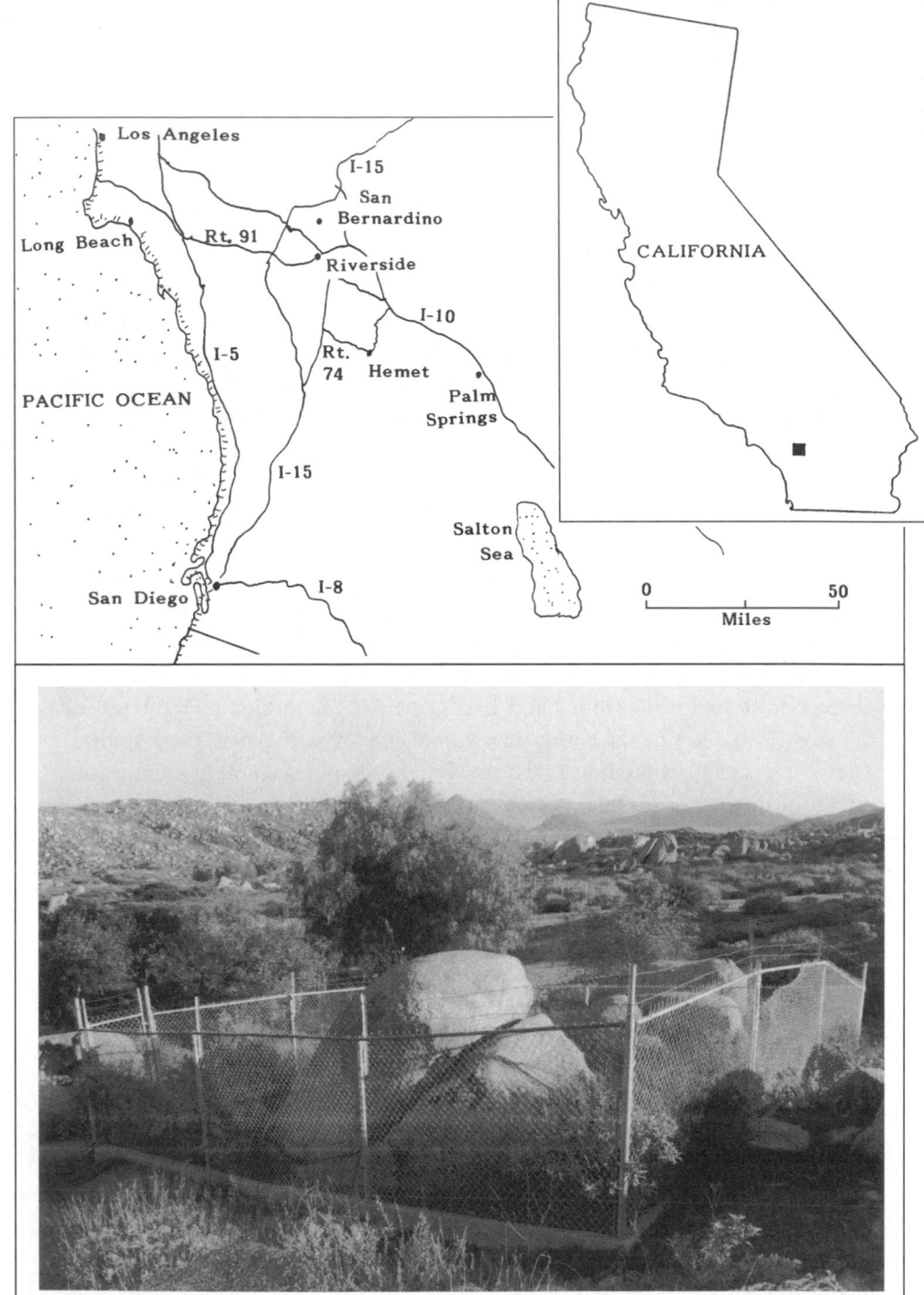

Total Magnetic Field/Inclination Angle
Nothing peculiar was evident at this site.

Further Investigations in Area
Keep your ears tuned to any strange sounds coming from the Los Angeles basin. If you do hear anything inexplicable, give me a call!

MAZE STONE
Hemet, California

Site Synopsis
At the end of a narrow canyon is a large boulder with a large maze pattern pecked into the stone. No other designs of this type are in the immediate area. No one knows when or why this pattern was placed here. Archaeologists aren't even sure *who*'s responsible.

Location
From downtown Los Angeles, take Interstate 10 east toward Palm Springs. About 25 miles east of Riverside exit south to Hemet. Once in Hemet take Florida Avenue (Route 74) west, turning right (north) on California Avenue. Stay on California for about three miles. At the end of the road there's a large fence. Park well off the road and follow the asphalt trail up to the stone.

Considerations
Several homeowners have complained about visitors blocking their driveways. If you don't want to be ticketed or towed, then don't park on anyone's property or in their driveway. This can be tricky, as there are few places near the entranceway fence to park. You may have to park a mile down the road and walk up.

The Maze Stone sits behind two fences. Please exercise the usual restraint when visiting this intriguing site.

History/Background
The setting is striking at this place. The stone is at the base of a narrow canyon, and the maze pattern faces due east on the side of a large boulder. North of here the canyon opens up to the Lakeview Mountains, which can be seen in the distance. To the south is a spectacular, open-plain view. All around the boulder are blocks of stone. They line the ridges; they sit clustered around the lower slopes. As the sun sets and a purple haze takes over, it's easy to confuse the stones for beings—they bear a striking resemblance to shadowy figures! Intriguingly, the selection of a boulder near the foot of a sloping canyon has similarities with other petroglyph sites. Along the southeastern plain of

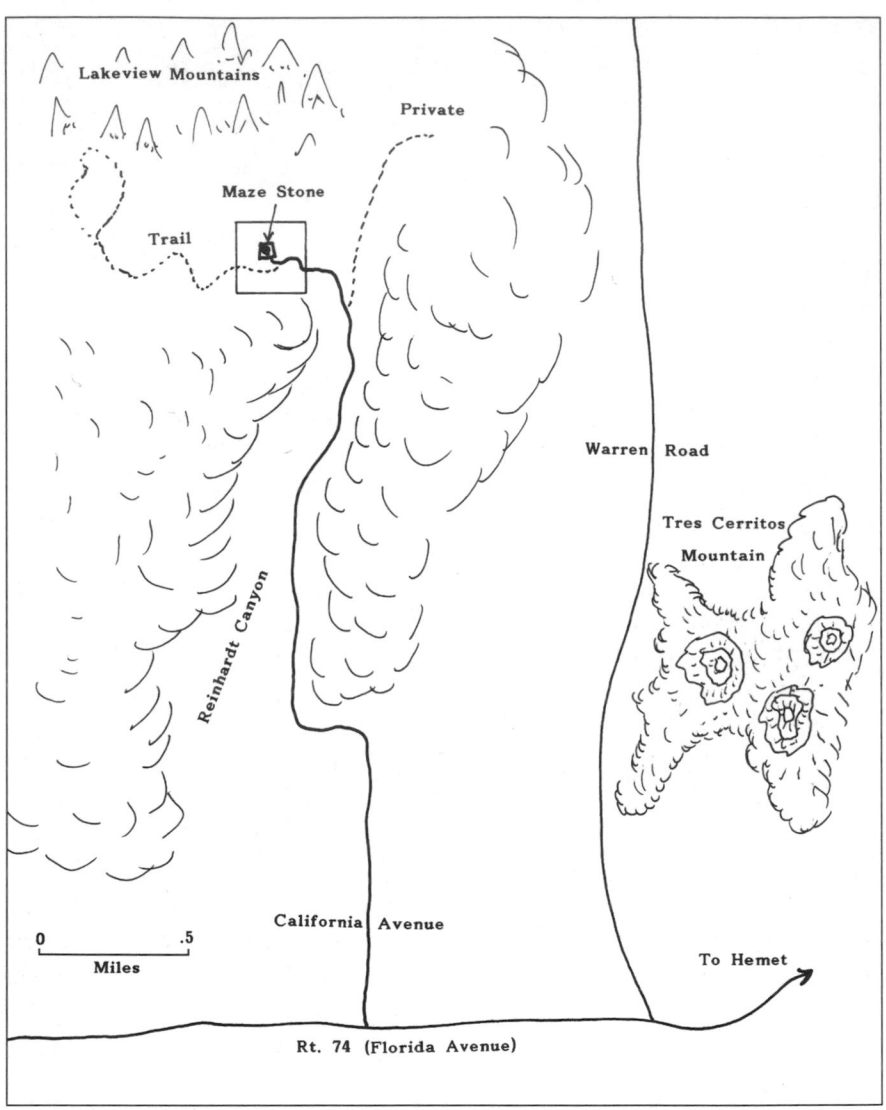

Maze Stone location, Hemet, California

Colorado, for example, researchers have found many petroglyphs along the foot slopes of hills and canyons. They rarely found glyphs on top of a hill or at the valley's lowest point—only along the foot-slope area! Researchers speculate that the Colorado petroglyphs guided people along an ancient trail system through the many canyons in the region. Perhaps the Maze Stone was carved to guide people through some ceremony.

The maze-style grid was pecked out of the base boulder with an instru-

The fence-enclosed Maze Stone, near Hemet, California. Very little archaeological survey work has been done in the canyon where this stone sits. The answer to who pecked out this maze, and why, may lie under one of the many boulders strewn about the area.

ment—stone or metal—that was harder than the rock matrix. A lot of work went into this project. But for what reason?

I thought the site would reveal a host of geomagnetic aberrations. Many base-line measurements were taken in and around the stone. There were no deviations within the canyon or at the stone.

This stone, the setting, and the design must have served some ritualistic purpose. In other parts of the world, maze petroglyphs are associated with fertility rites, particularly with the symbolic rebirth of life at springtime. It is interesting to note the placement of the maze pattern at Hemet: it faces east, toward the spring equinox, which occurs on March 21, while a canyon wall blocks watching the actual sunrise on that day—perhaps the ridge-top where the sun makes its entry over the canyon on the narrow valley is marked in some way? Clearly the carvers of the maze had a variety of flat boulders and orientations to choose from. Yet they chose this particular stone and carved an east-facing maze. This entire canyon and ridge must be thoroughly explored with these key concepts in mind.

While this type of pattern is unique in the area—the style of the maze seems to have more in common with ancient civilizations far to the south in Mexico—nonetheless, within the broad region of Southern California there

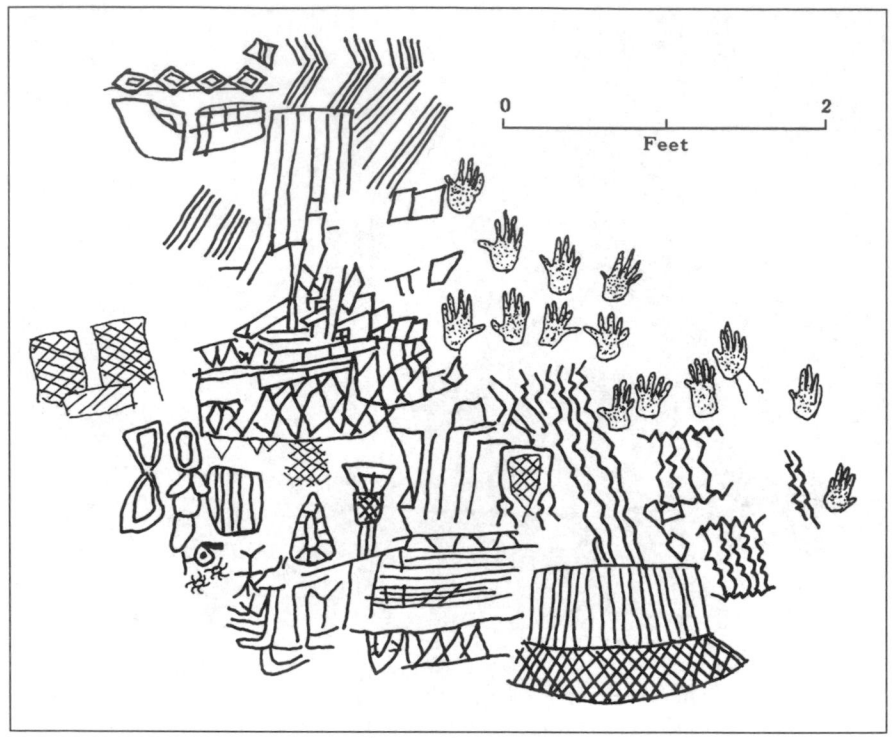

Ancient puberty rites rendered in red paint, near Perris, California;
note the drawn hands.

are some similarities. Far to the southeast, near the Fort Mohave Reservation near Needles, is a prehistoric maze of shallow ditches. Anthropologists believe that the labyrinth was constructed to confuse evil spirits who attempted to follow dead warriors down the Colorado River. The maze pattern allowed the Mojave dead to continue onward—since *their* ancestors constructed the site—while the bad spirits got hopelessly confused.

Maybe the Hemet Maze Stone has something to do with funerary rites? If so, then there could be burials in the vicinity.

Contact Person(s)/Organization

Unfortunately, there are no researchers who are actively engaged in cracking the mystery of this site. Interested parties may do well to speak with Hemet's older population regarding this stone. My experience in the town was rather disappointing: few younger folk even knew what I was talking about!

Total Magnetic Field/Inclination Angle

The many measurements taken at this site revealed nothing unusual.

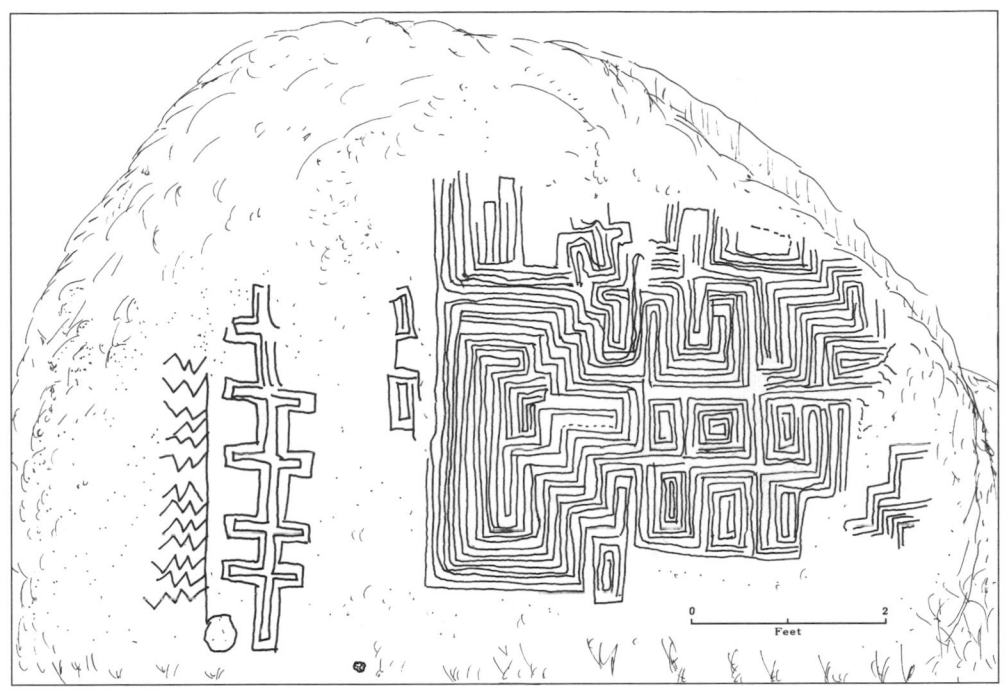

Maze-pattern boulder, painted in red, Green Valley, near Poway, California.
The meaning of these symbols is unknown.

Further Investigations in Area

As I alluded to earlier, this canyon needs a comprehensive investigation with respect to astronomically aligned stones. I recommend that interested hikers first scout out both canyon ridge-tops—due east and due west. If there *is* an association with the rising/setting sun during the equinox then there should be marker stones of some type: cairns, standing stones, circles of stone, etc. Next, a detailed survey of the entire canyon would be in order. Before attempting such work, however, do get permission from the many local landowners who have been buying up this spectacular property!

Due west of Hemet, near the town of Perris, is a sandstone cave located near a desert spring. In this cave are the red marks and symbols of an early people who lived nearby. Strange swirls, chevrons, and, most intriguingly, handprints decorate the walls of this cave. It is believed that this cave was used to initiate young girls into womanhood during or after their first menstruation. It's called a puberty rites cave.

Some 60 miles due south as the crow flies, in Green Valley, near Poway, is a boulder with similar maze patterns, although in this case the maze is painted in red.

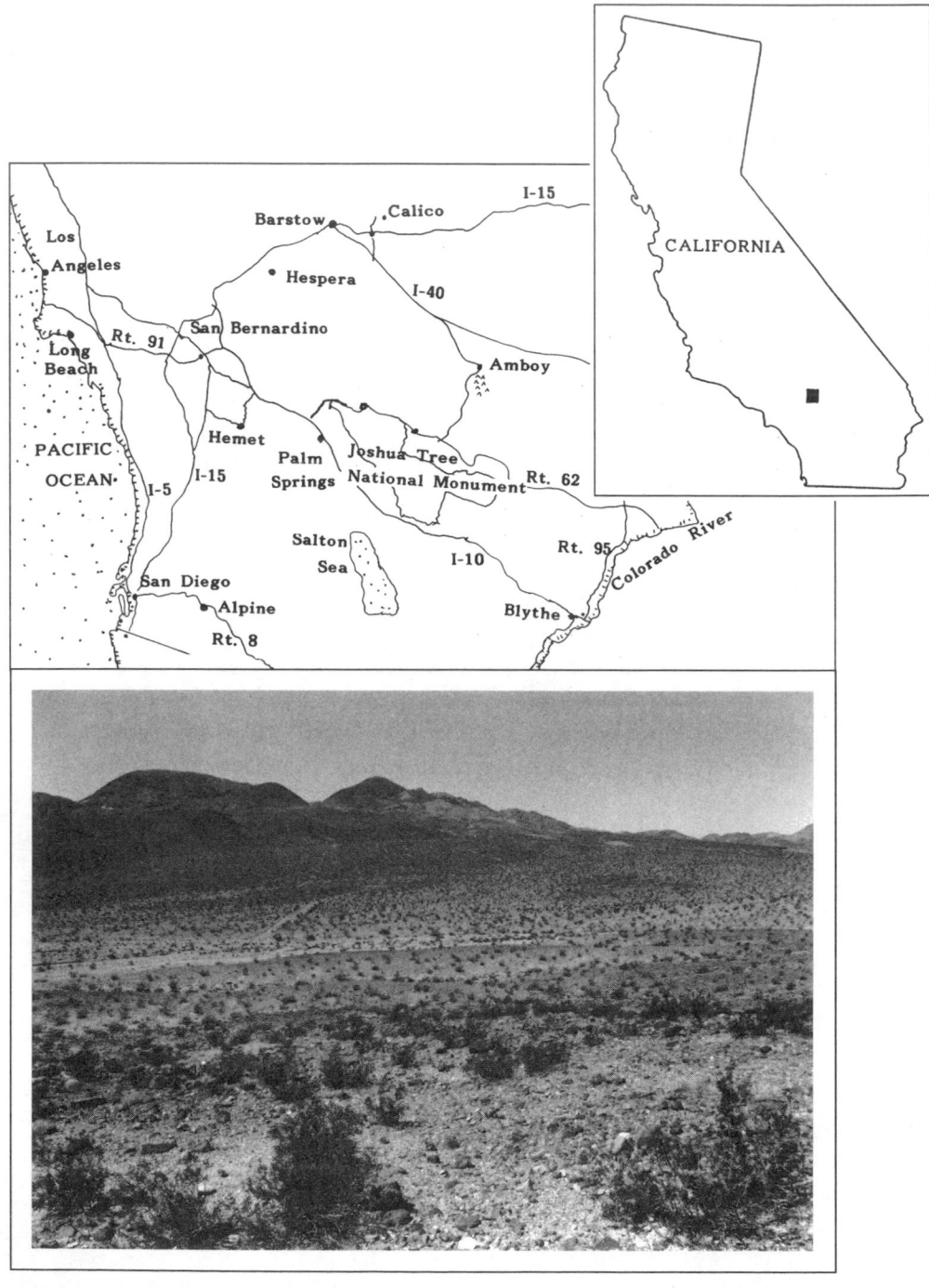

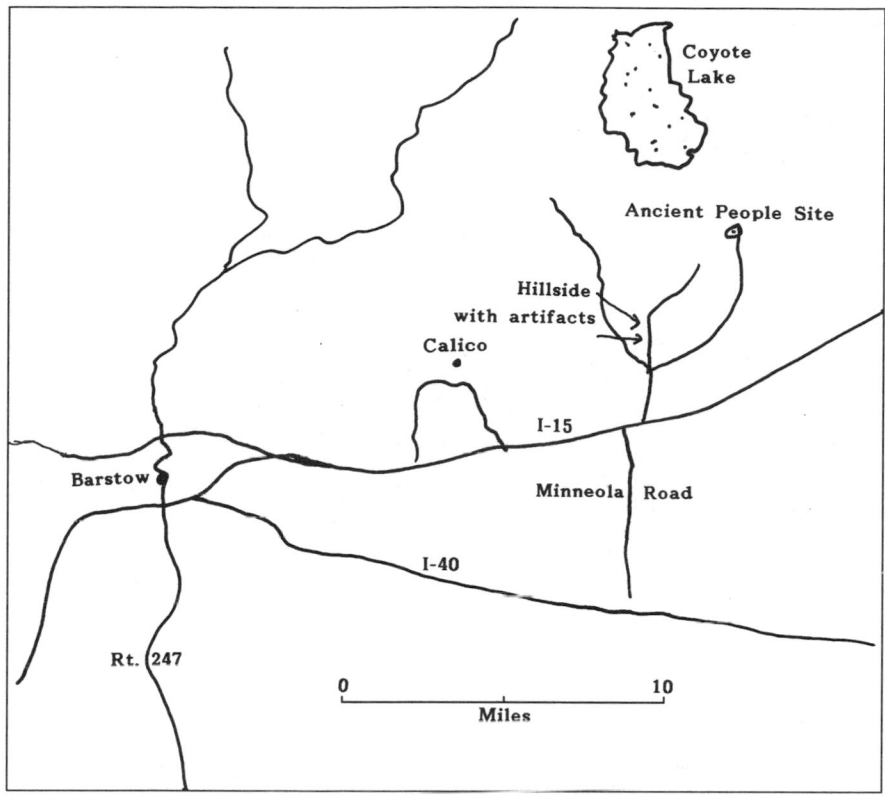

Detail of Ancient People site, near Calico, California

ANCIENT PEOPLE
Calico, California

Site Synopsis
At the base of the Calico Mountains in Southern California is an archaeological site that has been a source of major controversy since the 1960s. Some researchers claim ancient peoples hunted here over 200,000 years ago. If this is so, it would completely upset everything archaeologists know and understand about human evolution.

Location
From Los Angeles, take Interstate 15 for about 130 miles to Barstow. About 15 miles east of Barstow is a north end turnoff to Minneola Road. Exit here and follow the road signs to the Calico Early Man Site.

Considerations

The site is open only on the first Monday of each month from 10:30 A.M. to 4:30 P.M. On holiday Mondays, it's open the next day, Tuesday. It's closed all other days.

The new hours of operation severely limits access to this amazing yet desolated site. I suggest you call in advance. Considering the peculiar hours, you may want to hedge your bets and plan on staying for more than a few days. If your travel plans cannot be tailored around this site I recommend the drive anyway, just to see the general terrain and to walk in the surrounding fields, where early man supposedly flourished.

Be prepared to travel over a long stretch of gravel road. A combination of government budget shutdowns and an inexplicable lack of public interest has forced limited viewing hours on this remarkable site.

Any desert travel demands a good supply of water and food, just in case you do break down or have a flat. A CB radio is also a good idea out here. Make sure your car is in good working order. Stretches of secondary roads are quite desolate—if you happened to get stuck, you might not see another vehicle for hours. Be careful.

History/Background

Eleven thousand years ago, Southern California was a completely different place. As the last remains of Ice Age glaciers were melting into slush, vast areas of the below-sea-level landscape were covered with glacial lakes that lapped against huge forests of pine trees. Mastodons, giant sloths, camels, and other large creatures called this luxuriant, water-filled region paradise. And so did the early waves of Paleo Indian hunters, who successfully slaughtered great quantities of these prehistoric megafauna.

Today, where ice-cold water provided a bountiful home for the early ancestors of the American Indian, there is nothing but desert. With no more ice to feed them, over the next 10 centuries the lake waters dried up, leaving a parched desert terrain almost completely devoid of moisture. The worldwide climate change that ended the Ice Age spurred this massive evaporation.

According to the traditional interpretation of the peopling of America, sometime around 12,000 to 15,000 years ago, when most of the world's oceans were locked up in glaciers, the land bridge between Siberia and Alaska was exposed. It is assumed that hordes of Asians trekked across this former ocean strait and said hello to the New World. If so, then they were following game animals. Tangible evidence for this hypothesis rests solely with finds from central New Mexico. A number of years ago, near the town of Clovis, archaeologists uncovered evidence of these ancient hunters. They found a particular type of projectile point—arrow or spearhead—associated with a

A few of the many stones found along the ground near the Calico site. Were these stones cut and shaped by ancient peoples 40,000 to 200,000 years ago, or did they naturally split and cleave due to erosion? While most archaeologists believe these stones were not made as tools, Louis Leakey and other researchers who have dug the site adamantly insist the finds represent a group of Native Americans completely unknown to the modern world.

mastodon kill site. The artifact, now known in the literature as the "Clovis point," dated to over 11,500 years ago.

Nothing older than this site has ever been conclusively uncovered in the Americas, although there are many sites suspected of being older, generating great controversy. From a rigid point of view there is little conclusive evidence at Calico. But doubt lingers among those who have worked the ancient site.

The Calico controversy began in the late 1950s when Ruth De Ette Simpson, an employee of the San Bernardino County Museum, found some oddly shaped rocks near the Calico Mountains, about 15 miles east of Barstow. She thought they resembled prehistoric African stone tools, similar to those from Olduvai Gorge she had read about in the *National Geographic Magazine.*

The types of artifacts found in East Africa are collectively known as chopper tools, small stones that have been bashed along the sides to give them a cutting edge. At Olduvai Gorge in Tanzania, over 1.9 million years ago, groups of prehumans chipped stone pebbles into shapes known as scrapers, choppers, and hammerstones. The tools were used to butcher game.

A few years after Simpson's discovery, the world-famous paleontologist Louis Leakey was a visiting lecturer at the University of California, Riverside. Simpson showed Leakey the stones. He immediately saw the value of the stones and set out for Calico to look for a place to dig.

Leakey was at the height of his career. His long and hard work at Olduvai Gorge in East Africa had revealed the presence of an early type of upright pre-human. Almost single-handedly, he had rewritten our understanding of the early development of humans.

Even a casual reading of Louis Leakey's Olduvai Gorge reports indicates a man who knew what he was doing. Leakey spent over 20 years excavating the East African site before issuing a report on the matter. His writings are filled with pages of minutiae: dozens of site maps, scores of line illustrations of stone chopper tools, and the like. Leakey knew the methods and techniques of archaeology. He understood the value of detail, but he also knew what he was looking for.

Scan the rocky terrain at Olduvai and everything looks the same. That is, until you are trained to see what others miss: Leakey had an uncanny ability to walk along an ancient shoreline or streambed and find a rodent tooth. Years of field work trained his eye to see what others routinely missed. He did the same at the Calico site. His assumptions at Calico got him into academic hot water, and he never recovered from it.

When Leakey and colleagues issued the first preliminary report on Calico after four years of excavation, all hell broke loose. In the report the team wrote that the principal excavation dug to a depth of 13 feet "yielded more than 170 specimens in . . . undisturbed deposits. We consider them to be unquestionably the result of human activity."[22]

Well, so far, no problem. But it gets better:

> The whole assemblage has a very primitive appearance, but this is only to be expected in view of the probable age of the deposit from which it has been excavated. Geologists and geomorphologits who have examined the site are of the opinion that the age . . . is over 40,000 years but probably less than 120,000 years.[23]

Yeow! Up until then the earliest date for humans in the New World was 11,500 years. Now here was Dr. Louis Leakey claiming that American archaeologists had missed the boat by perhaps 110,00 years! Anticipating skepticism, Leakey and crew took pains to excavate pits near the main site to see if they could find other "stone tools." Nothing was found within the randomly selected pits that looked remotely like human-made artifacts. The main criticism of the Calico "tools" was that they were naturally cracked rocks that just happened to look worked. In other words, researchers who heard about the early

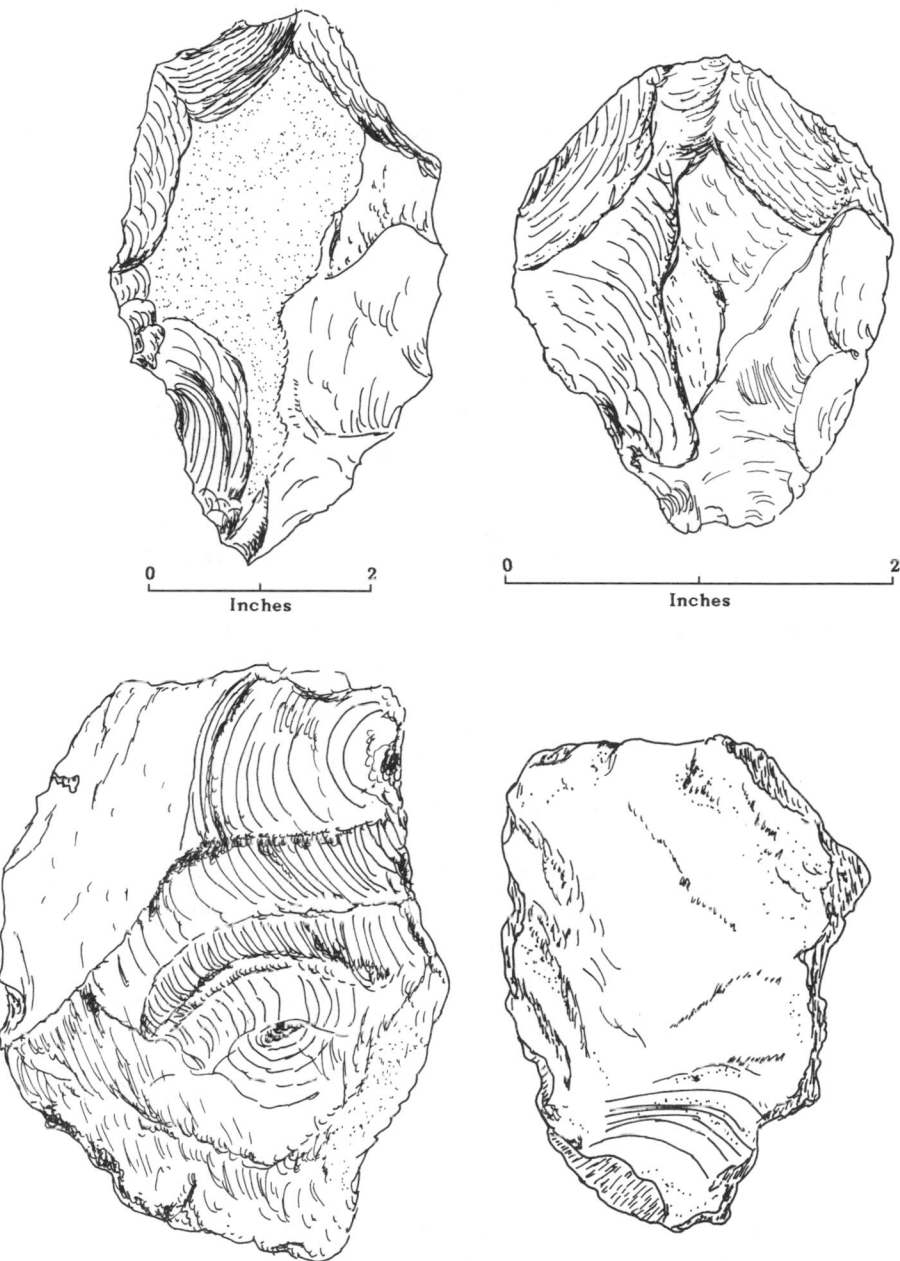

Top: Artifacts excavated at Olduvai Gorge in Tanzania that were made over half a million years ago. Bottom: According to Dr. Louis Leakey these stones, among others, were made by an early form of human at the Calico, California, site. The associated geology in which these seemingly "worked" stones were found dates from 40,000 to 200,000 years ago. The Calico stones share several characteristics of toolmaking: ideal and directed cleavage, a striking platform, concentric ripples throughout, and a bulblike scar and percussion form. (After L. S. B. Leakey, Olduvai Gorge and Cultural Resource Guide: Calico Early Man Archaeological Site)

dates at the site, but never bothered to look, claimed that the wind or other natural erosion factors led to the stones' shape.

Then, in 1980, Drs. James Bischoff, Richard Ku, and Roy Shlemon examined the Leakey tools for calcium carbonate "cement" that often encrusts artifacts. Using a technique known as uranium-thorium dating (which involves the half-life isotope decay of uranium 235 into lead 207, and thorium 232 into lead 208), the scientists discovered that the *cement* was over 200,000 years old, which meant the artifacts were even older!

But not everyone accepts this data. Twenty years after Leakey's initial report on the Calico site the debate continues to rage. Most archaeologists vehemently deny that anything of substance was ever found at Calico. Others have simply looked the other way and gone on with their own research. Leakey went to his grave in 1972 convinced that he was right and that eventually American archaeologists would "come around." So far, they haven't. In fact, the buzz in archaeological circles is that Leakey certainly knew his Olduvai Gorge material, but that he didn't know squat about American stone tools. Some scientists even say privately that the great man was probably affected by old age or suffering some form of dementia when he was excavating Calico.

Calico is a fascinating and challenging site. Anyone who takes the time to visit this barren, desolate area asks the obvious question: Are these slivers of stone, with seemingly sharpened cutting edges, artifacts or not? When you go I suggest you stop near the gated entranceway to the main site, right by the town landfill, and walk up the nearby hillside. Walk in areas of water runoff, where there would be a stream during the rainy winter months, and look for artifacts that have an unnatural shape to them. Look for stones that seem to have been changed or worked by people. Look for curved fractures in obsidian. Look for hand-sized stones that are edged or flaked. In short, look for small stone objects that would be useful to cut animal hides, or shaped stone that could be used to bash the skull of some animal to get to the creamy brains. Chances are you have found evidence of some very ancient people of America! But remember: Leave all stones, bones, and suspected tools in place. Take only pictures, not objects. Future archaeologists, once they recognize the value of Calico, will need these surface finds to fully articulate the site. Also, it's a federal offense to take any archaeological remnant off government-owned land.

Why look around the Calico desert? If there really were people coming here for over 200,000 years, there must be evidence of a whole series of ancient cultures in this area. The raw material, stone, is right. The ancient lake that was here was right—lakes beckon wildlife. And large animals coming to drink means you're going to have hunters following them. This area is perfect for raw material. It still has exactly the right stone for making very sharp spearheads and arrows.

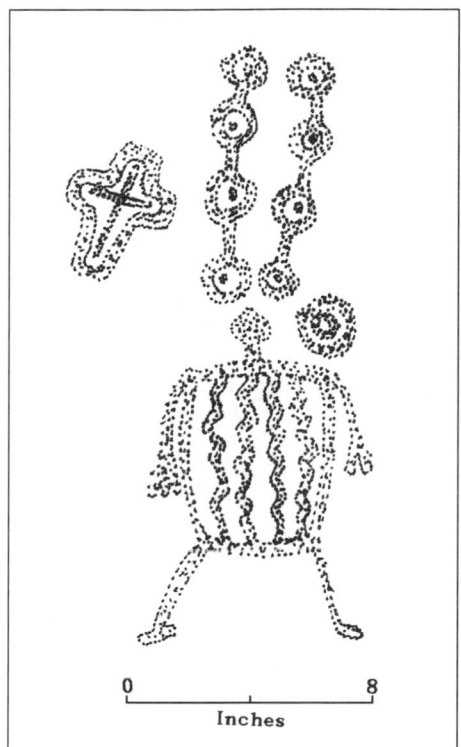

Detail of a pecked-image petroglyph, Black Canyon, northwest of Barstow, California

0   8

Inches

At Calico either we have an amazing collection of natural stones that were shaped by the wind and water or we have stones shaped by some group or culture from very long ago. Chances are the place was used over and over by different groups over vastly different time periods. Whatever the case, this site demands further exploration and analysis, but unfortunately contemporary American archaeologists—few if any with the expertise of recognizing artifacts from so long ago—tell us there's nothing in Calico. Some researchers have even stated publicly that the site is worthless, because the reputed artifacts look nothing like anything found at any other Native American site. Of course, it doesn't take a Ph.D. to realize that if these stones really are tools from over 100,000 to 200,000 years ago, then they *should* look different!

If the 200,000-year figure is correct and if the stone finds at Calico are indeed artifacts, then one way to explain their age is to think back to the *Gigantopithecus* idea that was proposed earlier in this chapter. If this so-called "extinct" creature, or some variant of this being, came to North America half a million years ago, then it seems likely there *may* be a connection with the Calico finds in the extreme southeastern sector of California. The most likely candidate for their makeup would be the ancestral Bigfoot. Curiously, over the past 100 years dozens of the "large, hairy man" stories have surfaced throughout California's major mountain systems, including those in the central and southern portions of the state.

It behooves us to find the Bigfoot, now confined to the remote mountains of California, to see if these beings use any kind of tools and if they are related in some way to the Calico finds. The antiquity of the Calico site would explain a lot in terms of the early type of hominid that perhaps used and worked that facility so long ago.

Louis Leakey will be vindicated. It's only a matter of time. The early-man site at Calico is real and very old. Study the illustrations in this section and then walk the fields with book in hand. No doubt you will find examples of tools made and used thousands if not hundreds of thousands of years ago. But which species of early human made them?

Contact Person(s)/Organization
The Bureau of Land Management
Barstow Resource Area
150 Coolwater Land
Barstow, California 92311
(619) 256-3591

Total Magnetic Field/Inclination Angle
Nothing significant was found at this site.

Further Investigations in Area
About 30 miles northwest of Barstow, deep within Black Canyon, are several strangely pecked images of crosses, braided circles, and humanoid figures. The site doubtless dates to a prehistoric period when the nearby Harper Lake was filled with life-giving water. To get there from Barstow take Route 58 west for above seven miles. Bear right on Santa Fe Avenue. Stay on Santa Fe for a little more than three miles. Turn right on Black Canyon Road. In about 15 miles Black Mountain will be on your right. Five miles beyond leads to Inscription Canyon. Look for the petroglyphs on the side of the road.

Southeast of the Calico Hills near the town of Daggett, just off old Route 66, are the remains of a massive lava flow. Coming from the Pisgah Crater, the hardened black lava is a present-day reminder of the continuous eruption of pyroclastic effluent that scorched the region millions of years ago.

Farther east along the road is a cinder cone crater near the town of Amboy. This classically shaped cone resulted from years of fiery embers disseminating into the air.

Moving south from Amboy, on the road to Twentynine Palms are a series of weird mounds. There are a multitude of these conical, earthen creations. Nearby is the dried-up Bristol Lake. These mounds are the result of salt-

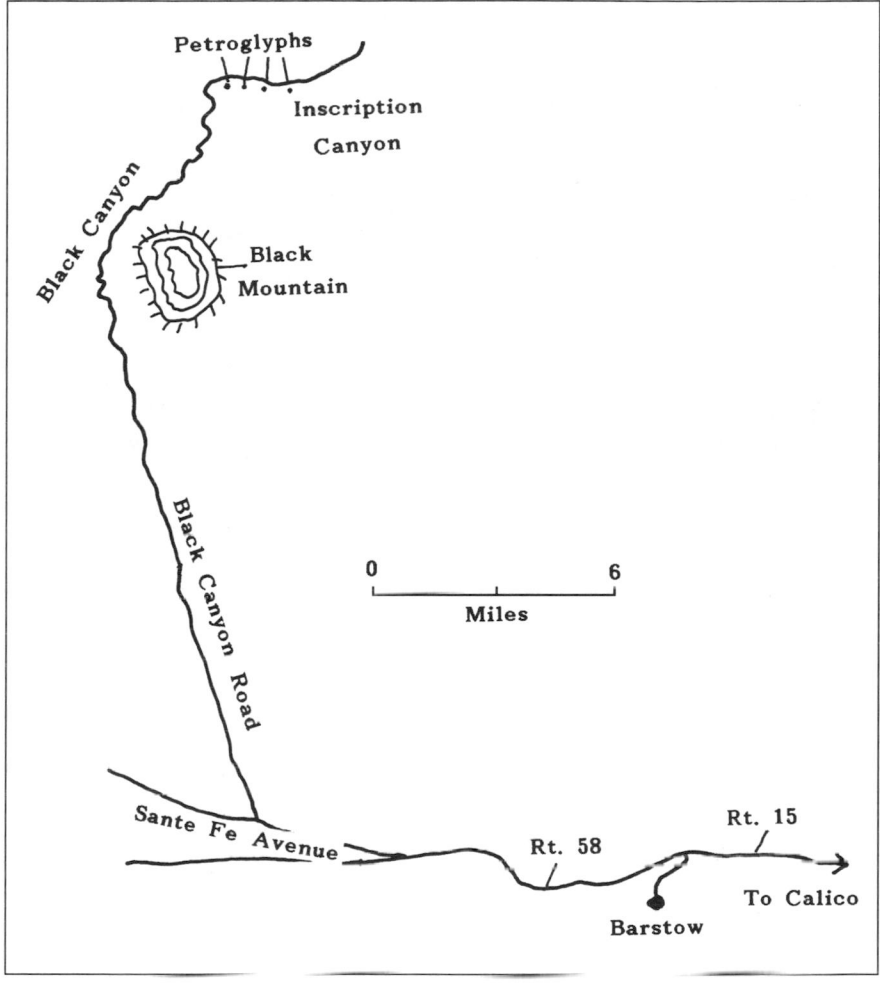

Location of Black Canyon petroglyphs, northwest of Barstow, California

mining operations along the lake. That, combined with some nice wind erosion, has created a wonderful spectacle. Stop and look.

GIANT DESERT CARVINGS
North of Blythe, California

Site Synopsis

Deep in the southeastern California desert near the Arizona border several large figures are emerging from the earth. The ancient inhabitants of the region scraped away the dark tan desert gravel to reveal the light earth underneath.

The largest of the figures is a 94-foot-tall man with outstretched arms.

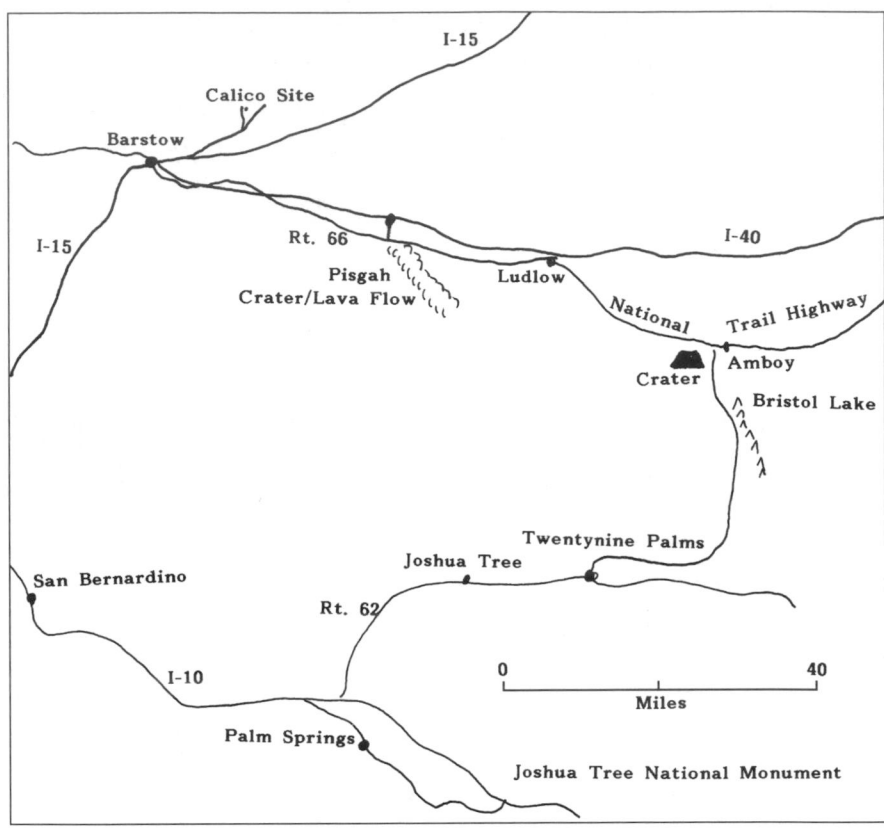

Lava flows, craters, and possible mounds south of Calico, California

Nearby is a four-legged animal that measures almost 50 feet across. A symbol of a spiral is at the animal's feet. Who made these patterns, and when? Why were they made?

Location

Known as the Desert Intaglios (an *intaglio* is a cutting or engraving in stone), they are about 15 miles north of Blythe. Take Interstate 10 out of Blythe, traveling north on Route 95 to the monument marker. Turn left (west) onto the dirt-gravel road. The first two figures are four tenths of a mile up the road on your right (north). Park and follow the trail to them. The next large figure is three tenths of a mile west of the first stop. Park and follow the trail north to the figure.

If you have time, visit the site to the south of here. It's not marked and it's not fenced in (see illustration).

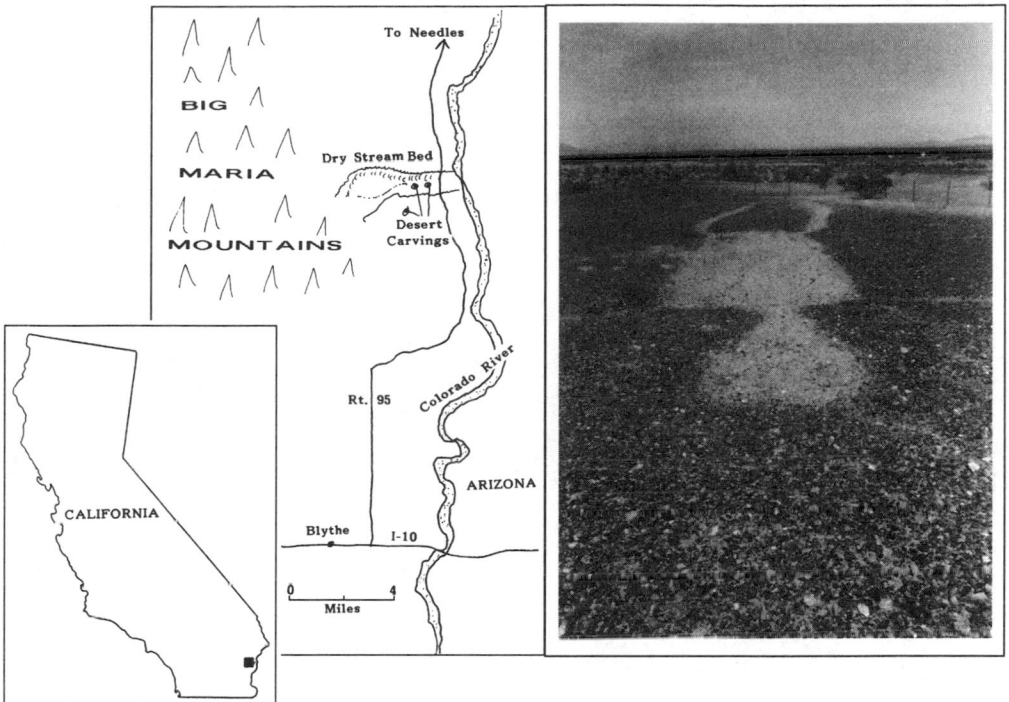

Considerations

As with all archaeological sites, take only pictures. Leave all stones, fossils, and artifacts in place. Don't even think about climbing the fence. There's already enough damage to these sites.

After a ground visit, the best possible way to see these unusual figures is from the air. A small airfield just outside of Blythe is a great place to rent a plane for a few passes over the site.

History/Background

The carvings were first spotted by a pilot in the 1930s. While the carvings can be seen from the ground, they were unknown in this region until air travel. Local Indians claimed ignorance of their origin or meaning. This has led to all sorts of speculation about UFOs, ancient astronauts, and weird cultures putting these things in place. It's very possible that the natives simply refused to say what they knew. That said, some contemporary anthropologists believe the giant figures honor the local Yuman people's creation myth.

In any event, this site is a must-see. Get there early in the morning when

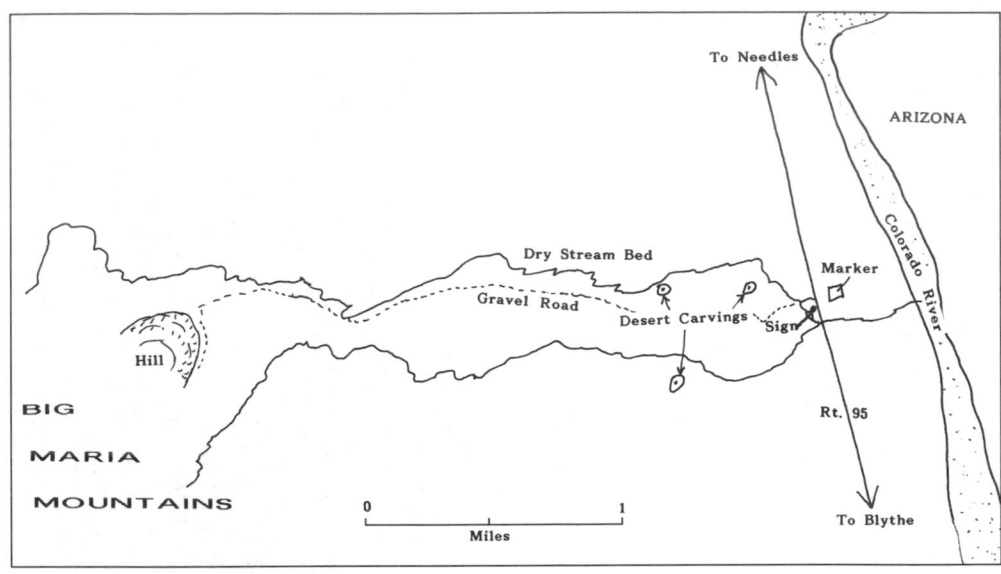

Detail of Giant Desert Carvings, north of Blythe, California

the sun isn't so hot. I also recommend a spring or fall visit, rather than a summer one. If summer is your only option, then wear a wide-brim hat, sunglasses, and try to arrive at sunrise.

The largest figure here is over 167 feet long while the smallest is about 95 feet. Three of the figures have been fenced in to protect them from locals who like to ride Jeeps across the forms.

So what's going on here? The Colorado River is about a mile to the east. The figures are perched near the edge of a steep embankment. It's likely that in ancient times the embankment was a bit farther away, given years of erosion. The embankment leads down to an intermittently dried-out stream that is fed from the Big Maria Mountains to the west. At one time this must have been a major stream feeding the Colorado. The very shape and width of the channel suggests that.

The first white explorers in the region noted that the Colorado River flooded its banks every spring. Soon after, many of the tribes living along the floodplain planted beans, maize, and melons in the thick, nutrient-rich soil. The entire area east of the Giant Carvings site was a perfect area for planting; it must have supported a large population.

The striking thing about these figures is their orientation. The artists who made these images had a large canvas on which to work, and could have placed them in any position. Yet, upon study, we see that the first manlike figure's

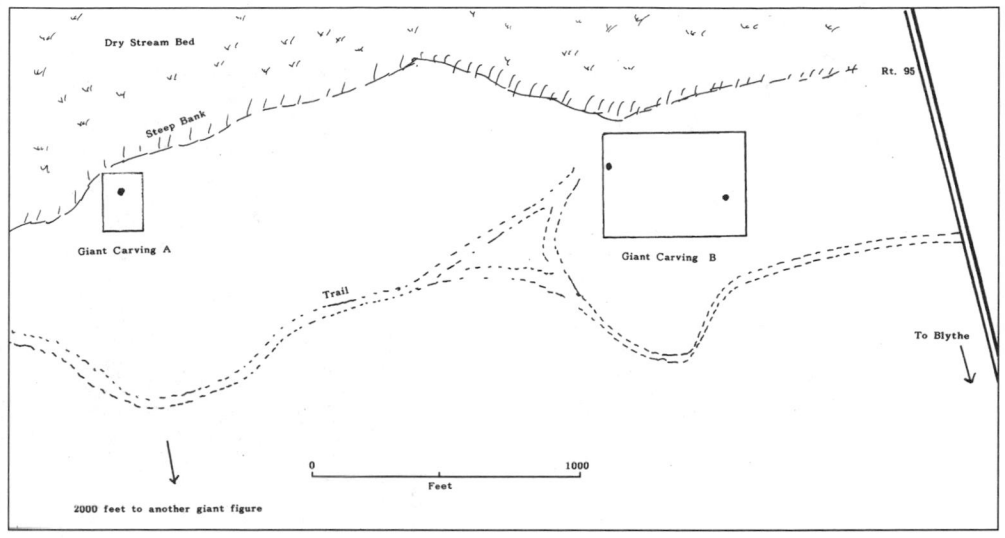

Detail of Giant Desert Carvings, north of Blythe, California

head is pointing to the north while the second image's head is pointing to the south (see illustration). Furthermore, the animal and spiral (a coiled serpent, in some viewers' minds) are aligned west-east. Clearly, orientation was important to the designers of this site. But why? Perhaps they were following the earth spirit?

Another peculiar thing about this site is that the carvings were definitely not made for surface dwellers—people on the ground. Yet there are no mountains to view these images from. Even the closest hill—about a half-mile away—is at the wrong viewing angle. You can't see anything. And farther away still—at the Big Maria Mountains—the images are too tiny to understand.

These intaglios could have been made for something hovering overhead, but not too far overhead—perhaps around 500 to 2,000 feet. Beyond that the images are meaningless. So what hovers at that altitude besides the imagination and UFOs intent on abduction? Birds of prey, such as the eagle and a host of other spirits within the cosmology of the people who took the trouble to make these delicate figures. These giant figures seem to be an offering of some type.

Until a detailed archaeological survey is carried out in the vicinity, it is difficult to say who constructed this site and when. But the geomagnetic measurements I obtained may shed some light as to the figure placements.

This gigantic humanoid figure was made by moving aside the sun-scorched brown stones to reveal the tan ground below. Native Americans interviewed in the 1930s, soon after these images were spotted from a plane, claimed no knowledge of their origin. Either they were keeping sacred information to themselves—a distinct possibility—or the figures were made long before the native population started farming the area.

Contact Person(s)/Organization

The Bureau of Land Management is responsible for the upkeep of these structures. For more information contact:
The Bureau of Land Management
1695 Spruce Street
Riverside, California 92507
(714) 351-6394

Further information on this site can be obtained from:

The Colorado River Reservation: Mohave (Hamakhava), Chemehuevi (Newewe), Hopi, Navajo (Diné)
Colorado River Tribes Administrative Office
Route 1, Box 23 B
Parker, Arizona 85344
(602) 669-9211

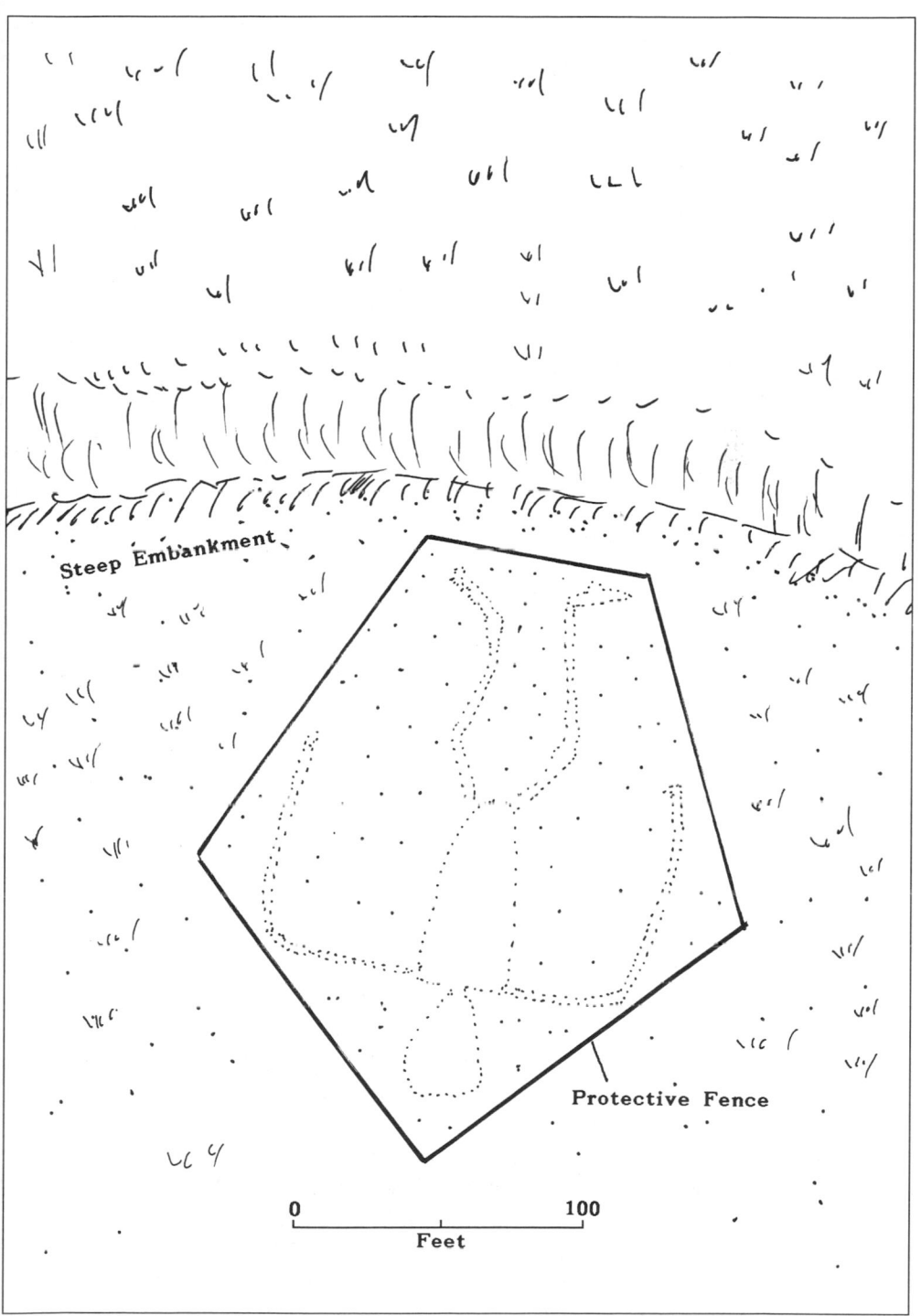

Steep Embankment

Protective Fence

0   100

Feet

Giant Desert Intaglio, Carving A

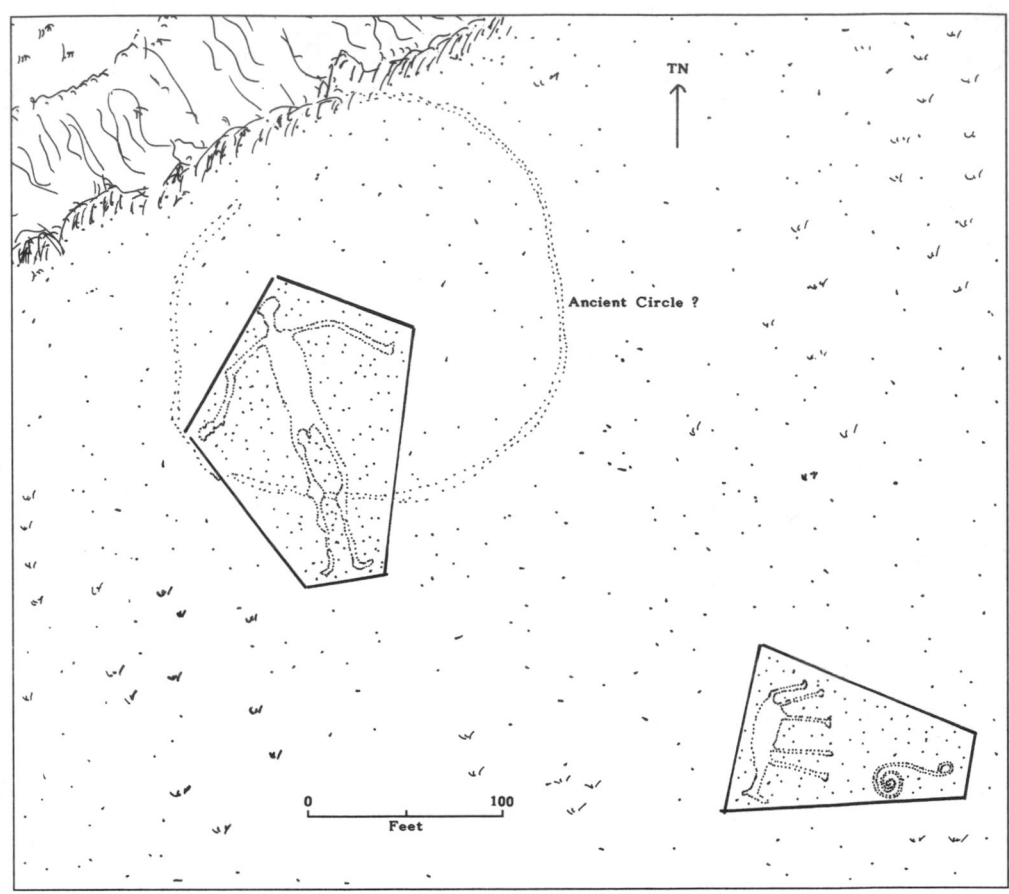

Giant Desert Intaglio, Carving B

Total Magnetic Field/Inclination Angle

This is an interesting site with respect to geomagnetic flux. In general, I found that the total magnetic field directly over the figures was significantly lower than at any other place on the plain. As I got closer to each figure the magnetic field shifted downward by almost 200 milligauss units. This same pattern was repeated at each giant intaglio. Nowhere else in the area did I get a magnetic flux "depression." This suggests that whoever carved these figures knew exactly where they should be placed. They were not randomly set down on the high area above the nearby stream; rather, a concerted effort took advantage of a natural aberration in the earth's magnetic field. But why? Perhaps to experience an altered state of mind via the differing secretion rates of the pineal gland's neurotransmitters.

Some of the large figures north of Blythe, California, include a spiral and some type of animal. The Big Maria Mountains are in the distance.

Further Investigations in Area

Another set of giant carved figures can be found at Providence Mountains State Park, north of here, about 40 miles west of the Colorado River.

Highway 78 going south from Blythe has some of the most interesting terrain. You can feel the presence of Indians here. In fact, east of Ripley, toward the Colorado River plateau, are another set of strange desert carvings.

Just north of Glamis, along the east side of Highway 78, are many earthen mounds and caves. Stop along the roadside, particularly near dried-out streambeds, and scan the terrain with a good pair of binoculars.

Farther south are roadside markers that say things like "Indian Trail." It's a powerful place of strangely unique landforms and mountains.

West of El Centro, just south of Ocotillo, are the remains of a cairn burial site reputedly over 22,000 years old. For years scholars have been arguing over the age of this site. Soon after data on it was published a scathing attack claimed that the dating techniques of the original researchers were faulty.[24] Based on other Yuha cairn burials in the Colorado Desert, the date should have been around 5,000 years ago. The final date has yet to be determined.

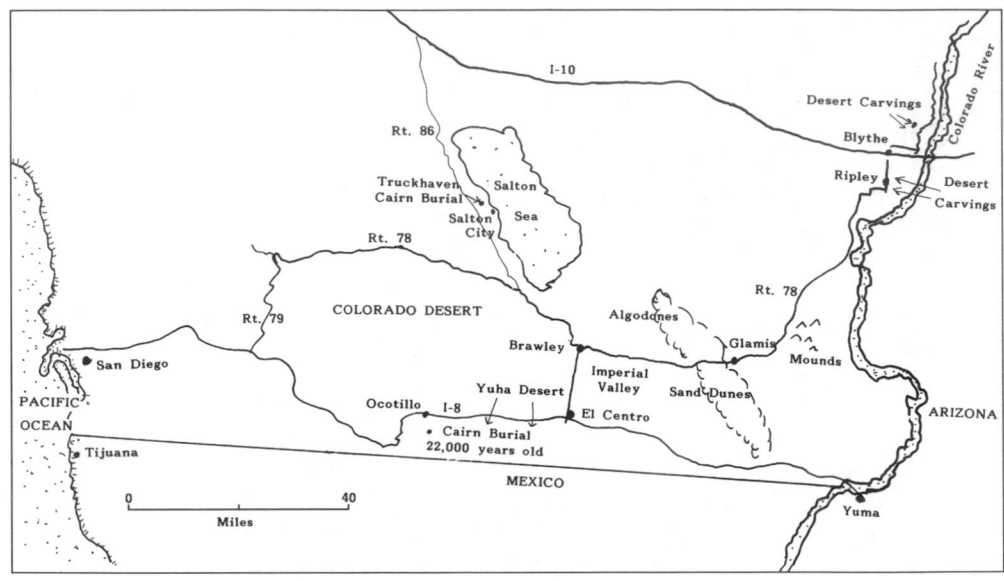

Mysterious sites south of Blythe, California: desert figures, mounds, cairn burial sites

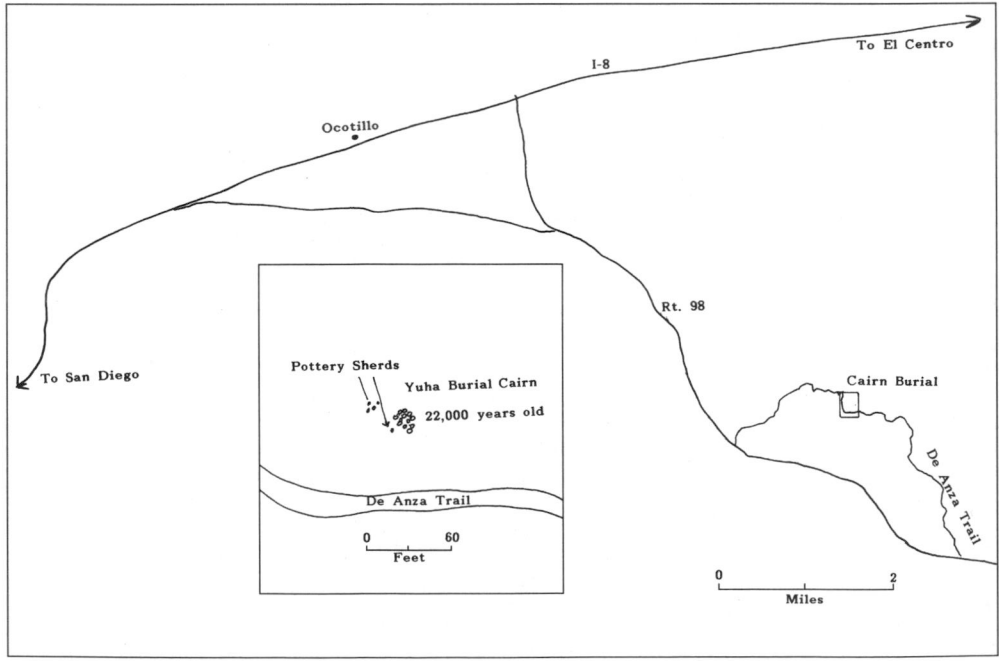

Detail of Yuha burial cairn south of Ocotillo, California. Scientists are still debating the antiquity of the burial, which may date to 22,000 years ago.

FIVE

Mysterious Finale

Amazing things happen to those who are aware of their surroundings. Some see the mystical in the mundane and others feel magic in the air. It all depends on the ability to recognize and appreciate hidden peculiarities. Those who see the world in grains of sand and heaven in wildflowers are forever in touch with their sense of place. They are not in conflict with the land they live on. Rather, they daily experience the collective awe of a much grander power about them.

The Pacific coastal states are a marvelous place to search for the unusual. While geologically active and still growing in population, the region tenaciously clings to mysteries, be they lava tubes strewn with forgotten symbols or giant desert figures understood only from high above.

Visiting all of these mysterious places takes determination and the ability to tolerate frustration. Some of the sites described here are easier to get to than others. A few experiences, like seeing a Bigfoot or going on a vision quest, demand things beyond map and text locations: luck, good timing, and a major attitude adjustment help.

While healthy skepticism is in order, allow yourself time to "commune" with a site. A quick "in-out, been-there, done-that" mind-set doesn't work. Getting to know a place means finding out as much information about it as you can and then going there to slowly and completely absorb it.

When you walk the trails to the sites listed here, when you climb into the caves or visit the beaches, when you search for sea serpents or treasure, remember to leave only footprints and to take only pictures. Stealing a piece of mystery, be it a bone, stone, petroglyph, or any other type of artifact, may not only be illegal under federal law, but it often upsets a higher order.

The value of such places is their ability to inform and astonish generations of people who have not yet seen them. Of course, the many remaining Native Americans in the Pacific Northwest and elsewhere would argue the case on a more spiritual level. Regardless of your religious beliefs, it is wise to listen to a people who have thousands of years of direct experience in the region. Destroy not what you have little understanding of; there may be a reality and consequence associated with such action that is entirely different from your own. Tread lightly in this spiritual domain. It's not as easily dismissed as you may think.

This third book in this field guide series is merely the start of a journey through a land we think we know so well. There's a mysterious world out there filled with adventure, excitement, and unusual phenomena. Join me on future trips, which are guaranteed to amuse, confuse, and rekindle your sense of youthful wonder.

Notes

1. Introduction

1. Salvatore M. Trento. *Field Guide to Mysterious Places of the West* (Boulder, Colorado: Pruett Publishing, 1994).
2. Salvatore M. Trento. *Field Guide to Mysterious Places of Eastern North America* (New York: Owl Books, 1997).

2. Washington

1. Salvatore Michael Trento. *Field Guide to Mysterious Places of the West* (Boulder, Colorado: Pruett Publishing, 1994).
2. M. Eells. "Traditions of the *Deluge* Among the Tribes of the Northwest," *American Antiquarian* 1 (1878), 70–72.
3. Paul L. Weis and William L. Newman. *The Channeled Scablands of Eastern Washington* (Cheney, Washington: Eastern Washington University Press, 1989), 11.
4. Ibid., 14.
5. Ibid., 14.
6. Ibid., 14.
7. James D. Keyser. *Indian Rock Art of the Columbia Plateau* (Seattle: University of Washington Press, 1992), 94.
8. Greg Long. "Machinelike Underground Sounds and UFO Phenomena." *International UFO Reporter* (November/December 1989), 17.

3. Oregon

1. Stuart Warren and Ted Long-Ishikawa. *Oregon Handbook* (Chico, California: Moon Publications, 1995), 20.

2. *Tales of the Neahkahnie Treasure* (Tillamook, Oregon: Tillamook County Pioneer Museum, 1991), 2–3.

3. See "The Oak Island Treasure" in Salvatore M. Trento, *Field Guide to Mysterious Places of Eastern North America* (New York: Owl Books, 1997).

4. Cited in Ron Warfield, *A Guide to Crater Lake* (Crater Lake Natural History Association, 1985), 10, 12.

5. Donald M. Hines. *Magic in the Mountains, The Yakima Shaman: Power and Practice* (Issaquah, Washington: Great Eagle Publishing, 1993), 80–81.

6. Partial data obtained from Chris Banta, *Seeing Is Believing?* (Agoura Hills, California: Funhouse Press, 1995).

7. John Litster. *Notes and Data* (Gold Hill, Oregon: Ernie & Irene Cooper, 1960).

8. Details from the Pilots' newsletter, *Acorde Report*, vol. 5, no. 6, February 1978. Medford, Oregon, as reproduced in Banta, *Seeing Is Believing?*, 1995, 112.

9. Litster, *Notes and Data* (1960).

10. Cited in Warren and Long-Ishikawa, *Oregon Handbook*, 1995, 488.

11. Ibid., 488–489.

4. Califorinia

1. Colin F. Taylor, ed., et al. *Native American Myths and Legends* (New York: Smithmark Publishers, 1994), 90–91.

2. Robert Michael Pyle. *Where Bigfoot Walks* (Boston: Houghton Mifflin, 1995), 132–133.

3. Ibid., 133.

4. Ibid., 133.

5. Cited in John Green, *Encounters with Bigfoot* (Blaine, Washington: Hancock House Publishers, 1994), 4.

6. Ibid., 4.

7. Ibid., 4.

8. Grover S. Krantz, *Big Footprints* (Boulder, Colorado: Johnson Books, 1992), 144.

9. Ibid., 144–145.

10. Ibid., 165–166.

11. Data adapted from Green, *Ecnounters with Bigfoot* (1994), 64.

12. Cited in Charles Burress, "Unraveling the Old Mystery of East Bay Walls," *San Francisco Chronicle*, 31 December 1984, 5

13. Salvatore M. Trento. *Field Guide to Mysterious Places of the West* (Boulder, Colorado: Pruett Publishing, 1994), 37–40.

14. Ibid., 136.

15. Colin F. Taylor et al. *Native American Myths and Legends* (New York: Smithmark Publishers, 1994), 89.

16. Trento, *Field Guide . . . West*, 227–230.

17. From the entrance sign at the site: A History of the Mystery Spot.

18. Tomi Kay Lussier. *Big Sur: A Complete History and Guide* (Cambria, California: Lussier and Big Sur Productions, 1993), 41.

19. Andrew W. Berg. "Formation of Mima Mounds: A Seismic Hypothesis," *Geology* 18 (1990), 281.

20. Trento, *Field Guide . . . West*, 39.
21. Ibid.
22. L. S. B. Leakey, Ruth De Ette Simpson, and Thomas Clements. "Archaeological Excavations in the Calico Mountains, California: Preliminary Report," *Science* 160 (May 31, 1968), 1022.
23. Ibid.
24. Phillip J. Wilke. "Cairn Burials of the California Deserts," *American Antiquarian* 1 (1978), 44.

Bibliography

Allen, John Eliot. "New Publication Provides Details on 202 Largest of Oregon's Lakes." *The Oregonian*, 31 October 1985.

Alt, David D., and Hyndman, Donald W. *Roadside Geology of Northern California*. Missoula, Montana: Mountain Press, n.d.

——. *Roadside Geology of Oregon*. Missoula, Montana: Mountain Press, 1994.

——. *Roadside Geology of Washington*. Missoula, Montana: Mountain Press, 1993.

Anderson, Ian. "Humming Fish Disturbs the Peace." *New Scientist*, 12 September 1985, 64.

Banta, Chris. *Seeing Is Believing?* Agoura Hills, California: Funhouse Press, 1995.

Barnes, G. W. "The Hillocks or Mound-Formations of San Diego, California." *American Naturalist* 13 (1879): 565–71.

Bates, Betsy. "85-million-year-old Sea Serpent Surfaces in Museum Basement." *Los Angeles Herald Examiner*, 17 January 1988.

Begley, Sharon, et al. "Do You Hear What I Hear?" *Newsweek*, 3 May 1993.

Bell, Hugh Stevens. "Armored Mud Balls: Their Origin, Properties, and Role in Sedimentation." *Journal of Geology* 48 (1940): 1–31.

Berg, Andrew W. "Formation of Mima Mounds: A Seismic Hypothesis." *Geology* 18 (1990): 281.

Bishop, William Henry. "Southern California." *Harpers New Monthly Magazine* 65 (October 1882): 713–28.

Bliss, Loren. *Ancient Afro-European Penetration in the Pacific Northwest*. Privately published. Federal Way, Washington, 1977.

Bower, Bruce. "Flakes, Breaks, and the First Americans." *Science News* 131 (1987): 172.

Brown, Robert, ed. *Science for All*, vol. 1–5. London: Cassell, Petter, Galpin & Co., n.d.

Bryant, William Cullen, ed. *Picturesque America*, vol. 1 and 2. New York: D. Appleton and Company, 1874.

Burress, Charles. "Unraveling the Old Mystery of East Bay Walls." *San Francisco Chronicle*, 31 December 1984.

Campbell, Marius R. "Natural Mounds." *Journal of Geology* 14 (1906): 708–17.

Carter, George F. "California as an Island." *The Masterkey* 38 (1964): 74–78.

Chamberlain, Rebecca. *Poverty Hill*. Personal Communication, March 1995.

Chever, Edward E. "The Indians of California." *American Naturalist* 4 (May 1870): 129–48.

Childress, David Hatcher. *Lost Cities of North and Central America*. Stelle, Illinois: Adventures Unlimited Press, 1992.

Chitwood, Larry. "Central Oregon's Underground World Filled with Wind That Roars, Whistles." *The Oregonian*, 31 October 1985.

Chong, Linda. "Commerce Becomes Reluctant Boom Town," *Los Angeles Herald Examiner*, 17 January 1988.

Corliss, William R., comp. *Anomalies in Geology*. Glen Arm, Maryland: The Sourcebook Project, 1989.

———. *Inner Earth*. Glen Arm, Maryland: The Sourcebook Project, 1991.

———. *Neglected Geological Anomalies*. Glen Arm, Maryland: The Sourcebook Project, 1990.

———. *Science Frontiers*. Glen Arm, Maryland: The Sourcebook Project, 1994.

———. *Unknown Earth*. Glen Arm, Maryland: The Sourcebook Project, 1980.

Cox, George W., and Hunt, Jodee. "Form of Mima Mounds in Relation to Occupancy by Pocket Gophers." *Journal of Mammalogy* 71 (1990): 90.

Cox, George W., and Gakahu, Christopher G. "Formation of Mima Mounds in the Kenya Highlands: A Test of the Dalquest-Scheffer Hypothesis," *Journal of Mammalogy* 65 (1984): 149.

Crosby, Harry. *The Cave Paintings of Baja California*. La Jolla, California: Copley Books, 1979.

Cultural Resource Guide: Calico Early Man Archeological Site. Yermo, California: Friends of Calico Early Man Site, n.d.

Dana, James D. *The Geological Story*. New York: Ivison, Blakeman, Taylor and Company, 1875.

De Colange, Leo, ed. *The Picturesque World*, vol. 1 and 2. Boston: Estes & Lariat, 1879.

De Nadaillac, Marquis. *Prehistoric America*. New York: G. P. Putnam's Sons, 1901.

Eargle, Dolan H., Jr. *California Indian Country*. San Francisco: Trees Company Press, 1992.

———. *The Earth Is Our Mother*. San Francisco: Trees Company Press, 1993.

Eberly, Vince. *The Runic Stone*. Personal Communication, March 1995.

Edwards, S. C. "Concretions." *Rocks and Minerals* 20 (1945): 99.

Eells, M. "Traditions of the 'Deluge' Among the Tribes of the Northwest." *American Antiquarian* 1 (1878): 70–72.

Essig, E. O. "The Ruppia Balls of Little Borax Lake." *Scientifc Monthly* 66 (1948): 467.

Geological Excursions in Southern California. Riverside, California: Geological Society of America, Cordilleran Section Meeting, UCR Campus Museum, 1971.

Gordon, David G. "What Is That?" *Oceans* 20 (August 1987): 44.

Grant, Campbell. *Rock Art of the American Indian.* New York: Thomas Y. Crowell Company, 1967.

———. *The Rock Paintings of the Chumash* (reprint). Santa Barbara, California: Santa Barbara Museum of National History, 1993.

Green, John. *Sasquatch: The Apes Among Us.* Blaine, Washington: Hancock House Publishers, 1978.

———. *Encounters with Bigfoot.* Blaine, Washington: Hancock House Publishers, 1994.

Harpers Weekly 17, 28 June 1873.

Hines, Donald M. *Magic in the Mountains, The Yakima Shaman: Power and Practice.* Issaquah, Washington: Great Eagle Publishing, 1993.

The House of Mystery: The Oregon Vortex (pamphlet). Gold Hill, Oregon: Oregon Vortex, n.d.

Howe, Carrol B. *Ancient Modocs of California and Oregon.* Portland, Oregon: Binford & Mort Publishing, 1994.

Hull, Tupper. "Salvager Gets into Hot Water over Sunken Galleon Filled with Treasures," *Los Angeles Herald Examiner,* 17 January 1988.

Hunt, Charles Butler. *Death Valley.* Berkeley: University of California Press, 1975.

Ingersoll, Ernest. "In the Wahlamet Valley of Oregon." *Harpers New Monthly Magazine* 65 (October 1882): 764–71.

Jackson, Ruth A. *Combing the Coast.* San Francisco: Chronicle Books, 1985.

Jones, Alan G., and Savage, Peter J. "North American Central Plains Conductivity Anomaly Goes East." *Geophysical Research Letters* 13 (1986): 685.

Jordan, David Starr. "A Miocene Catastrophe." *Natural History* 20 (1920): 18–22.

Juillerat, Lee. *Captain Jack's Stronghold: Historic Trail Booklet.* Tule Lake, California: Lava Beds Natural History Association, 1992.

Keel, John A. *The Complete Guide to Mysterious Beings.* New York: Doubleday, 1994.

Kerr, Richard A. "New Gravity Anomalies Mapped from Old Data," *Science* 215 (1982): 1220.

Kesseli, John E. "Rock Streams in the Sierra Nevada, California." *Geographical Review* 31 (1941): 203–27.

Keyser, James D. *Indian Rock Art of the Columbia Plateau.* Seattle, University of Washington Press, 1992.

Krantz, Grover S. *Big Footprints.* Boulder, Colorado: Johnson Books, 1992.

Lambert, David. *The Field Guide to Early Man.* New York: Facts on File, 1987.

Larsen, Charlie and Jo. *Lava Beds Caves.* Vancouver, Washington: ABC Publishing, 1990.

Lava River Cave (pamphlet). Bend, Oregon: Northwest Interpretive Association and Deschutes National Forest, 1985.

Leakey, L. S. B., Simpson, Ruth De Ette, and Clements, Thomas. "Archaeological Excavations in the Calico Mountains, California: Preliminary Report." *Science* 160 (31 May 1968): 1022–23.

Leakey, L. S. B. *Olduvai Gorge, 1951–1961, Volume I: A Preliminary Report on the Geology and Fauna*. Cambridge, England: Cambridge University Press, 1965.

Leakey, M. D. *Olduvai Gorge, 1960–1963, Volume 3: Excavations in Beds I and II*. Cambridge, England: Cambridge University Press, 1971.

Leary, Kevin. "Sausalito's Weird Hum Is Back." *San Francisco Chronicle* 29 July 1985.

Litster, John. *The Oregon Vortex*, 4th ed. Gold Hill, Oregon: Ernie & Irene Cooper, 1960.

Long, Greg. "Machinelike Underground Sounds and UFO Phenomena." *International UFO Reporter*, November/December 1989, 17.

Lussier, Tomi Kay. *Big Sur: A Complete History and Guide*. Cambria, California: Lussier and Big Sur Productions, 1993.

McRae, Bill, and Jewell, Judy. *Pacific Northwest*. Hawthorn, Australia: Lonely Planet Publications, 1995.

Morgan, Neil. *The Pacific States*. New York: Time Incorporated, 1967.

"Nature's Hidden Power Line." *Science Digest* 90 (October 1982): 18.

Nelson, Byron. *Our Home Forever*. Hoopa, California: Hupa Tribe, 1994.

Norris, Robert M., and Webb, Robert W. *Geology of California*. New York: John Wiley & Sons, 1976.

Peet, Stephen D. *Ancient Monuments and Ruined Cities*. Chicago: Office American Antiquarian, 1904.

Peterson, Natasha. *Sacred Sites*. Chicago: Contemporary Books, 1988.

Pyle, Robert Michael. *Where Bigfoot Walks*. Boston: Houghton Mifflin, 1995.

Queenan, Charles F. *Long Beach and Los Angeles*. Northridge, California: Windsor Publications, 1986.

Rubenstein, Steve. "Detours on the Trail of Mysterious Hum." *San Francisco Chronicle*, 25 September 1985.

Satterfield, Archie, and Lyons, Dianne J. Boulerice. *Washington Handbook*. Chico, California: Moon Publications, 1994.

Scheffer, Victor B. "The Mystery of the Mima Mounds." *Scientifcic Monthly* 65 (1947): 283–94.

Schoolcraft, Henry Rowe. *History of the Indian Tribes of the United States*. Philadelphia: J. B. Lippincott, 1857.

"Sea Serpents Seen off California Coast." *ISC Newsletter* 2 (Winter, 1983): 9.

"Sea Serpent Sightings Substantiated by British Columbia Scientists." *Baltimore Sun*, 30 July 1992.

Sharp, Robert P., and Glazner, Allen F. *Geology Underfoot in Southern California*. Missoula, Montana: Mountain Press, 1993.

Simon, C. "Deep Crust Hints Meteoritic Impact." *Science News* 121 (1982): 69.

Smith, Peter J. "Can Honeycomb Weathering be ET?" *Nature* 301 (1983): 291.

Tales of the Neahkahnie Treasure. Tillamook, Oregon: Tillamook County Pioneer Museum, 1991.

Taylor, Colin F., ed., et al. *Native American Myths and Legends*. New York: Smithmark Publishers, 1994.

Thayer, William M. *Marvels of the New West*. Norwich, Connecticut: Henry Bill Publishing Company, 1888.

Todd, J. E. "Log-Like Concretions and Fossil Shores." *American Geologist* 17 (1896): 347.

Towle, James N. "The Anomalous Geomagnetic Variation Field and Geoelectric Structure Associated with the Mesa Butte Fault System, Arizona." *Geological Society of America Bulletin* 95 (1984): 221.

Trento, Salvatore M. *Field Guide to Mysterious Places of the West.* Boulder, Colorado: Pruett Publishing, 1994.

———. *Field Guide to Mysterious Places of Eastern North America.* New York: Henry Holt, 1997.

Vaughan, Ralph E. "The Calico Controversy." *Ancient American* 2 (September/ October 1994): 16–18.

Warfield, Ron. *A Guide to Crater Lake: The Mountain That Used to Be.* Crater Lake National Monument: Crater Lake Natural History Association, 1985.

Warren, Stuart, and Long-Ishikawa, Ted. *Oregon Handbook.* Chico, California: Moon Publications, 1995.

Weir, Kim. *Northern California Handbook.* Chico, California: Moon Publications, 1994.

Weis, Paul L., and Newman, William L. *The Channeled Scablands of Eastern Washington: The Geologic Story of the Spokane Flood.* Cheney, Washington: Eastern Washington University Press, 1989.

Whitney, Dudley J. "San Joaquin Valley Hog Wallows." *Scientific Monthly* 66 (1948): 356–57.

Wilke, Phillip J. "Cairn Burials of the California Deserts." *American Antiquity* 43 (1978): 444.

Williams, Henry T. *Williams' Illustrated Pacific Tourist Guide Across the Continent.* New York: Henry T. Williams, 1879.

Index